New Perspectives on

MICROSOFT® EXCEL 2002

Brief Bonus Edition

JUNE JAMRICH PARSONS

DAN OJA

ROY AGELOFF
University of Rhode Island

PATRICK CAREY
Carey Associates, Inc.

THOMSON
COURSE TECHNOLOGY

Australia • Canada • Mexico • Singapore • Spain • United Kingdom • United States • Japan

New Perspectives on Microsoft® Excel 2002—Brief Bonus Edition
is published by Course Technology.

Managing Editor:
Rachel Crapser

Senior Product Manager:
Kathy Finnegan

Senior Product Manager:
Amanda Shelton

Product Manager:
Karen Stevens

Associate Product Manager:
Brianna Germain

Editorial Assistant:
Abbey Reider

Senior Marketing Manager:
Rachel Stephens

Developmental Editor:
Jane Pedicini

Production Editor:
Christine Gatliffe

Composition:
GEX Publishing Services

Text Designer:
Meral Dabcovich

Cover Designer:
Efrat Reis

COPYRIGHT © 2004 Course Technology, a division of Thomson Learning, Inc. Thomson Learning™ is a trademark used herein under license.

Printed in the United States of America

2 3 4 5 6 7 8 9 BM 08 07 06 05 04

For more information, contact Course Technology, 25 Thomson Place, Boston, Massachusetts, 02210.

Or find us on the World Wide Web at: www.course.com

ALL RIGHTS RESERVED. No part of this work covered by the copyright hereon may be reproduced or used in any form or by any means—graphic, electronic, or mechanical, including photocopying, recording, taping, Web distribution, or information storage and retrieval systems—without the written permission of the publisher.

For permission to use material from this text or product, contact us by
Tel (800) 730-2214
Fax (800) 730-2215
www.thomsonrights.com

Disclaimer
Course Technology reserves the right to revise this publication and make changes from time to time in its content without notice.

ISBN 0-619-21421-X

New Perspectives Preface

Course Technology is the world leader in information technology education. The New Perspectives Series is an integral part of Course Technology's success. Visit our Web site to see a whole new perspective on teaching and learning solutions.

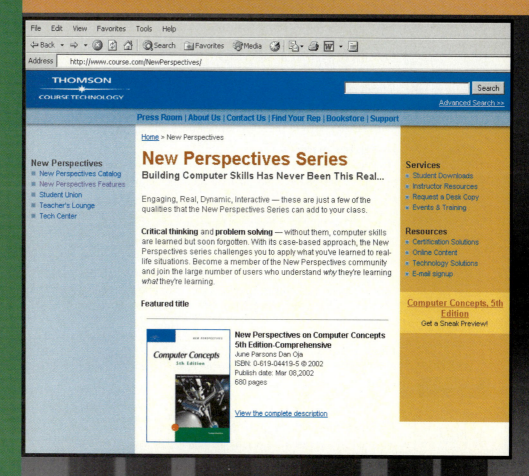

New Perspectives—Building Computer Skills Has Never Been This Real

Why New Perspectives will work for you.

Critical thinking and **problem solving**—without them, computer skills are learned but soon forgotten. With its **case-based** approach, the New Perspectives Series challenges students to apply what they've learned to real-life situations. Become a member of the New Perspectives community and watch your students not only **master** computer skills, but also **retain** and carry this **knowledge** into the world.

New Perspectives catalog
Our online catalog is never out of date! Go to the Catalog link on our Web site to check out our available titles, request a desk copy, download a book preview, or locate online files.

Complete system of offerings
Whether you're looking for a Brief book, an Advanced book, or something in between, we've got you covered. Go to the Catalog link on our Web site to find the level of coverage that's right for you.

Instructor materials
We have all the tools you need—data files, solution files, figure files, a sample syllabus, and ExamView, our powerful testing software package.

How well do your students know Microsoft Office?
Experience the power, ease, and flexibility of SAM XP and TOM. These innovative software tools provide the first truly integrated technology-based training and assessment solution for your applications course. Click the Tech Center link to learn more.

Get certified
If you want to get certified, we have the titles for you. Find out more by clicking the Teacher's Lounge link.

Interested in online learning?
Enhance your course with rich online content for use through MyCourse 2.0, WebCT, and Blackboard. Go to the Teacher's Lounge to find the platform that's right for you.

Your link to the future is at www.course.com/NewPerspectives

What you need to know about this book.

- Student Online Companion takes students to the Web for additional work.
- ExamView testing software gives you the option of generating a printed test, LAN-based test, or test over the Internet.
- New Perspectives Labs provide students with self-paced practice on computer-related topics.
- This edition expands the coverage of worksheet manipulation. Students learn how to add, remove, rename, and move worksheets.
- Students will appreciate the in-depth explanation of cells and cell references, as they learn about absolute, relative, and mixed references and how to correctly apply them in formulas.
- This Bonus edition presents instructors with a choice in coverage of Excel functions. Excel Tutorial 2 is financially oriented and designed to provide more in-depth coverage of formulas and functions. Alternatively, the new bonus tutorial (located in the back of the book) offers a simple and streamlined introduction to basic formulas and functions.
- This Bonus edition includes an added reference that highlights common Excel functions.

"I particularly like the Excel spreadsheet that goes with the functions reference material. It helps the 'reader' visualize a function and if the 'reader' does not understand it, he/she can study it (or evaluate the formulas) and the references to specific cells."
IdaLynn Gedde
Arapahoe Community College

"The workbook used as an example in Tutorial 1 and the exercises conform to standard business usage, and the story that wraps the tutorial is both interesting and valid to today's business environment."
Eric Johnston,
Vatterott College

"The material is presented in a clear and concise manner; very well organized and detailed. The end-of tutorial exercises are very good; they reinforce the the concepts that were presented in the tutorials."
Donna Occhifinto,
County College of Morris

CASE	TROUBLE?	SESSION 1.1	QUICK CHECK	RW
Tutorial Case Each tutorial begins with a problem presented in a case that is meaningful to students. The case sets the scene to help students understand what they will do in the tutorial.	**TROUBLE? Paragraphs** These paragraphs anticipate the mistakes or problems that students may have and help them continue with the tutorial.	**Sessions** Each tutorial is divided into sessions designed to be completed in about 45 minutes each. Students should take as much time as they need and take a break between sessions.	**Quick Check Questions** Each session concludes with conceptual Quick Check questions that test students' understanding of what they learned in the session.	**Reference Windows** Reference Windows are succinct summaries of the most important tasks covered in a tutorial. They preview actions students will perform in the steps to follow.

www.course.com/NewPerspectives

TABLE OF CONTENTS

Preface	iii
Microsoft Office XP	**OFF 1**
Read This Before You Begin	OFF 2

Introducing Microsoft Office XP — OFF 3
Preparing Promotional Materials for Delmar Office Supplies

Exploring Microsoft Office XP	OFF 4
Integrating Programs	OFF 7
Starting Office Programs	OFF 9
Switching Between Open Programs and Files	OFF 12
Using Personalized Menus and Toolbars	OFF 13
Using Speech Recognition	OFF 15
Saving and Closing a File	OFF 16
Opening a File	OFF 18
Printing a File	OFF 20
Getting Help	OFF 21
Exiting Programs	OFF 23
Quick Check	OFF 23
Review Assignments	OFF 23
Quick Check Answers	OFF 24

Microsoft Excel 2002	
Level Tutorials I	**EX 1.01**
Read This Before You Begin	EX 1.02

Tutorial 1 — EX 1.03

Using Excel to Manage Financial Data
Creating an Income Statement

SESSION 1.1	**EX 1.04**
Introducing Excel	EX 1.04
Understanding Spreadsheets	EX 1.04
Parts of the Excel Window	EX 1.05
Navigating in a Workbook	EX 1.08
Navigating Within a Worksheet	EX 1.08
Navigating Between Worksheets	EX 1.11
Opening and Saving a Workbook	EX 1.12
Working with Ranges	EX 1.15
Selecting Ranges	EX 1.15
Other Selection Techniques	EX 1.17
Moving a Selection of Cells	EX 1.18
Session 1.1 Quick Check	EX 1.19
SESSION 1.2	**EX 1.20**
Entering Information into a Worksheet	EX 1.20
Entering Text	EX 1.20
Entering Dates	EX 1.21
Entering Values	EX 1.21
Entering Formulas	EX 1.22
Working with Rows and Columns	EX 1.26
Inserting a Row or Column	EX 1.26
Clearing or Deleting a Row or Column	EX 1.27
Increasing the Width of a Column or the Height of a Row	EX 1.29
Editing Your Worksheet	EX 1.31
Working in Edit Mode	EX 1.31
Undoing an Action	EX 1.32
Working with Worksheets	EX 1.33
Adding and Removing Worksheets	EX 1.33
Renaming a Worksheet	EX 1.35
Moving a Worksheet	EX 1.35
Printing a Worksheet	EX 1.36
Session 1.2 Quick Check	EX 1.37
Review Assignments	EX 1.37
Case Problems	EX 1.38
Lab Assignments	EX 1.42
Internet Assignments	EX 1.44
Quick Check Answers	EX 1.44

Tutorial 2 — EX 2.01

Working with Formulas and Functions
Analyzing a Mortgage

SESSION 2.1	**EX 2.02**
Working with Excel Functions	EX 2.02
Function Syntax	EX 2.03
Financial Functions	EX 2.05
Inserting a Function	EX 2.06
Copying and Pasting Formulas	EX 2.10
Relative and Absolute References	EX 2.14
Session 2.1 Quick Check	EX 2.16
SESSION 2.2	**EX 2.16**
Filling in Formulas and Values	EX 2.16
Copying Formulas	EX 2.17
Filling a Series	EX 2.18
Filling In Dates	EX 2.19
Using Excel's Logical Functions	EX 2.21
Using the AutoSum Button	EX 2.25
Using Excel's Date Functions	EX 2.27
Session 2.2 Quick Check	EX 2.29
Review Assignments	EX 2.29
Case Problems	EX 2.31
Internet Assignments	EX 2.36
Quick Check Answers	EX 2.36

Tutorial 3 — EX 3.01

Developing a Professional-Looking Worksheet
Formatting a Sales Report

SESSION 3.1	**EX 3.02**
Formatting Worksheet Data	EX 3.02
Using the Formatting Toolbar	EX 3.03
Copying Formats	EX 3.06
Using the Format Cells Dialog Box	EX 3.07
Working with Fonts and Colors	EX 3.09
Aligning Cell Contents	EX 3.11
Indenting and Wrapping Text	EX 3.12
Other Formatting Options	EX 3.14
Working with Cell Borders and Backgrounds	EX 3.14
Adding a Cell Border	EX 3.14
Setting the Background Color and Pattern	EX 3.18
Session 3.1 Quick Check	EX 3.20
SESSION 3.2	**EX 3.21**
Formatting the Worksheet	EX 3.21
Merging Cells into One Cell	EX 3.21
Hiding Rows and Columns	EX 3.22

Formatting the Sheet Background	EX 3.23
Formatting Sheet Tabs	EX 3.24
Clearing and Replacing Formats	EX 3.25
Using Styles	EX 3.28
Creating a Style	EX 3.28
Applying a Style	EX 3.29
Using AutoFormat	EX 3.31
Formatting the Printed Worksheet	EX 3.32
Opening the Print Preview Window	EX 3.32
Defining the Page Setup	EX 3.33
Working with Headers and Footers	EX 3.35
Working with the Print Area and Page Breaks	EX 3.37
Session 3.2 Quick Check	EX 3.40
Review Assignments	EX 3.41
Case Problems	EX 3.42
Internet Assignments	EX 3.46
Quick Check Answers	EX 3.46

Tutorial 4   EX 4.01

Working with Charts and Graphics
Charting Sales Data for Vega Telescopes

SESSION 4.1	**EX 4.02**
Excel Charts	EX 4.02
Creating a Chart with the Chart Wizard	EX 4.03
Choosing a Chart Type	EX 4.04
Choosing a Data Source	EX 4.06
Choosing Chart Options	EX 4.08
Choosing the Chart Location	EX 4.10
Moving and Resizing an Embedded Chart	EX 4.13
Updating a Chart	EX 4.14
Creating a Pie Chart	EX 4.14
Rotating the Pie Chart	EX 4.16
Exploding a Slice of a Pie Chart	EX 4.17
Session 4.1 Quick Check	EX 4.19
SESSION 4.2	**EX 4.19**
Modifying a Chart	EX 4.19
Editing the Data Source	EX 4.19
Changing the Chart Location	EX 4.22
Changing Chart Options	EX 4.23
Formatting Chart Elements	EX 4.23
Formatting Chart Text	EX 4.24
Inserting New Chart Text	EX 4.25
Working with Colors and Fills	EX 4.27
Using a Graphic Image as a Background	EX 4.30
Changing the Axis Scale	EX 4.32
Working with Three Dimensional Charts	EX 4.33
Using the Drawing Toolbar	EX 4.35
Displaying the Drawing Toolbar	EX 4.36
Working with AutoShapes	EX 4.36
Formatting an AutoShape	EX 4.38
Printing Your Charts	EX 4.40
Session 4.2 Quick Check	EX 4.42
Review Assignments	EX 4.42
Case Problems	EX 4.43
Internet Assignments	EX 4.47
Quick Check Answers	EX 4.48

Creating Web Pages with Excel   WEB 1
Publishing Workbooks to the Web

Publishing a Non-Interactive Web Site	WEB 2
Setting the Publishing Options	WEB 2
Publishing the Web Page	WEB 4
Publishing an Interactive Web Site	WEB 6
Publishing the Web Page	WEB 6
Working with the Published Page	WEB 7
Review Assignments	WEB 8

Microsoft Excel 2002
Bonus Tutorial 2   B-EX 2.01
Read This Before You Begin   B-EX 2.02

Tutorial 2   B-EX 2.03

Creating a Worksheet
Producing a Sales Comparison Report for MSI

SESSION 2.1	**B-EX 2.04**
Developing Worksheets	B-EX 2.04
Planning the Worksheet	B-EX 2.04
Building the Worksheet	B-EX 2.05
Entering Labels	B-EX 2.05
Entering Data	B-EX 2.07
Using the AutoSum Button	B-EX 2.09
Entering Formulas	B-EX 2.10
Copying a Formula Using the Fill Handle	B-EX 2.11
Copying a Formula Using Relative References	B-EX 2.12
Copying a Formula Using an Absolute Reference	B-EX 2.13
Absolute Versus Relative Cell References	B-EX 2.14
Copying Cell Contents Using the Copy-and-Paste Method	B-EX 2.15
Renaming the Worksheet	B-EX 2.17
Saving the New Workbook	B-EX 2.17
Session 2.1 Quick Check	B-EX 2.18
SESSION 2.2	**B-EX 2.18**
Excel Functions	B-EX 2.18
AVERAGE Function	B-EX 2.20
MAX Function	B-EX 2.22
MIN Function	B-EX 2.22
Building Formulas by Pointing	B-EX 2.22
Testing the Worksheet	B-EX 2.23
Spell Checking the Worksheet	B-EX 2.24
Improving the Worksheet Layout	B-EX 2.24
Changing Column Width	B-EX 2.24
Inserting a Row or Column into a Worksheet	B-EX 2.26
Using the Undo Button	B-EX 2.27
Moving a Range Using the Mouse	B-EX 2.28
Using AutoFormat	B-EX 2.29
Previewing the Worksheet Using Print Preview	B-EX 2.30
Centering the Printout	B-EX 2.32
Adding Headers and Footers	B-EX 2.33
Setting the Print Area	B-EX 2.35
Documenting the Workbook	B-EX 2.36
Adding Cell Comments	B-EX 2.36
Displaying and Printing Worksheet Formulas	B-EX 2.38
Session 2.2 Quick Check	B-EX 2.39
Review Assignments	B-EX 2.40
Case Problems	B-EX 2.41
Internet Assignments	B-EX 2.45
Quick Check Answers	B-EX 2.45

Bonus Excel Functions Reference	**B-EX R1**
Index	**1**
Task Reference	**9**
File Finder	**15**

Acknowledgments

We would like to thank the many people whose invaluable contributions made this book possible. First, thanks to our reviewers: Rory DeSimone, University of Florida; Michael Feiler, Merritt College; Eric Johnston, Vatterott College; Mary McIntosh, Red River College; Donna Occhifinto, County College of Morris; and IdaLynn Gedde, Arapahoe Community College. At Course Technology we would like to thank Rachel Crapser, Managing Editor; Kathy Finnegan, Senior Product Manager; Brianna Germain, Associate Product Manager; Christine Gatliffe, Production Editor; John Bosco, Manuscript Quality Assurance Manager; and Marianne Broughey, Harris Bierhoff, and John Freitas, Quality Assurance Testers. A special thanks to Jane Pedicini, Development Editor, for her dedication and hard work in completing this text.

June Jamrich Parsons

Dan Oja

Roy Ageloff

Patrick Carey

www.course.com/NewPerspectives

New Perspectives on

MICROSOFT® OFFICE XP

TUTORIAL 1   OFF 3

Introducing Microsoft Office XP

Delmar Office Supplies	
Exploring Microsoft Office XP	4
Starting Office Programs	9
Using Personalized Menus and Toolbars	13
Saving and Closing a File	16
Opening a File	18
Printing a File	20
Getting Help	21
Exiting Programs	23

Read This Before You Begin

To the Student

Data Disks
To complete this tutorial and the Review Assignments, you need one Data Disk. Your instructor will either provide you with the Data Disk or ask you to make your own.

If you are making your own Data Disk, you will need **one** blank, formatted high-density disk. You will need to copy a set of files and/or folders from a file server, standalone computer, or the Web onto your disk. Your instructor will tell you which computer, drive letter, and folder contain the files you need. You could also download the files by going to www.course.com and following the instructions on the screen.

The information below shows you which folder goes on your disk, so that you will have enough disk space to complete the tutorial and Review Assignments:

Data Disk 1
Write this on the disk label:
Data Disk 1: Introducing Office XP
Put this folder on the disk:
Tutorial.01

When you begin the tutorial, be sure you are using the correct Data Disk. Refer to the "File Finder" chart at the back of this text for more detailed information on which files are used in the tutorial. See the inside front or inside back cover of this book for more information on Data Disk files, or ask your instructor or technical support person for assistance.

Using Your Own Computer
If you are going to work through this tutorial using your own computer, you need:

- **Computer System** Microsoft Windows 98, NT, 2000 Professional, or higher must be installed on your computer. This book assumes a typical installation of Microsoft Office XP.

- **Data Disk** You will not be able to complete this tutorial or Review Assignments using your own computer until you have your Data Disk.

Visit Our World Wide Web Site
Additional materials designed especially for you are available on the World Wide Web.
Go to www.course.com/NewPerspectives.

To the Instructor

The Data Disk Files are available on the Instructor's Resource Kit for this title. Follow the instructions in the Help file on the CD-ROM to install the programs to your network or standalone computer. For information on creating the Data Disk, see the "To the Student" section above.

You are granted a license to copy the Data Disk Files to any computer or computer network used by students who have purchased this book.

OBJECTIVES

In this tutorial you will:

- Explore the programs that comprise Microsoft Office
- Explore the benefits of integrating data between programs
- Start programs and switch between them
- Use personalized menus and toolbars
- Save and close a file
- Open an existing file
- Print a file
- Get Help
- Close files and exit programs

INTRODUCING MICROSOFT OFFICE XP

Preparing Promotional Materials for Delmar Office Supplies

CASE

Delmar Office Supplies

Delmar Office Supplies, a company in Wisconsin founded by Nicole Delmar in 1996, sells recycled office supplies to businesses and home-based offices around the world. The demand for quality recycled papers, reconditioned toner cartridges, and renovated office furniture has been growing each year. Nicole and all her employees use Microsoft Office XP, which provides everyone in the company the power and flexibility to store a variety of information, create consistent documents, and share data. In this tutorial, you'll review some of the latest documents the company's employees have created using Microsoft Office XP.

Exploring Microsoft Office XP

Microsoft Office XP, or simply **Office**, is a collection of the most popular Microsoft programs: Word, Excel, PowerPoint, Access, and Outlook. Each Office program contains valuable tools to help you accomplish many tasks, such as composing reports, analyzing data, preparing presentations, and compiling information.

Microsoft Word 2002, or simply **Word**, is a **word processing program** you use to create text documents. The files you create in Word are called **documents**. Word offers many special features that help you compose and update all types of documents, ranging from letters and newsletters to reports, fliers, faxes, and even books—all in attractive and readable formats. You also can use Word to create, insert, and position figures, tables, and other graphics to enhance the look of your documents. Figure 1 shows a business letter that a sales representative composed with Word.

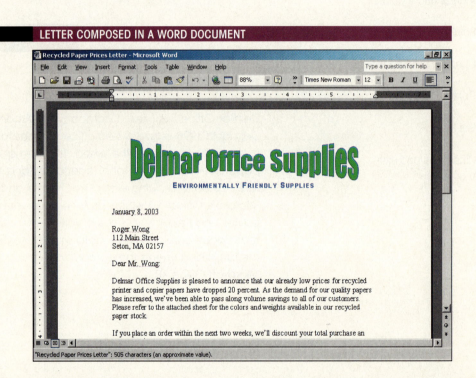

Figure 1 — LETTER COMPOSED IN A WORD DOCUMENT

Microsoft Excel 2002, or simply **Excel**, is a **spreadsheet program** you use to display, organize, and analyze numerical information. You can do some of this in Word with tables, but Excel provides many more tools for performing calculations than Word does. Its graphics capabilities also enable you to display data visually. You might, for example, generate a pie chart or bar chart to help readers quickly see the significance of and the connections between information. The files you create in Excel are called **workbooks**. Figure 2 shows an Excel workbook with a line chart that the Operations Department uses to track the company's financial performance.

INTRODUCING MICROSOFT OFFICE XP   OFF 5

| Figure 2 | FINANCIAL DATA IN AN EXCEL WORKBOOK |

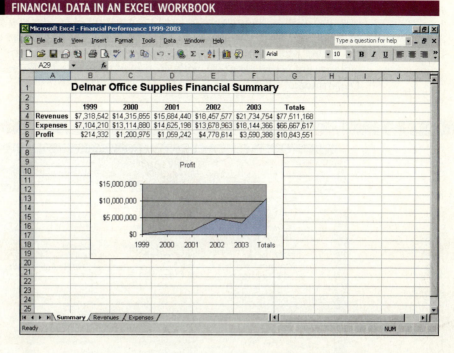

Microsoft PowerPoint 2002, or simply PowerPoint, is a presentation graphics program you use to create a collection of "slides" that can contain text, charts, pictures, and so on. The files you create in PowerPoint are called presentations. You can show these presentations on your computer monitor, project them onto a screen as a slide show, print them, share them over the Internet, or display them on the World Wide Web. You also can use PowerPoint to generate presentation-related documents such as audience handouts, outlines, and speakers' notes. Figure 3 shows an effective slide presentation the Sales Department created with PowerPoint to promote the latest product line.

| Figure 3 | SLIDE PRESENTATION CREATED IN POWERPOINT |

Microsoft Access 2002, or simply **Access**, is a **database program** you use to enter, organize, display, and retrieve related information. The files you create in Access are called **databases**. With Access you can create data entry forms to make data entry easier, and you can create professional reports to improve the readability of your data. Figure 4 shows a table in an Access database with customer names and addresses compiled by the Sales Department.

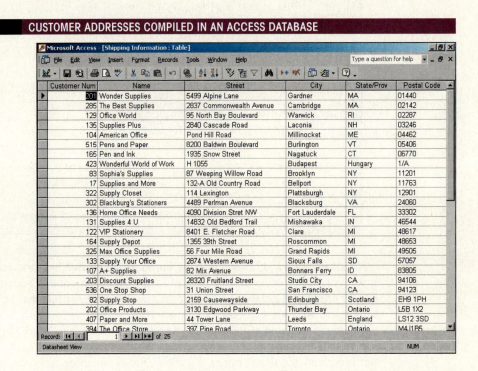

Figure 4: CUSTOMER ADDRESSES COMPILED IN AN ACCESS DATABASE

Microsoft Outlook 2002, or simply **Outlook**, is an **information management program** you use to send, receive, and organize e-mail; plan your schedule; arrange meetings; organize contacts; create a to-do list; and jot down notes. You also can use Outlook to print schedules, task lists, or phone directories and other documents. Figure 5 shows how Nicole Delmar uses Outlook to plan her schedule and create a to-do list.

INTRODUCING MICROSOFT OFFICE XP

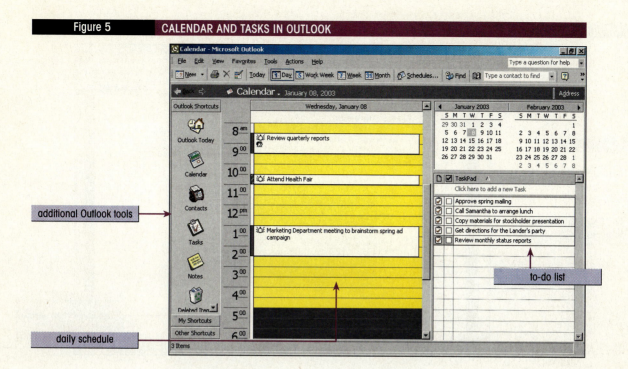

Figure 5: CALENDAR AND TASKS IN OUTLOOK

Although each Office program individually is a strong tool, their potential is even greater when used together.

Integrating Programs

One of the main advantages of Office is **integration**, the ability to share information between programs. Integration ensures consistency and accuracy, and it saves time because you don't have to re-enter the same information in several Office programs. The staff at Delmar Office Supplies uses the integration features of Office daily, including the following examples:

- The Accounting Department created an Excel bar chart on the last two years' fourth-quarter results, which they inserted into the quarterly financial report, created in Word. They added a hyperlink to the Word report that employees can click to open the Excel workbook and view the original data. See Figure 6.

Figure 6   WORD DOCUMENT WITH AN EXCEL CHART

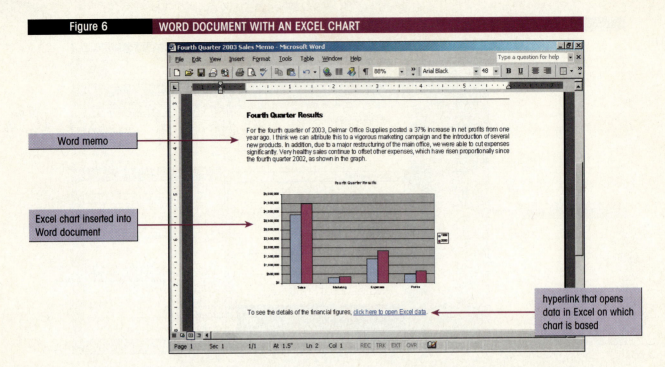

- An Excel pie chart of sales percentages by divisions of Delmar Office Supplies can be duplicated on a PowerPoint slide. The slide is part of the Operations Department's presentation to stockholders. See Figure 7.

Figure 7   POWERPOINT PRESENTATION WITH AN EXCEL CHART

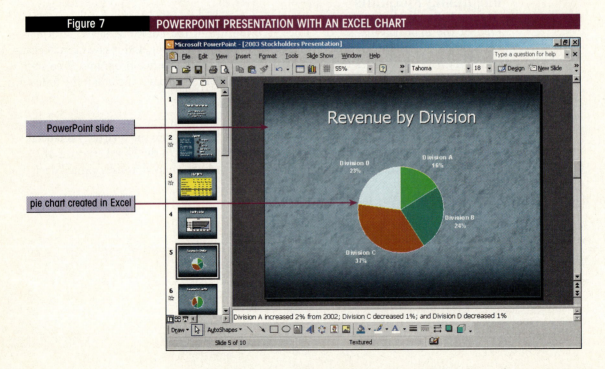

- An Access database or an Outlook contact list that stores the names and addresses of customers can be combined with a form letter that the Marketing Department created in Word, to produce a mailing promoting the company's newest products. See Figure 8.

6. Click the blank area above the vertical scroll box to move up one full screen, and then click the blank area below the vertical scroll box to move down a full screen.

7. Click the **vertical scroll box** and drag it to the top of the scroll bar to again change the area of the worksheet being displayed in the window.

You can also use the Go To dialog box and the Name box to jump directly to a specific cell in the worksheet, whether the cell is currently visible in the workbook window or not. Try this now.

To use the Go To dialog box and Name box:

1. Press the **F5** key to open the Go To dialog box.

2. Type **K55** in the Reference text box, and then click the **OK** button. Cell K55 is now the active cell.

3. Click the **Name** box, type **E6**, and then press the **Enter** key. Cell E6 becomes the active cell.

4. Press **Ctrl + Home** to make cell A1 the active cell.

Navigating Between Worksheets

A workbook is usually composed of several worksheets. The workbook shown in Figure 1-8 contains three worksheets (this is the default for new blank workbooks) labeled Sheet1, Sheet2, and Sheet3. To move between the worksheets, you click the sheet tab of the worksheet you want to display.

To move between worksheets:

1. Click the **Sheet2** tab. Sheet2, which is blank, appears in the workbook window. Notice that the Sheet2 tab is now white with the name "Sheet2" in a bold font. This is a visual indicator that Sheet2 is the active worksheet.

2. Click the **Sheet1** tab to return to the first sheet in the workbook.

Some workbooks will contain so many worksheets that some sheet tabs will be hidden from view. If that is the case, you can use the tab scrolling buttons located in the lower-left corner of the workbook window to scroll through the list of sheet tabs. Figure 1-9 describes the actions of the four tab scrolling buttons. Note that clicking the tab scrolling buttons does not change the active sheet; clicking the tab scrolling buttons allows you to view the other sheet tabs in the workbook. To change the active sheet, you must click the sheet tab itself.

| Figure 1-9 | TAB SCROLLING BUTTONS |

first sheet — last sheet
previous sheet — next sheet

Now that you have some basic skills navigating through a worksheet and a workbook, you can begin working with Mike's financial records. Some of the figures from the Lawn Wizards' April income statement have already been entered in an Excel workbook.

Opening and Saving a Workbook

There are several ways of accessing a saved workbook. To open a workbook, you can click the Open command on Excel's File menu or you can click the Open button found on the Standard toolbar. You can also click the Workbooks link found in the Task Pane (if the Task Pane is visible to you). Any of these methods will display the Open dialog box. Once the Open dialog box is displayed, you have to navigate through the hierarchy of folders and drives on your computer or network to locate the workbook file.

Mike has saved the income statement with the filename "Lawn1." Locate and open this file now.

To open the Lawn1 workbook:

1. Place your Excel Data Disk in the appropriate drive.

   TROUBLE? If you don't have a Data Disk, you need to contact your instructor or technical support person who will either give you one or give you instructions for creating your own. You can also review the instructions on the Read This Before You Begin page located at the front of this book.

2. Click the **Open** button on the Standard toolbar. The Open dialog box is displayed. See Figure 1-10.

| Figure 1-10 | OPEN DIALOG BOX |

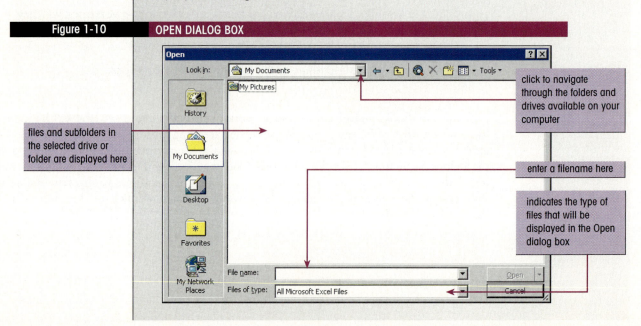

3. Click the **Look in** list arrow to display the list of available drives. Locate the drive that contains your Data Disk. This text assumes your Data Disk is a 3½-inch disk in drive A.

4. Click the drive that contains your Data Disk. A list of documents and folders on your Data Disk appears in the list box.

5. In the list of file and folder names, double-click **Tutorial.01**, double-click **Tutorial** to display the contents of the folder, and then click **Lawn1**.

6. Click the **Open** button (you could also have double-clicked Lawn1 to open the file). The workbook opens, displaying the income figures in the Sheet1 worksheet. Note that if the Task Pane was previously visible, it has now disappeared. See Figure 1-11.

Figure 1-11 **LAWN1 WORKBOOK**

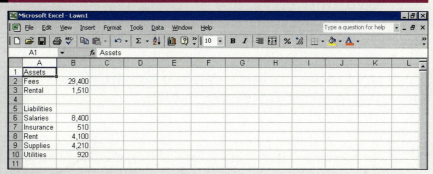

TROUBLE? In true accounting terminology, the word "Revenues" should be used in this income statement instead of the word "Assets," and the word "Expenses" should be used instead of the word "Liabilities." If requested by your instructor, you can change these terms to reflect accounting practices. Making this change will cause discrepancies between your screen and the figures and text references throughout the rest of this tutorial; however, such discrepancies will not interfere with your ability to complete the tasks in the tutorial.

Sometimes you will want to open a new blank workbook. Excel allows you to have several workbooks open at the same time. To create a new blank workbook, you can click the New button on the Standard toolbar.

Before going further in the Lawn1 workbook, you should make a copy of the file with a new name. This will allow you to go back to the original version of the file if necessary.

Mike suggests that you save the file with the name "Lawn2."

To save the workbook with a different name:

1. Click **File** on the menu bar, and then click **Save As**. The Save As dialog box opens with the current workbook name in the File name text box. Note that the Tutorial folder on your Data Disk is automatically opened, so you do not have to navigate through your computer's hierarchy of folders and drives.

2. Click immediately to the right of "Lawn1" in the File name text box, press the **Backspace** key, and then type **2**.

3. Make sure that "Microsoft Excel Workbook" is displayed in the Save as type list box. See Figure 1-12.

Figure 1-12 SAVE AS DIALOG BOX

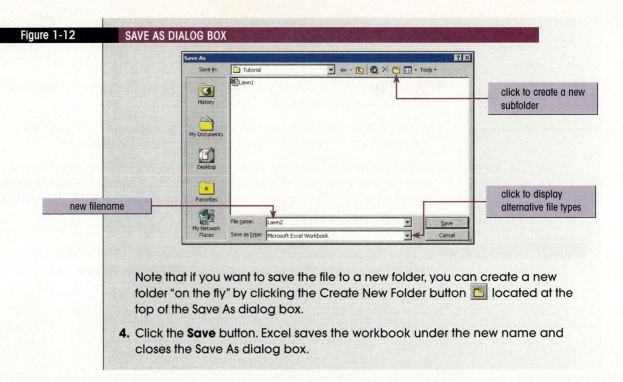

Note that if you want to save the file to a new folder, you can create a new folder "on the fly" by clicking the Create New Folder button located at the top of the Save As dialog box.

4. Click the **Save** button. Excel saves the workbook under the new name and closes the Save As dialog box.

By default, Excel saves the workbooks in Microsoft Excel Workbook format. If you are creating a report that will be read by applications other than Excel (or versions of Excel prior to Excel 2002), you can select a different type from the Save as type list box in the Save (or Save As) dialog box.

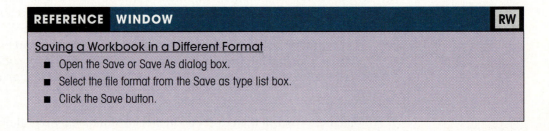

REFERENCE WINDOW

Saving a Workbook in a Different Format
- Open the Save or Save As dialog box.
- Select the file format from the Save as type list box.
- Click the Save button.

Figure 1-13 displays a partial list of the other formats you can save your workbook as. You can add other formats by running the Excel 2002 or Office XP installation program. Note that some of the formats described in Figure 1-13 save only the active worksheet, not the entire workbook.

Figure 1-13 SOME OF THE FILE FORMATS SUPPORTED BY EXCEL

FORMAT	DESCRIPTION
CSV (Comma delimited)	Saves the active worksheet as a text file with columns separated by commas
DBF2, DBF3, DBF4	Saves the active worksheet as a dBASE table in the different versions of dBASE
Formatted Text (Space delimited)	Saves the active worksheet as a text file with columns separated by spaces
Microsoft Excel 2.1, 3.0, 4.0 Worksheet	Saves the workbook in the earliest versions of Excel
Microsoft Excel 5.0, 95, 97, 2000 Workbook	Saves the workbook in an earlier version of Excel
Text (Tab delimited)	Saves the active worksheet as a text file with columns separated by tabs
Web Archive	Saves the workbook as a Web site, enclosed within a single file
Web Page	Saves the workbook in HTML format, suitable for use as a Web page
WK1, WK2, WK3	Saves the active worksheet as a Lotus 1-2-3 spreadsheet
WK4 (1-2-3)	Saves the workbook as a Lotus 1-2-3 document
WQ1	Saves the active worksheet as a Quattro Pro spreadsheet
XML Spreadsheet	Saves the workbook in XML format, suitable for use in Web queries

In this text you will use only the Microsoft Excel Workbook format.

Working with Ranges

The data in the Lawn2 workbook contains the assets and liabilities for Lawn Wizards during the month of April, 2003. Mike would like to include this information in a title at the top of the worksheet. To make room for the title, you have to move the current content down a few rows. To move a group of cells in a worksheet, you have to first understand how Excel handles cells.

A group of worksheet cells is called a **cell range**, or **range**. Ranges can be either adjacent or nonadjacent. An **adjacent range** is a single rectangular block such as all of the data entered in cells A1 through B10 of the Lawn2 workbook. A **nonadjacent range** is comprised of two or more separate adjacent ranges. You could view the Lawn2 workbook as containing two non-adjacent ranges: the first range, cell A1 through cell B3, contains the company's assets, and the second range, cell A5 through cell B10, displays the company's liabilities.

Just as a cell reference indicates the location of the cell on the worksheet, a range reference indicates the location and size of the range. For adjacent ranges, the range reference identifies the cells in the upper-left and lower-right corners of the rectangle, with the individual cell references separated by a colon. For example, the range reference for Mike's income statement is A1:B10. If the range is nonadjacent, a semicolon separates the rectangular blocks, such as A1:B3;A5:B10, which refers to data in Mike's income statement, but does not include the blank row (row 4), which separates the assets from the liabilities.

Selecting Ranges

Working with ranges of cells makes working with the data in a worksheet easier. Once you know how to select ranges of cells, you can move and copy the data anywhere in the worksheet or workbook.

> **REFERENCE WINDOW**
>
> **Selecting Adjacent or Nonadjacent Ranges of Cells**
>
> To select an adjacent range of cells:
> - Click a cell in the corner of the rectangle that comprises the adjacent range.
> - Press and hold down the left mouse button, and drag the pointer through the cells you want selected.
> - Release the mouse button.
>
> To select a nonadjacent range of cells:
> - Select an adjacent range of cells.
> - Press and hold down the Ctrl key, and then select another adjacent cell range.
> - With the Ctrl key still pressed, continue to select other cell ranges until all of the ranges are selected.
> - Release the mouse button and the Ctrl key.

Next you'll select the adjacent range A1 through B10.

To select the range A1:B10:

1. Click cell **A1** (if necessary) to make it the active cell, and then press and hold down the left mouse button.

2. With the mouse button still pressed, drag the pointer to cell **B10**.

3. Release the mouse button. All of the cells in the range A1:B10 are now highlighted, indicating that they are selected. See Figure 1-14.

Figure 1-14 SELECTING RANGE A1:B10

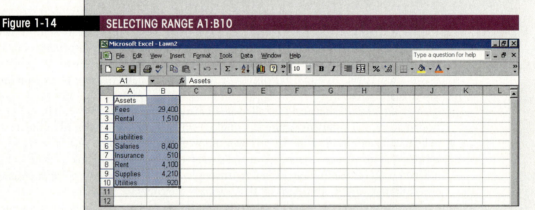

To deselect the range, you can click any cell in the worksheet.

4. Click cell **C1** to deselect the range.

To select a nonadjacent range, you begin by selecting an adjacent range, and then you press and hold down the Ctrl key and select other adjacent ranges. Release the Ctrl key and the mouse button when you are finished. Next you'll select the assets and then select the liabilities in the income statement.

To select the nonadjacent range A1:B3;A5:B10:

1. Select the range **A1:B3**.

2. Press and hold down the **Ctrl** key.

3. Select the range **A5:B10**. See Figure 1-15.

| Figure 1-15 | SELECTING THE NONADJACENT RANGE A1:B3;A5:B10 |

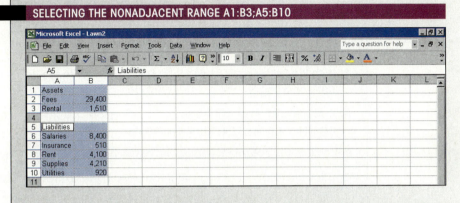

4. Click any cell in the worksheet to deselect the range.

Other Selection Techniques

To select a large range of data, Excel will automatically scroll horizontally or vertically to display additional cells in the worksheet. Selecting a large range of cells using the mouse drag technique can be slow and frustrating. For this reason, Excel provides keyboard shortcuts to quickly select large blocks of data without having to drag through the worksheet to select the necessary cells. Figure 1-16 describes some of these selection techniques.

Figure 1-16	OTHER RANGE SELECTION TECHNIQUES
TO SELECT...	**ACTION**
A large range of cells	Click the first cell in the range, press and hold down the Shift key, and then click the last cell in the range. All of the cells between the first and last cell are selected.
All cells on the worksheet	Click the Select All button, the gray rectangle in the upper-left corner of the worksheet where the row and column headings meet.
All cells in an entire row or column	Click the row or column heading.
A range of cells containing data	Click the first cell in the range, press and hold down the Shift key, and then double-click the side of the active cell in which you want to extend the selection. Excel extends the selection up to the first empty cell.

Try some of the techniques described in Figure 1-16 using the income statement.

To select large ranges of cells:

1. Click cell **A1** to make it the active cell.

2. Press and hold down the **Shift** key, and then click cell **B10**. Note that all of the cells between A1 and B10 are selected.

> **TROUBLE?** If the range A1:B10 is not selected, try again, but make sure you hold down the Shift key while you click cell B10.
>
> 3. Release the Shift key.
> 4. Click cell **A1** to remove the selection.
> 5. Press and hold down the **Shift** key, and move the pointer to the bottom edge of cell A1 until the mouse pointer changes to ⇖.
> 6. Double-click the bottom edge of cell **A1**. The selection extends to cell A3, the last cell before the blank cell A4.
> 7. With the Shift key still pressed, move the pointer to the right edge of the selection until, once again, the pointer changes to ⇖.
> 8. Double-click the right edge of the selection. The selection extends to the last non-blank column in the worksheet.
> 9. Click the **A** column heading. All of the cells in column A are selected.
> 10. Click the **1** row heading. All of the cells in the first row are selected.

Moving a Selection of Cells

Now that you know various ways to select a range of cells, you can move the income statement data to another location in the worksheet. To move a cell range, you first select it and then position the pointer over the selection border and drag the selection to a new location. Copying a range of cells is similar to moving a range. The only difference is that you must press the Ctrl key while you drag the selection to its new location. A copy of the original data appears at the location of the pointer when you release the mouse button.

You can also move a selection to a new worksheet in the current workbook. To do this, you press and hold down the Alt key and then drag the selection over the sheet tab of the new worksheet. Excel will automatically make that worksheet the active sheet, so you can drag the selection into its new location on the worksheet.

Next you'll move the cells in the range A1:B10 to a new location, beginning at cell A5.

> ### To move the range A1:B10 down four rows:
>
> 1. Select the range **A1:B10**.
> 2. Move the pointer over the bottom border of the selection until the pointer changes to ⇖.
> 3. Press and hold down the left mouse button, and then drag the selection down four rows. A ScreenTip appears indicating the new range reference of the selection. See Figure 1-17.

Figure 1-17 MOVING A SELECTION TO THE RANGE A5:B14

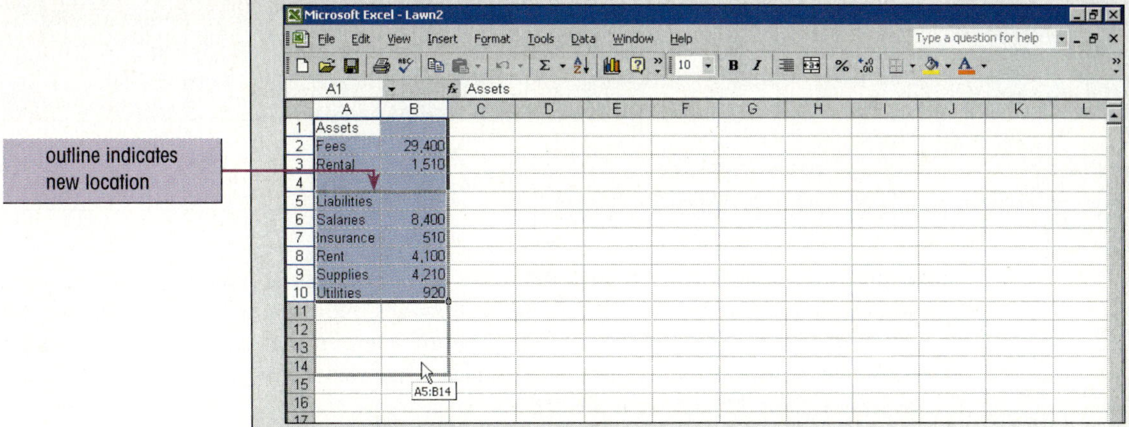

outline indicates new location

4. When the ScreenTip displays "A5:B14", release the left mouse button. The income statement is now moved to range A5:B14.

5. Click cell **A1** to remove the selection.

At this point, you have made space for a title and other information to be placed above the income statement. In the next session you will learn how to enter the new text into the worksheet, as well as how to edit the contents already there.

To exit Excel:

1. Click **File** on the menu bar, and then click **Exit**.

2. When Excel prompts you to save your changes, click the **Yes** button. Excel saves the changes to the workbook and closes.

Session 1.1 QUICK CHECK

1. A(n) ___Cell___ is the place on the worksheet where a column and row intersect.

2. Cell ___D2___ refers to the intersection of the fourth column and second row.

3. What combination of keys can you press to make A1 the active cell in the worksheet? *Control Home*

4. To make Sheet2 the active worksheet, you *Click Sheet2 Tab.*

5. Describe the two types of cell ranges in Excel.

6. What is the cell reference for the rectangular group of cells that extends from cell A5 down to cell F8?

7. Describe how you move a cell range from the Sheet1 worksheet to the Sheet2 worksheet.

SESSION 1.2

In this session, you will enter text and values into a worksheet. You will also enter formulas using basic arithmetic operators. You will use Excel's edit mode to change the value in a cell. You will insert rows and columns into a worksheet and modify the width of a column. You will insert, delete, and move worksheets, and you will rename sheet tabs. Finally, you will create a hard copy of your workbook by sending its contents to a printer.

Entering Information into a Worksheet

In the previous session, you learned about the different parts of Excel's workbook window, and you learned how to work with cells and cell ranges. Now you will enter some new information in Mike's April income statement. The information that you enter in the cells of a worksheet can consist of text, values, or formulas. Mike wants you to enter text that describes the income statement located on Sheet1.

Entering Text

Text entries include any combination of letters, symbols, numbers, and spaces. Although text is sometimes used as data, text is more often used to describe the data contained in the workbook. For example, the range A5:A14 of the income statement indicates the various asset and liability categories.

To enter text in a worksheet, you click the cell in which you want the text placed and then type the text you want entered. Excel automatically aligns text with the left edge of the cell. Mike wants you to enter the text labels "Lawn Wizards" in cell A1 and "Income Statement" in cell A2.

To enter labels in cell A1 and A2:

1. If you took a break after the previous session, make sure Excel is running and the Lawn2 workbook is open.
2. Verify that Sheet1 is the active worksheet in the Lawn2 workbook.
3. Click cell **A1** if necessary to make it the active cell.
4. Type **Lawn Wizards** and then press the **Enter** key.
5. In cell A2, type **Income Statement** and then press the **Enter** key. See Figure 1-18.

   TROUBLE? If you make a mistake as you type, you can correct the error with the Backspace key. If you realize you made an error after pressing the Enter key, reenter the text by repeating Steps 3 through 5.

Figure 1-18   **ADDING NEW TEXT TO THE INCOME STATEMENT**

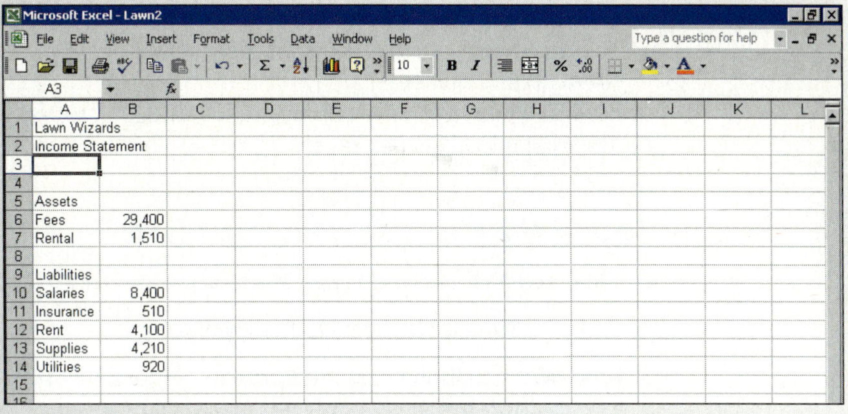

Note that even though you entered text in cells A1 and A2, the text appears to flow into cells B1 and B2. When you enter a text string longer than the width of the active cell, Excel will display the additional text if the cells to the right of the active cell are blank. If those cells are not blank, then Excel will truncate the display (though the entire text is still present in the cell). As you will see later, you can increase the width of the column if the text is cut off.

Entering Dates

Dates are treated as separate from text in Excel. As you will learn later, Excel includes several special functions and commands to work with dates. For example, you can insert a function that will calculate the number of days between two dates (you will learn more about this in the next tutorial). To enter a date, separate the parts of the date with a slash or hyphen. For example, the date April 1, 2003 can be entered as either "4/1/2003" or "1-Apr-2003".

You can also enter the date as the text string "April 1, 2003", in which case Excel might automatically convert the text to "1-Apr-2003". You can change the format used by Excel to display dates by changing the cell's format. You will learn about date formats in Tutorial 3.

Mike wants the date "4/1/2003" to appear in cell A3.

To insert the date in cell A3:

1. Verify that cell A3 is the active cell.

2. Type **4/1/2003** and then press the **Enter** key.

   TROUBLE? Your system may be set up to display dates using the mm/dd/yy format; therefore, you may see the date displayed as 4/1/03 rather than 4/1/2003.

Entering Values

Values are numbers that represent a quantity of some type: the number of units in an inventory, stock prices, an exam score, and so on. Values can be numbers such as 378 and 25.275, or negative numbers such as –55.208. Values can also be expressed as currency ($4,571.25) or percentages (7.5%). Dates and times are also values, though that fact is hidden from you by the way Excel displays date information.

As you type information into a cell, Excel determines whether the information you have entered can be treated as a value. If so, Excel will automatically recognize the value type and right-align the value within the cell. Not all numbers are treated as values. For example, Excel treats a telephone number (1-800-555-8010) or a Social Security number (372-70-9654) as a text entry.

Mike would like to add a miscellaneous category to the list of monthly liabilities. In April, the total miscellaneous expenses incurred by Lawn Wizards totaled $351.

To add the miscellaneous expenses:

1. Click cell **A15** and then type **Misc** as the category.

2. Press the **Tab** key to move to the next column.

3. Type **351** and then press the **Enter** key. Figure 1-19 shows the new entry in the income statement.

Figure 1-19   ADDING A NEW CATEGORY AND VALUE TO THE INCOME STATEMENT

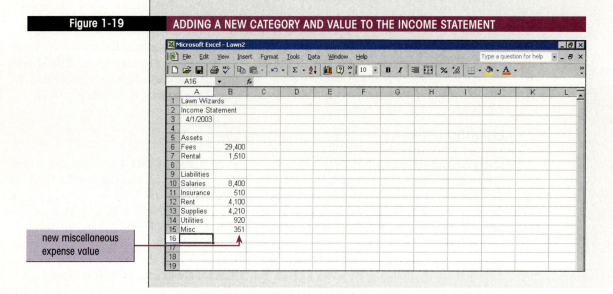

new miscellaneous expense value

Entering Formulas

A **formula** is an expression that is used to calculate a value. You can enter a formula by typing the expression into the active cell, or in special cases Excel will automatically insert the formula for you. Excel formulas always begin with an equal sign (=) followed by an expression that calculates a value. If you do not start with an equal sign, Excel will treat the expression you enter as text. The expression can contain one or more **arithmetic operators**, such as +, −, *, or /, that are applied to either values or cells in the workbook. Figure 1-20 gives some examples of Excel formulas.

Figure 1-20 ARITHMETIC OPERATORS USED IN FORMULAS

ARITHMETIC OPERATION	ARITHMETIC OPERATOR	EXAMPLE	DESCRIPTION
Addition	+	=10+A5 =B1+B2+B3	Adds 10 to the value in cell A5 Adds the values of cells B1, B2, and B3
Subtraction	–	=C9–B2 =1–D2	Subtracts the value in B2 from the value in cell C9 Subtracts the value in cell D2 from 1
Multiplication	*	=C9*B9 =E5*0.06	Multiplies the value in cell C9 by the value in cell B9 Multiplies the value in cell E5 by 0.06
Division	/	=C9/B9 =D15/12	Divides the value in cell C9 by the value in cell B9 Divides the value in cell D15 by 12
Exponentiation	^	=B5^3 =3^B5	Raises the value in cell B5 to the third power Raises 3 to the power specified in cell B5

REFERENCE WINDOW

Entering a Formula
- Click the cell where you want the formula value to appear.
- Type = and then type the expression that calculates the value you want.
- For formulas that include cell references, such as B2 or D78, you can type the cell reference or you can use the mouse or arrow keys to select each cell.
- When the formula is complete, press the Enter key.

If an expression contains more than one arithmetic operator, Excel performs the calculation in the order of precedence. The **order of precedence** is a set of predefined rules that Excel follows to unambiguously calculate a formula by determining which operator is applied first, which operator is applied second, and so forth. First, Excel performs exponentiation (^). Second, Excel performs multiplication (*) or division (/). Third, Excel performs addition (+) or subtraction (-).

For example, because multiplication has precedence over addition, the formula *=3+4*5* has the value 23. If the expression contains two or more operators with the same level of precedence, Excel applies them going from left to right in the expression. In the formula *=4*10/8*, Excel first multiplies 4 by 10 and then divides the product by 8 to return the value 5.

You can add parentheses to a formula to make it easier to interpret or to change the order of operations. Excel will calculate any expression contained within the parentheses before any other part of the formula. The formula *=(3+4)*5* first calculates the value of *3+4* and then multiplies the total by *5* to return the value *35* (note that without the parentheses, Excel would return a value of *23* as noted in the previous paragraph). Figure 1-21 shows other examples of Excel formulas in which the precedence order is applied to return a value.

Figure 1-21 — EXAMPLES ILLUSTRATING ORDER OF PRECEDENCE RULES

FORMULA VALUE A1=10, B1=20, C1=3	ORDER OF PRECEDENCE RULE	RESULT
=A1+B1*C1	Multiplication before addition	70
=(A1+B1)*C1	Expression inside parentheses executed before expression outside	90
=A1/B1+C1	Division before addition	3.5
=A1/(B1+C1)	Expression inside parentheses executed before expression outside	.435
=A1/B1*C1	Two operators at same precedence level, leftmost operator evaluated first	1.5
=A1/(B1*C1)	Expression inside parentheses executed before expression outside	.166667

The Lawn2 workbook contains the asset and liability values for various categories, but it doesn't include the total assets and liabilities, nor does it display Lawn Wizards' net income (assets minus liabilities) for the month of April. Mike suggests that you add formulas to calculate these values now.

To calculate the total assets for the month of April:

1. Click cell **A8** to make it the active cell.
2. Type **Total** and then press the **Tab** key twice.
3. In cell C8, type **=B6+B7** (the income from fees and rental for the month).

   Note that as you type in the cell reference, Excel surrounds each cell with a different colored border that matches the color of the cell reference in the formula. As shown in Figure 1-22, Excel surrounds cell B6 with a blue border matching the blue used for the cell reference. Green is used for the B7 cell border and cell reference.

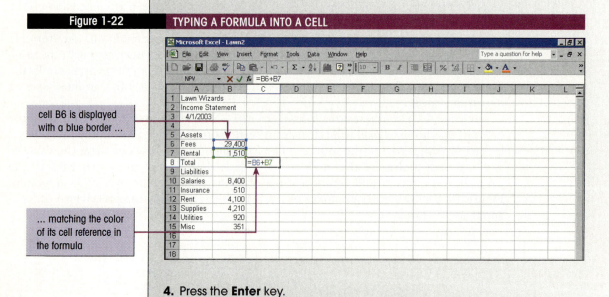

Figure 1-22 — TYPING A FORMULA INTO A CELL

cell B6 is displayed with a blue border ...

... matching the color of its cell reference in the formula

4. Press the **Enter** key.

   The total assets value displayed in cell C8 is 30,910.

You can also enter formulas interactively by clicking each cell in the formula rather than typing in the cell reference. Using this approach reduces the possibility of error caused by typing in an incorrect cell reference.

To enter a formula by pointing and clicking:

1. Click cell **A16** to make it the active cell.

2. Type **Total** and then press the **Tab** key twice.

   TROUBLE? Note that when you started to type the word "Total" in cell A16, Excel automatically completed it for you. Since some worksheets will repeat the same word or phrase several times within a row or column, this AutoComplete feature can save you time.

3. In cell C16, type **=** and then click cell **B10**. Excel automatically inserts the reference to cell B10 into your formula.

4. Type **+** and then click cell **B11**.

5. Type **+** and then click cell **B12**.

6. Continue to select the rest of the liabilities in the range B13:B15, so that the formula in cell C16 reads **=B10+B11+B12+B13+B14+B15**. Do not type an equal sign after you click cell B15.

7. Press the **Enter** key. The total liabilities value "18,491" appears in cell C16.

   Now you can calculate the net income for the month of April.

8. In cell A18, enter **Net Income** and then press the **Tab** key twice.

9. In cell C18, enter the formula **=C8−C16** by clicking to select the cell references, and then press the **Enter** key. Figure 1-23 shows the completed formulas in the income statement.

Figure 1-23 **TOTAL ASSETS, LIABILITIES, AND NET INCOME**

	A	B	C
1	Lawn Wizards		
2	Income Statement		
3	4/1/2003		
4			
5	Assets		
6	Fees	29,400	
7	Rental	1,510	
8	Total		30,910
9	Liabilities		
10	Salaries	8,400	
11	Insurance	510	
12	Rent	4,100	
13	Supplies	4,210	
14	Utilities	920	
15	Misc	351	
16	Total		18,491
17			
18	Net Income		12,419
19			
20			

Working with Rows and Columns

Mike examines the worksheet and points out that it is difficult to separate the assets from the liabilities. He would like you to insert a blank row between row 8 and row 9. You could do this by moving the cell range A9:C18 down one row, but there is another way. Excel allows you to insert rows or columns into your worksheet.

Inserting a Row or Column

To insert a new row, you select a cell in the row where you want the new row placed. You then select Rows from the Insert menu. Excel will shift that row down, inserting a new blank row in its place. Inserting a new column follows the same process. Select a cell in the column where you want the new column inserted, and click Columns on the Insert menu. Excel will shift that column to the right, inserting a new blank column in its place.

To insert multiple rows or columns, select multiple cells before applying the Insert command. For example, to insert two new blank rows, select two adjacent cells in the same column, and click Rows on the Insert menu. To insert three new blank columns, select three adjacent cells in the same row, and click Columns on the Insert menu.

You can also insert individual cells within a row or column (rather than an entire row or column). To do this, select the range where you want the new cells placed, and click Cells on the Insert menu. Excel provides four options:

- **Shift cells right**: Inserts new blank cells into the selected region, and moves the selected cells to the right. The new cells will have the same number of rows and columns as the selected cells.
- **Shift cells down**: Inserts new blank cells into the selected region, and moves the selected cells down. The new cells will have the same number of rows and columns as the selected cells.
- **Entire row**: Inserts an entire blank row.
- **Entire column**: Inserts an entire blank column.

You can also insert rows and columns by right-clicking the selected cells and choosing Insert on the shortcut menu. This is equivalent to clicking the Cells command on the Insert menu.

REFERENCE WINDOW | RW

Inserting New Cells Into a Worksheet

To insert a new column or row in the worksheet:
- Select a cell where you want to insert the new column or row.
- Click Insert on the menu bar, and then click Columns or Rows; or right-click the selected cell and then click Insert on the shortcut menu.
- Click the Entire column or Entire row option button.

To insert new cells into the worksheet:
- Select the cell range where you want to insert the new cells.
- Click Insert on the menu bar, and then click Cells; or right-click the selected cell and then click Insert on the shortcut menu.
- Click the Shift cells right option button to move the selected cells to the right, or click the Shift cells down button to move the selected cells down.

Now that you have seen how to insert new cells into your worksheet, you'll insert three new blank cells into the range A9:C9.

To insert three new cells into the worksheet:

1. Select the range **A9:C9**.

2. Click **Insert** on the menu bar, and then click **Cells**.

3. Click the **Shift cells down** option button, if necessary. See Figure 1-24.

Figure 1-24   INSERT DIALOG BOX

4. Click the **OK** button.

   Excel inserts new blank cells in the range A9:C9 and shifts the rest of the income statement down one row.

   TROUBLE? Excel displays an Insert Options button on the lower-right corner of cell C9. You can use this button to define how the new cells should be formatted. You will learn about formatting in Tutorial 3.

When you insert a new row, the formulas in the worksheet are automatically updated to reflect the changing position. For example, the formula for Net Income has changed from =C8–C16 to =C8–C17 to reflect the new location of the total liabilities cell. You will learn more about how formulas are adjusted in Tutorial 2.

Clearing or Deleting a Row or Column

Mike wants to make one further change to the income statement. He wants to consolidate the supplies and miscellaneous categories into one entry. Your first task will be to remove the current contents of the range A14:B14 (the supplies category). Excel provides two ways of removing data. One way, called **clearing**, simply deletes the contents of the cells. To clear the contents of a cell, you use either the Delete key or the Clear command on the Edit menu. Clearing the contents of a cell does not change the structure of the workbook; that is, the row is not removed from the worksheet. Do not press the spacebar to enter a blank character in an attempt to clear a cell's content. Excel treats a blank character as text, so even though the cell appears to be empty, it is not.

To remove the supplies category data:

1. Select the range **A14:B14**.

2. Press the **Delete** key. The text and values in the range A14:B14 are cleared.

   Now you can enter the text for the supplies and miscellaneous category.

3. In cell A14, type **Supplies & Misc.** and then press the **Tab** key.

   Now enter the total for the new category.

4. In cell B14, type **4,561** and then press the **Enter** key.

   TROUBLE? Do not worry that the Supplies & Misc category label in cell A14 appears to be cut off. The adjacent cell is no longer empty, and cell A14 is not wide enough to display the entire text entry. You will correct this problem shortly.

Now you need to delete the miscellaneous category from the income statement. Excel provides similar options for deleting rows, columns, and cells as it does for inserting them. To delete a row, column, or cell from the worksheet, you first select the cell or range and then click Delete on the Edit menu (you can also right-click the selected range and choose Delete on the shortcut menu). Excel provides you with the following delete options:

- **Shift cells left**   Deletes the selected cells and shifts cells from the right into the selected region
- **Shift cells up**   Deletes the selected cells and shifts cells from the bottom up into the selected region
- **Entire row**   Deletes the entire row
- **Entire column**   Deletes the entire column

Because you no longer need the miscellaneous category, you will delete the cell range A16:C16.

To delete the cell range A16:C16:

1. Select the range **A16:C16**.

2. Click **Edit** on the menu bar, and then click **Delete**.

3. Select the **Shift cells up** option button if necessary, and then click the **OK** button. Excel deletes the contents of the cell range and moves the cells below up one row. See Figure 1-25.

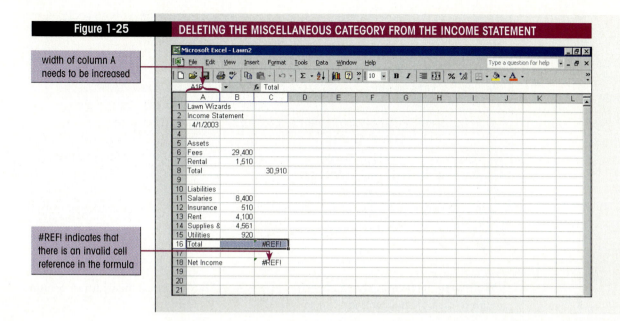

Figure 1-25 DELETING THE MISCELLANEOUS CATEGORY FROM THE INCOME STATEMENT

width of column A needs to be increased

#REF! indicates that there is an invalid cell reference in the formula

Mike immediately sees two problems. One problem is that the text entry in cell A14 is cut off. The second is that the liabilities total in cell C16 and the net income in cell C18 have been replaced with *#REF!* The *#REF!* entry is Excel's way of indicating that there is an invalid cell reference in a formula. Because Excel cannot calculate the formula's value, Excel displays this text as a warning. The invalid cell reference occurred when the miscellaneous total was deleted. Since that cell no longer exists, any formula that is based on that cell, such as the formula that calculates the liability, will return an error message, and since the total liability now returns an error message, the formula for the net income on which the total liability value is based also returns an error.

So you need to do two things: 1) increase the width of column A so that no text is truncated, and 2) revise the formula in cell C16 to remove the error message. First you will change the width of column A.

Increasing the Width of a Column or the Height of a Row

Excel provides several methods for changing the width of a column or the height of a row. You can click the dividing line of the column or row, or you can drag the dividing line to change the width of the column or the height of the row. You can also double-click the border of a column heading, and the column will increase in width to match the length of the longest entry in the column. Widths are expressed either in terms of the number of characters or the number of screen pixels.

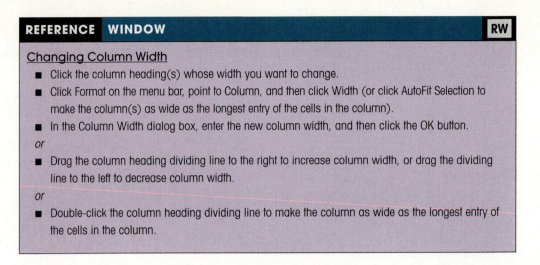

REFERENCE WINDOW

Changing Column Width
- Click the column heading(s) whose width you want to change.
- Click Format on the menu bar, point to Column, and then click Width (or click AutoFit Selection to make the column(s) as wide as the longest entry of the cells in the column).
- In the Column Width dialog box, enter the new column width, and then click the OK button.

or

- Drag the column heading dividing line to the right to increase column width, or drag the dividing line to the left to decrease column width.

or

- Double-click the column heading dividing line to make the column as wide as the longest entry of the cells in the column.

You'll drag the dividing line between columns A and B to increase the width of column A enough to display the complete text in cell A14.

To increase the width of column A:

1. Move the mouse pointer to the dividing line between the column A and column B headings until the pointer changes to ↔.

2. Click and drag the pointer to the right to a length of about **15** characters (or 110 pixels).

3. Release the mouse button. The entire text in cell A14 should now be visible. See Figure 1-26.

Figure 1-26   INCREASING THE WIDTH OF COLUMN A

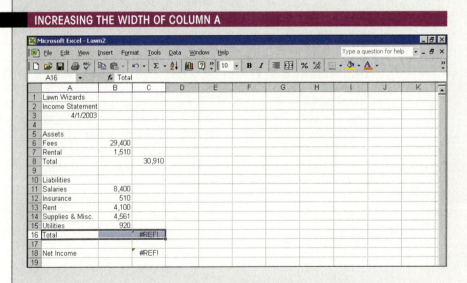

TROUBLE? If the text in cell A14 is still truncated, drag the dividing line further to the right.

Editing Your Worksheet

When you work in Excel you might make mistakes that you want to correct or undo. You have an error in the Lawn2 workbook of an invalid cell reference in cell C16. You could simply delete the formula in cell C16 and reenter the formula from scratch. However, there may be times when you will not want to change the entire contents of a cell, but merely edit a portion of the entry. For example, if a cell contains a large block of text or a complicated formula, you might not want to retype the text or formula completely. Instead, you can edit a cell by either selecting the cell and then clicking in the Formula bar to make the changes or by double-clicking the cell to open the cell in **edit mode**.

Working in Edit Mode

When you are working in edit mode or editing the cell using the Formula bar, some of the keys on your keyboard act differently than they do when you are not editing the content of a cell. For example, the Home, Delete, Backspace, and End keys do not move the insertion point to different cells in the worksheet; rather they move the insertion point to different locations within the cell. The Home key, for example, moves the insertion point to the beginning of whatever text has been entered into the cell. The End key moves the insertion point to the end of the cell's text. The left and right arrow keys move the insertion point backward and forward through the text in the cell. The Backspace key deletes the character immediately to the left of the insertion point, and the Delete key deletes the character at the location of the insertion point. Once you are finished editing the cell, press the Enter key to leave editing mode or to remove the insertion point from the Formula bar.

> **REFERENCE WINDOW** RW
>
> **Editing a Cell**
> - Double-click the cell to begin edit mode; click the cell and press the F2 key to begin edit mode; or click the cell and then click in the Formula bar.
> - Use the Home, End, ←, or → keys to move the insertion point within the cell's content. Use the Delete and Backspace keys to erase characters.
> - Press the Enter key when finished, or if you are working in the Formula bar, click the Enter button.

Now you'll use edit mode to change the formula in cell C16.

To edit the formula in cell C16:

1. Double-click cell **C16**.

   An insertion point appears in the cell, indicating where new text will be inserted into the current cell expression. Note that the formula appears fine except for the *+#REF!* at the end of the expression. See Figure 1-27. This notation indicates that the cell reference used in the formula no longer points to a valid cell reference. In this case, the cell referenced was deleted. You can fix the error by deleting the *+#REF!* from the formula.

Figure 1-27 — EDITING THE FORMULA IN CELL C16

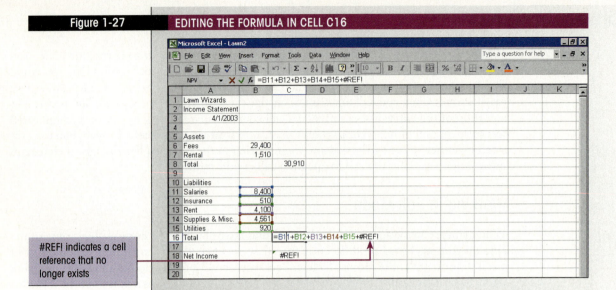

#REF! indicates a cell reference that no longer exists

2. Press the **End** key to move the blinking insertion point to the end of the cell.

3. Press the **Backspace** key six times to delete *+#REF!* from the formula.

4. Press the **Enter** key. The value 18,491 appears in cell C16, and the net income for the company is 12,419.

If you make a mistake as you type, you can press the Esc key or click the Cancel button on the Formula bar to cancel all changes you made while in edit mode.

Undoing an Action

Another way of fixing a mistake is to undo the action. Undoing an action cancels it, returning the workbook to its previous state. To undo an action, click the Undo button located on the Standard toolbar. As you work, Excel maintains a list of your actions, so you can undo most of the actions you perform on your workbook during your current session. To reverse more than one action, click the list arrow next to the Undo button and click the action you want to undo from the list. To see how this works, use the Undo button to remove the edit you just made to cell C16.

To undo your last action:

1. Click the **Undo** button on the Standard toolbar. The value *#REF!* appears again in cells C16 and C18 indicating that your last action, editing the formula in cell C16, has been undone.

If you find that you have gone too far in undoing your previous actions, you can go forward in the action list and redo those actions. To redo an action, you click the Redo button on the Standard toolbar. Use the Redo button now to return the formula in cell C16 to its edited state.

To redo your last action:

1. Click the **Redo** button on the Standard toolbar. The edited formula has been reinserted into cell C16 and the value 18,491 again appears in the cell.

   TROUBLE? If you don't see the Redo button, click the Toolbar Options button located on the right edge of the Standard toolbar, and then click to repeat the delete (the Redo button will now appear on the toolbar). You can also click the Repeat Delete command on the Edit menu (you might have to wait a few seconds for Excel to display the full Edit menu). After you undo an action, the Repeat command changes to reflect the action that has been undone so you can choose to repeat the action if undoing the action does not give you the result you want.

Through the use of edit mode and the Undo and Redo buttons, you should be able to correct almost any mistake you make in your Excel session.

Working with Worksheets

By default, Excel workbooks contain three worksheets labeled Sheet1, Sheet2, and Sheet3. You can add new worksheets or remove old ones. You can also give your worksheets more descriptive names. In the Lawn2 workbook, there is no data entered in the Sheet2 or Sheet3 worksheets. Mike suggests that you remove these sheets from the workbook.

Adding and Removing Worksheets

To delete a worksheet, you first select its sheet tab to make the worksheet the active sheet; then right-click the sheet tab and choose Delete from the shortcut menu. Try this now by deleting the Sheet2 and Sheet3 worksheets.

To delete the Sheet2 and Sheet3 worksheets:

1. Click the **Sheet2** tab to make Sheet2 the active sheet.
2. Right-click the sheet tab, and then click **Delete** on the shortcut menu. Sheet2 is deleted and Sheet3 becomes the active sheet.
3. Right-click the **Sheet3** tab, and then click **Delete**.

   There is now only one worksheet in the workbook.

After you have deleted the two unused sheets, Mike informs you that he wants to include a description of the workbook content and purpose. In other words, Mike wants to include a **documentation sheet**, a worksheet that provides information about the content and purpose of the workbook. A documentation sheet can be any information that you feel is important, for example, the name of the person who created the workbook or instructions on how to use the workbook. A documentation sheet is a valuable element if you intend to share the workbook with others. The documentation sheet is often the first worksheet in the workbook, though in this case Mike wants to place it at the end of the workbook.

To insert a new worksheet, you can either use the Insert Worksheet command or the right-click method. Using either method will insert a new worksheet before the active sheet.

To insert a new worksheet in the workbook:

1. Click **Insert** on the menu bar.

2. Click **Worksheet**. A new worksheet with the name "Sheet2" is placed at the beginning of your workbook.

Mike wants the documentation sheet to include the following information:

- The company name
- The date the workbook was originally created
- The person who created it
- The purpose of the workbook

You'll add this information to the new sheet in the Lawn2 workbook.

To insert the documentation information in the new worksheet:

1. Click cell **A1** if necessary, and then type **Lawn Wizards**.

2. Click cell **A3**, type **Date:** and then press the **Tab** key.

3. Enter the current date using the date format, mm/dd/yyyy. For example, if the date is April 5, 2003, enter the text string "4/5/2003." Press the **Enter** key.

4. In cell A4, type **Created By:** and then press the **Tab** key.

5. Enter your name in cell B4, and then press the **Enter** key.

6. Type **Purpose:** in cell A5, and then press the **Tab** key.

7. In cell B5, type **To record monthly income statements for the Lawn Wizards**, and then press the **Enter** key.

8. Increase the width of column A to **15** characters. Figure 1-28 shows the completed documentation sheet (your sheet will display a different name and date).

Figure 1-28   CREATING A DOCUMENTATION SHEET

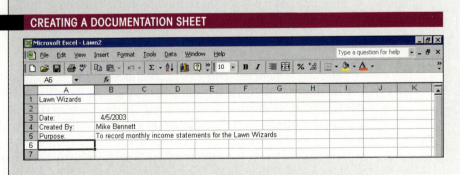

Renaming a Worksheet

The current sheet names "Sheet2" and "Sheet1" are not very descriptive. Mike suggests that you rename Sheet2 "Documentation" and Sheet1 "April Income". To rename a worksheet, you double-click the sheet tab to select the sheet name, and then you type a new name for the sheet.

Rename the sheet tabs using more meaningful names.

To rename the worksheets:

1. Double-click the **Sheet2** tab. Note that the name of the sheet is selected.
2. Type **Documentation** and then press the **Enter** key. The width of the sheet tab adjusts to the length of the name you type.
3. Double-click the **Sheet1** tab.
4. Type **April Income** and then press the **Enter** key.

Moving a Worksheet

Finally, Mike wants the Documentation sheet to appear last in the workbook. He feels that the actual data should be displayed first. To move the position of a worksheet in the workbook, you click the worksheet's sheet tab, and drag and drop it to a new location relative to the other worksheets.

You can create a copy of the entire worksheet by holding down the Ctrl key as you drag and drop the sheet tab. When you release the mouse button, a copy of the original worksheet will be placed at the new location, while the original sheet will stay at its initial position in the workbook.

REFERENCE WINDOW   RW

Moving or Copying a Worksheet
- Click the sheet tab of the worksheet you want to move (or copy).
- Drag the sheet tab along the row of sheet tabs until the small arrow appears in the desired location. To create a copy of the worksheet, press and hold down the Ctrl key as you drag the sheet tab to the desired location.
- Release the mouse button. Release the Ctrl key if necessary.

You'll move the Documentation sheet now.

To move the Documentation worksheet:

1. Click the **Documentation** tab to make it the active worksheet.
2. Click the **Documentation** tab again, and then press and hold down the left mouse button so the pointer changes to 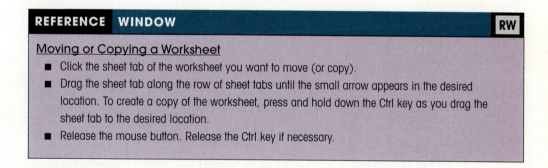. A small arrow appears in the upper-left corner of the sheet tab.
3. Drag the pointer to the right of the April Income tab, and then release the mouse button. The Documentation sheet is now the second sheet in the workbook.

Printing a Worksheet

Now that you are finished editing the Lawn2 workbook, you can create a hard copy of its contents for your records. You can print the contents of your workbook using either the Print command on the File menu or by clicking the Print button on the Standard toolbar. If you use the Print command, Excel displays a dialog box in which you can specify which worksheets you want to print, the number of copies, and the print quality (or resolution). If you click the Print button, you will not have a chance to set these options, but if you do not need to do so, clicking the Print button is a faster way of generating your output. Finally, you can also choose the Print Preview command on the File menu or click the Print Preview button on the Standard toolbar to see what your page will look like before it is sent to the printer. You can print directly from Print Preview.

If you are printing to a shared printer on a network, many other people might be sending print jobs at the same time you do. To avoid confusion, you will print the contents of both the Documentation sheet and the April Income sheet. You will use the Print command on the File menu since you need to print the entire workbook and not just the active worksheet (which is the default print setting). You will learn more about the Print Preview command in the next tutorial.

To print the contents of the Lawn2 workbook:

1. Click **File** on the menu bar, and then click **Print** to open the Print dialog box. See Figure 1-29.

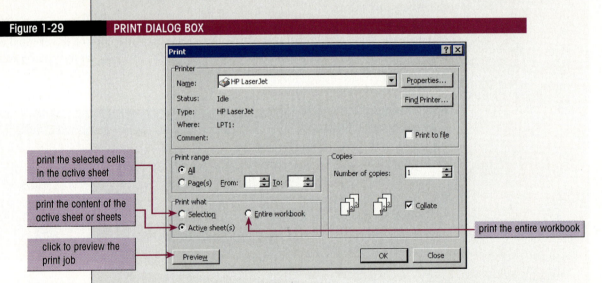

Figure 1-29 PRINT DIALOG BOX

- print the selected cells in the active sheet
- print the content of the active sheet or sheets
- click to preview the print job
- print the entire workbook

2. Click the **Name** list box, and then select the printer to which you want to print.

   Now you need to select what to print. To print the complete workbook, select the Entire workbook option button. To print the active worksheet, select the Active sheet(s) option button. To print the selected cells on the active sheet, click the Selection option button.

3. Click the **Entire workbook** option button.

4. Make sure "1" appears in the Number of copies list box, since you only need to print one copy of the workbook.

> **5.** Click the **OK** button to send the workbook to the printer.
>
> **TROUBLE?** If the workbook does not print, see your instructor or technical resource person for help.
>
> You have completed your work on the Lawn2 workbook, so you can save your changes and exit Excel.
>
> **6.** Click the **Save** button 💾 on the Standard toolbar, and then click the **Close** button ✕ on the title bar.

You give Mike the hard copy of the Lawn2 workbook. He will file the report for later reference. If he needs to add new information to the workbook or if he needs you to make further changes to the structure of the workbook, he will contact you.

Session 1.2 QUICK CHECK

1. Indicate whether Excel treats the following cell entries as a value, text, or a formula:
   a. 11/09/2003
   b. Net Income
   c. 321
   d. =C11*225
   e. 201-19-1121
   f. =D1-D9
   g. 44 Evans Avenue

2. What formula would you enter to divide the value in cell E5 by the value in cell E6?

3. What formula would you enter to raise the value in cell E5 to the power of the value in cell E6?

4. When you insert a new row into a worksheet, the selected cells are moved _____.

5. When you insert a new column into a worksheet, the selected cells are moved _____.

6. To change the name of a worksheet, double-click the _____.

7. Which key do you press to clear the contents of the active cell?

8. How does clearing a cell differ from deleting a cell?

REVIEW ASSIGNMENTS

Mike has another workbook in which he wants you to make some changes. This workbook contains the income and expense figures for May. Mike has already done some work on the file, but wants you to make some modifications and additions. To complete this task:

1. Start Excel and open the workbook **Income1** located in the Tutorial.01/Review folder on your Data Disk.

2. Save the workbook as **Income2** in the same folder.

3. Change the date in cell A3 to 5/1/2003.

4. Insert new cells in the range A12:C12, shifting the other cells down. In cell A12, enter the text "Rent". In cell B12, enter the value "4,100".

Explore 5. Edit the formula in cell C16 so that the formula includes the cost of rent in the liabilities total.

Explore 6. There is a mistake in the formula for the net income. Fix the formula so that it displays the difference between the assets and the liabilities in the month of May.

7. Move the income statement values in the range A5:C18 to the range C1:E14.

8. Resize the width of column C to 15 characters.

9. Insert a sheet named "Documentation" at the beginning of the workbook.

10. In the Documentation sheet, enter the following text:
    - Cell A1: Lawn Wizards
    - Cell A3: Date:
    - Cell B3: *Enter the current date*
    - Cell A4: Created By:
    - Cell B4: *Enter your name*
    - Cell A5: Purpose:
    - Cell B5: To record income and expenses for the month of May

11. Increase the width of column A in the Documentation worksheet to 20 characters.

12. Rename Sheet1 as **May Income**.

13. Delete Sheet2 and Sheet3.

14. Print the entire contents of the Income2 workbook.

15. Save and close the workbook, and then exit Excel.

CASE PROBLEMS

Case 1. Cash Flow Analysis at Madison Federal Lisa Wu is a financial consultant at Madison Federal. She is working on a financial plan for Tom and Carolyn Watkins. Lisa has a cash flow analysis for the couple, and she wants you to record this information for her. Here are the relevant financial figures:

Receipts
- Employment Income: 95,000
- Other Income: 5,000

Disbursements
- Insurance: 940
- Savings/Retirement: 8,400
- Living Expenses: 63,000
- Taxes: 16,300

Lisa wants you to calculate the total receipts and total disbursements and then to calculate the income surplus (receipts minus disbursements) in an Excel workbook that she has already started. To complete this task:

1. Open the **CFlow1** workbook located in the Tutorial.01/Cases folder on your Data Disk, and then save the workbook as **CFlow2** in the same folder.

2. Move the contents of the range A1:C12 to the range A3:C14.

3. Insert the text "Cash Flow Analysis" in cell A1.

4. Increase the width of column A to 130 pixels, the width of column B to 160 pixels, and the width of column C to 130 pixels.

5. Insert the financial numbers listed earlier into the appropriate cells in column C.

6. In cell C6, insert a formula to calculate the total receipts.

7. In cell C12, insert a formula to calculate the total disbursements.

8. Insert a formula to calculate the surplus in cell C14.

9. Rename Sheet1 as **Cash Flow**.

10. Insert a worksheet at the beginning of the workbook named "Documentation".

11. In the Documentation sheet, enter the following text:

    - Cell A1: Cash Flow Report
    - Cell A3: Date:
    - Cell B3: *Enter the current date*
    - Cell A4: Created By:
    - Cell B4: *Enter your name*
    - Cell A5: Purpose:
    - Cell B5: Cash flow analysis for Tom and Carolyn Watkins

12. Increase the width of column A in the Documentation worksheet to 20 characters.

13. Delete Sheet2 and Sheet3.

14. Print the contents of the entire workbook.

Explore 15. What would the surplus be if the couple's taxes increased to 18,500? Enter this value into the Cash Flow worksheet, and then print just the Cash Flow worksheet.

16. Save and close the workbook, and then exit Excel.

Case 2. Financial Report for EMS Industries Lee Evans is an agent at New Haven Financial Services. His job is to maintain financial information on stocks for client companies. He has the annual balance sheet for a company named EMS Industries in an Excel workbook and needs your help in finishing the workbook layout and contents. To complete this task:

1. Open the **Balance1** workbook located in the Tutorial.01/Cases folder on your Data Disk, and then save the workbook as **Balance2** in the same folder.

2. Select the cells A1:C2 and insert two new rows into the worksheet.

3. Insert the text "Annual Balance Sheet for EMS Industries" in cell A1.

4. Move the contents of the range A19:C33 to the range E3:G17.

5. Move the contents of the range B36:C38 to the range B19:C21.

6. Change the width of column B to 150 pixels, the width of column D to 20 pixels, and the width of column F to 150 pixels.

7. Insert a formula in cell C10 to calculate the total current assets, in cell C17 to calculate the total noncurrent assets, in cell G10 to calculate the total current liabilities, and in cell G17 to calculate the total noncurrent liabilities.

8. In cell C19, insert a formula to calculate the total of the current and noncurrent assets.

9. In cell C20, insert a formula to calculate the total of the current and noncurrent liabilities.

10. In cell C21, insert a formula to calculate the annual balance (the total assets minus the total liabilities).

11. Rename Sheet1 as **Annual Balance Sheet**.

12. Delete Sheet2 and Sheet3.

13. Insert a worksheet named "Documentation" at the front of the workbook.

14. Enter the following text into the Documentation sheet:
    - Cell A1: Annual Balance Report
    - Cell A3: Company:
    - Cell B3: EMS Industries
    - Cell A4: Date:
    - Cell B4: *Enter the current date*
    - Cell A5: Recorded By:
    - Cell B5: *Enter your name*
    - Cell A6: Summary:
    - Cell B6: Annual Balance Sheet

15. Increase the width of column A in the Documentation worksheet to 20 characters.

16. Print the entire contents of the workbook.

17. Save and close the workbook, and then exit Excel.

Case 3. Analyzing Sites for a New Factory for Kips Shoes Kips Shoes is planning to build a new factory. The company has narrowed the site down to four possible cities. Each city has been graded on a 1-to-10 scale for four categories: the size of the local market, the quality of the labor pool, the local tax base, and the local operating expenses. Each of these four factors is given a weight with the most important factor given the highest weight. After the sites are analyzed, the scores for each factor will be multiplied by their weights, and then a total weighted score will be calculated.

Gwen Sanchez has entered the weights and the scores for each city into an Excel workbook. She needs you to finish the workbook by inserting the formulas to calculate the weighted scores and the total overall score for each city. To complete this task:

1. Open the **Site1** workbook located in the Tutorial.01/Cases folder on your Data Disk, and then save the workbook as **Site2** in the same folder.

2. Switch to the Site Analysis sheet.

3. In cell B12, calculate the weighted Market Size score for Waukegan by inserting a formula that multiplies the value in cell B5 by the value in cell C5.

4. Insert formulas to calculate the weighted scores for the rest of the cells in the range B12:E15.

5. Insert formulas in the range B17:E17 that calculate the totals of the weighted scores for each of the four cities. Which city has the highest weighted score?

6. Switch to the Documentation sheet, and enter your name and the date in the appropriate location on the sheet.

7. Print the entire workbook.

Explore   8. Gwen reports that Brockton's score for market size should be 6 and not 5. Modify this entry in the table, and then print just the Site Analysis worksheet with the new total scores. Does this change your conclusions about which city is most preferable for the new factory?

9. Save and close the workbook, and then exit Excel.

Case 4. Cash Counting Calculator Rob Stuben works at a local town beach in Narragansett where a fee is collected for parking. At the end of each day, the parking attendants turn in the cash they have collected with a statement of the daily total. Rob is responsible for receiving the daily cash from each attendant, checking the accuracy of the daily total, and taking the cash deposit to the bank.

Rob wants to set up a simple cash counter using Excel, so that he can insert the number of bills of each denomination into a worksheet so the total cash is automatically computed. By a simple cash counter method, he only has to count and enter the number of one-dollar bills, the number of fives, and so on. To complete this task:

1. Save a new workbook with the name **CashCounter** in the Tutorial.01/Cases folder on your Data Disk.

Explore   2. In the workbook, create a worksheet named **Counter** with the following properties:
- All currency denominations (1, 5, 10, 20, 50, 100) should be listed in the first column of the worksheet.
- In the second column, you will enter the number of bills of each denomination, but this column should be left blank initially.
- In the third column, insert the formulas to calculate totals for each denomination, (that is, the number of bills multiplied by the denomination of each bill).
- In a blank cell at the bottom of the third column, which contains the formulas for calculating the totals of each denomination, a formula that calculates the grand total of the cash received should be entered.

3. Create a Documentation sheet. The sheet should include the title of the workbook, the date the workbook was created, your name, and the purpose of the workbook. Make this worksheet the first worksheet in the workbook.

4. Adjust the widths of the columns, if necessary. Delete any blank worksheets from the workbook.

Explore   5. On Rob's first day using the worksheet, the cash reported by an attendant was $1,565. Rob counted the bills and separated them by denomination. Enter the following values into the worksheet:
- 5 fifties
- 23 twenties
- 41 tens
- 65 fives
- 120 ones

6. Print the entire contents of your workbook.

Explore

7. On Rob's second day, the cash reported by an attendant was $1,395. Again, Rob counted the money and separated the bills by denomination. Clear the previous values, and then enter the new values for the distribution of the bills into the worksheet:

    - 2 hundreds
    - 4 fifties
    - 17 twenties
    - 34 tens
    - 45 fives
    - 90 ones

8. Print just the Counter worksheet.

9. Save and close the workbook, and then exit Excel.

LAB ASSIGNMENTS

The New Perspectives Labs are designed to help you master some of the key computer concepts and skills presented in each chapter of the text. If you are using your school's lab computers, your instructor or technical support person should have installed the Labs software for you. If you want to use the Labs on your home computer, ask your instructor for the appropriate software. See the Read This Before You Begin page for more information on installing and starting the Lab.

Each Lab has two parts: Steps and Explore. Use Steps first to learn and review concepts. Read the information on each page and do the numbered steps. As you work through the Lab, you will be asked to answer Quick Check questions about what you have learned. At the end of the Lab, you will see a Summary Report of your answers to the Quick Checks. If your instructor wants you to turn in this Summary Report, click the Print button on the Summary Report screen.

When you have completed Steps, you can click the Explore button to complete the Lab Assignments. You can also use Explore to practice the skills you learned and to explore concepts on your own.

SPREADSHEETS Spreadsheet software is used extensively in business, education, science, and humanities to simplify tasks that involve calculations. In this Lab you will learn how spreadsheet software works. You will use spreadsheet software to examine and modify worksheets, as well as to create your own worksheets.

1. Click the Steps button to learn how spreadsheet software works. As you proceed through the Steps, answer all of the Quick Check questions that appear. After you complete the Steps, you will see a Quick Check Summary Report. Follow the instructions on the screen to print this report.

2. Click the Explore button to begin this assignment. Click OK to display a new worksheet. Click File on the menu bar, and then click Open to display the Open dialog box. Click the file **Income.xls** and then press the Enter key to open the **Income and Expense Summary** workbook. Notice that the worksheet contains labels and values for income from consulting and training. It also contains labels and values for expenses

such as rent and salaries. The worksheet does not, however, contain formulas to calculate Total Income, Total Expenses, or Profit. Do the following:

a. Calculate the Total Income by entering the formula =SUM(C4:C5) in cell C6.
b. Calculate the Total Expenses by entering the formula =SUM(C9:C12) in C13.
c. Calculate Profit by entering the formula =C6-C13 in cell C15.
d. Manually check the results to make sure you entered the formulas correctly.
e. Print your completed worksheet showing your results.

3. You can use a spreadsheet to keep track of your grades in a class and to calculate your grade average. In Explore, click File on the menu bar, and then click Open to display the Open dialog box. Click the file **Grades.xls** to open the workbook. The worksheet contains the labels and formulas necessary to calculate your grade average based on four test scores. You receive a score of 88 out of 100 on the first test. On the second test, you score 42 out of 48. On the third test, you score 92 out of 100. You have not taken the fourth test yet. Enter the appropriate data in the **Grades.xls** worksheet to determine your grade average after taking three tests. Print out your worksheet.

4. Worksheets are handy for answering "what if" questions. Suppose you decide to open a lemonade stand. You're interested in how much profit you can make each day. What if you sell 20 cups of lemonade? What if you sell 100? What if the cost of lemons increases?

In Explore, open the file **Lemons.xls** and use the worksheet to answer questions a through d. Then print the worksheet for question e:

a. What is your profit if you sell 20 cups a day?
b. What is your profit if you sell 100 cups a day?
c. What is your profit if the price of lemons increases to $.07 and you sell 100 cups?
d. What is your profit if you raise the price of a cup of lemonade to $.30? (Lemons still cost $.07 and assume you sell 100 cups.)
e. Suppose your competitor boasts that she sold 50 cups of lemonade in one day and made exactly $12.00. On your worksheet adjust the cost of cups, water, lemons, and sugar, and the price per cup to show a profit of exactly $12.00 for 50 cups sold. Print this worksheet.

5. It is important to make sure the formulas in your worksheet are accurate. An easy way to test this is to enter 1's for all the values on your worksheet, then check the calculations manually. In Explore, open the file **Receipt.xls**, which contains a formula that calculates sales receipts. Enter "1" as the value for Item 1, Item 2, Item 3, and Sales Tax %. Now manually calculate what you would pay for three items that each cost $1.00 in a state where sales tax is 1% (.01). Do your manual calculations match those of the worksheet? If not, correct the formulas in the worksheet, and then print out a *formula report* of your revised worksheet.

6. In Explore, create your own worksheet showing your household budget for one month. Make up the numbers for the budget. Put a title at the top of the worksheet. Use formulas to calculate your total income and expenses for the month. Add another formula to calculate how much money you were able to save. Print a formula report of your worksheet. Also, print your worksheet showing realistic values for one month.

INTERNET ASSIGNMENTS

Student Union

The purpose of the Internet Assignments is to challenge you to find information on the Internet that you can use to create effective spreadsheets. The actual assignments are updated and maintained on the Course Technology Web site. Log on to the Internet and use your Web browser to go to the Student Union on the New Perspectives Series site at **www.course.com/NewPerspectives/studentunion**. Click the Online Companions link, and then click the link for this text.

QUICK CHECK ANSWERS

Session 1.1

1. cell
2. D2
3. Ctrl + Home
4. Click the Sheet2 tab.
5. Adjacent and nonadjacent. An adjacent range is a rectangular block of cells. A nonadjacent range consists of two or more separate adjacent ranges.
6. A5:F8
7. Select the cells you want to move, and then press and hold down the Alt key and drag the selection over the Sheet2 tab. When Sheet2 becomes the active sheet, continue to drag the selection to position it in its new location in the worksheet, and then release the left mouse button and the Alt key.

Session 1.2

1. a. value
   b. text
   c. value
   d. formula
   e. text
   f. formula
   g. text
2. =E5/E6
3. =E5^E6
4. down
5. to the right
6. sheet tab and then type the new name to replace the highlighted sheet tab name
7. Delete key
8. Clearing a cell deletes the cell's contents but does not affect the position of other cells in the workbook. Deleting a cell removes the cell from the worksheet, and other cells are shifted into the deleted cell's position.

TUTORIAL 2

WORKING WITH FORMULAS AND FUNCTIONS

Analyzing a Mortgage

OBJECTIVES

In this tutorial you will:

- Work with the Insert Function button
- Learn about Excel's financial functions
- Copy and paste formulas and functions
- Work with absolute and relative references
- Learn to use Excel's Auto Fill features
- Create logical functions
- Work with Excel's date functions

CASE

Prime Realty

You work as an assistant at Prime Realty (PR) selling real estate. One of the agents at PR, Carol Malloy, has asked you to help her develop an Excel workbook that calculates mortgages. The workbook needs to include three values: the size of the loan, the number of payments, and the annual interest rate. Using this information in the workbook, you will be able to determine the monthly payment needed to pay off the loan and the total cost of the mortgage over the loan's history. Carol wants the workbook to display a table showing the monthly payments with information describing how much of the payment is for interest and how much is applied toward the principal. Carol also wants the workbook to be flexible enough so that if a client intends on making additional payments, beyond the required monthly payment, the workbook will show how the cost of the loan and subsequent payments are affected.

In this tutorial, you will use Excel's financial functions to create the workbook for the mortgage calculations.

SESSION 2.1

In this session, you will learn about Excel's functions. You will insert functions and function arguments. You will copy and paste formulas and functions into your workbook. Finally, you will learn about absolute and relative references and how to insert them into your formulas.

Working with Excel Functions

Carol has already started the loan workbook. She has not entered any values yet, but she has entered some text and a documentation sheet. Open her workbook now.

To open Carol's workbook:

1. Start Excel and then open the **Loan1** workbook located in the Tutorial.02/Tutorial folder on your Data Disk.

2. On the Documentation sheet, enter your name in cell B3.

3. Click the **Mortgage** tab to make the sheet the active worksheet. See Figure 2-1.

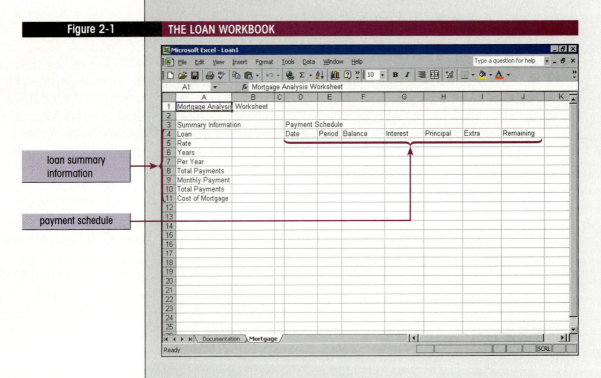

Figure 2-1 THE LOAN WORKBOOK

4. Save the workbook as **Loan2** in the Tutorial.02/Tutorial folder on your Data Disk.

The Mortgage worksheet is divided into two sections. The Summary Information section is the area in which you will enter the basic information about the loan, including the amount of the loan, the current interest rate, and the length of the mortgage. Figure 2-2 provides a description of the information that you will enter in the cells in that section.

Figure 2-2 CELLS IN THE SUMMARY INFORMATION SECTION

CELL	DESCRIPTION
B4	Enter the amount of the loan
B5	Enter the interest rate
B6	Enter the length of the mortgage in years
B7	Enter the number of periods (months) that the interest will be compounded each year
B8	Calculate the total number of periods in the loan
B9	Calculate the monthly payment
B10	Calculate the total payments on the loan
B11	Calculate the cost of the loan (total payments minus the amount of the loan)

The other section of the worksheet contains the payment schedule; it indicates how much is paid toward the principal and how much is paid in interest each month. The schedule also indicates the balance remaining on the loan each month. Figure 2-3 describes the values to be placed in each column.

Figure 2-3 COLUMNS IN THE PAYMENT SCHEDULE

COLUMN	DESCRIPTION
Date	Date that loan payment is due
Period	Loan payment period
Balance	Balance of loan remaining to be paid
Interest	Interest due
Principal	Portion of the monthly payment used to reduce the principal
Extra	Extra payments beyond the scheduled monthly payment
Remaining	Balance of loan remaining after the monthly payment

To make this worksheet operational, you need to use financial functions that are provided in Excel.

Function Syntax

In the previous tutorial you used formulas to calculate values. For example, the formula =*A1+A2+A3+A4* totals the values in the range A1:A4 and places the sum in the active cell. Although calculating sums this way for small ranges works fine, a formula that calculates the sum of 100 cells would be so large that it would become unmanageable. In Excel you can easily calculate the sum of a large number of cells by using a function. A **function** is a predefined, or built-in, formula for a commonly used calculation.

Each Excel function has a name and syntax. The **syntax** specifies the order in which you must enter the different parts of the function and the location in which you must insert commas, parentheses, and other punctuation. The general syntax for an Excel function is =FUNCTION(*argument1*, *argument2*, ...), where FUNCTION is the name of the Excel function, and *argument1*, *argument2*, and so on are **arguments**—the numbers, text, or cell references used by the function to calculate a value. Some arguments are **optional arguments** because they are not necessary for the function to return a value. If you omit an optional argument, Excel assumes a default value for it. By convention, optional arguments will appear in this text within square brackets along with the default value. For example, in the function =FUNCTION(*argument1*,[*argument2=value*]), the second argument is optional, and *value* is the default value assigned to *argument2* if a value is omitted from the argument list. A convention that you will follow in this text is to display function names in uppercase letters; however, when you enter formulas into your own Excel worksheets, you can use either uppercase or lowercase letters.

Excel supplies over 350 different functions organized into 10 categories:

- Database functions
- Date and Time functions
- Engineering functions
- Financial functions
- Information functions
- Logical functions
- Lookup functions
- Math functions
- Statistical functions
- Text and Data functions

You can learn about each function using Excel's online Help. Figure 2-4 describes some of the more important math and statistical functions that you may often use in your workbooks.

Figure 2-4   MATH AND STATISTICAL FUNCTIONS

FUNCTION	DESCRIPTION
AVERAGE(*values*)	Calculates the average value in a set of numbers, where *values* is either a cell reference or a collection of cell references separated by commas
COUNT(*values*)	Counts the number of cells containing numbers, where *values* is either a cell reference or a range of cell references separated by commas
MAX(*values*)	Calculates the largest value in a set of numbers, where *values* is either a cell reference or a range of cell references separated by commas
MIN(*values*)	Calculates the smallest value in a set of numbers, where *values* is either a cell reference or a range of cell references separated by commas
ROUND(*number, num_digits*)	Rounds a *number* to a specified number of digits, indicated by the *num_digits* arguments
SUM(*numbers*)	Calculates the sum of a collection of numbers, where *numbers* is either a cell or a range reference or a series of numbers separated by commas

For example, the SUM function calculates the total for the values in a range of cells. The SUM function has only one argument, the cell reference containing the values to be totaled. To calculate the total of the cells in the range A1:A100, you would insert the expression =SUM(A1:A100) into the active cell.

Functions can also be combined with formulas. For example, the expression =MAX(A1:A100)/100 returns the maximum value in the range A1:A100 and then divides the value by 100. One function can also be nested inside the other. The expression =ROUND(AVERAGE(A1:A100),1) uses the AVERAGE function to calculate the average of the values in the range A1:A100 and then uses the ROUND function to round the average value off to the first decimal place.

By combining functions and formulas, you can create very sophisticated expressions to handle almost any situation.

Financial Functions

In Carol's workbook, you will use one of Excel's financial functions to calculate information about the loan. Figure 2-5 describes a few of Excel's financial functions in more detail.

Figure 2-5 — FINANCIAL FUNCTIONS

FUNCTION	DESCRIPTION
FV(rate,nper,pmt,[pv=0],[type=0])	Calculates the future value of an investment based on periodic, constant payments, and a constant interest rate, where rate is the interest rate per period, nper is the number of periods, pmt is the payment per period, pv is the present value of the investment, and type indicates when payments are due (type=0 for payments at the end of each period, type=1 for payments at the beginning of each period)
IPMT(rate,per,nper pv,[fv=0],[type=0])	Calculates the interest payment for a given period for an investment based on period cash payments and a constant interest rate, where fv is the future value of the investment
PMT(rate,nper,pv,[fv=0],[type=0]	Calculates the payment for a loan based on constant payments and a constant interest rate
PPMT(rate,per,nper,pv,[fv=0],[type=0])	Calculates the payment on the principal for a given period for an investment based on period cash payments and a constant interest rate
PV(rate,nper,pmt,[fv=0],[type=0])	Calculates the present value of an investment

You need a function to calculate the monthly payment that will pay off a loan at a fixed interest rate. You can use Excel's PMT function to do just that. The syntax of the PMT function is PMT(*rate,nper,pv,[fv=0],[type=0]*) where *rate* is the interest rate per period of the loan, *nper* is the total number of periods, *pv* is the present value of the loan, *fv* is the future value, and *type* specifies whether the payment is made at the beginning of each period (*type=1*) or at the end of each period (*type=0*). Note that both the *fv* and *type* arguments are optional arguments. If you omit the *fv* argument, Excel assumes that the future value will be 0, in other words that the loan will be completely paid off. If you omit the *type* argument, Excel assumes a type value of 0 so that the loan is paid off at the end of each period.

For example, if Carol wanted to know the monthly payment for a $50,000 loan at 9% annual interest compounded monthly over 10 years, the arguments for the PMT function would be *PMT(0.09/12,10*12,50000)*. Note that the yearly interest rate is divided by the number of periods (months) for the interest rate per period. Similarly, the number of periods (months) is multiplied by the number of years in order to arrive at the total number of periods.

The value returned by the PMT function is –633.38, indicating that a client would have to spend $633.38 per month to pay off the loan in 10 years. Excel uses a negative value to indicate that the value is an expense rather than income.

You can also use the PMT function for annuities other than loans. For example, if you want to determine how much money to save at a 6% annual interest rate compounded monthly so that you will have $5000 at the end of five years, you use the following PMT function: =*PMT(0.06/12,5*12,0,5000)*. Note that the present value is 0 (since you are starting out with no money in the account) and the future value is 5000 (since that is the amount you want to have after 5 years). In this case, Excel will return a value of –71.66, indicating that you would have to invest $71.66 per month to achieve $5000 in your savings account after 5 years.

Inserting a Function

Carol wants to calculate the monthly payment for a 20-year loan of $150,000 at 7.5% annual interest compounded monthly. First you need to enter this information into the workbook. You also need to enter a formula that will calculate the total number of monthly payments.

To add the loan information:

1. Click cell **B4**, type **$150,000** and then press the **Enter** key. Even though you have added a dollar symbol in writing the loan amount, Excel still interprets cell B4 as a numeric value and not a text string.

2. In cell B5, type **7.5%** and then press the **Enter** key. Note that when you type a percentage into a worksheet cell, Excel interprets the percentage as a value. The actual value in cell B5 is 0.075; the value is just *formatted* to appear with the percent sign. You will learn more about how Excel formats numbers in the next tutorial.

3. In cell B6, type **20** and then press the **Enter** key.

4. In cell B7, type **12** since there are 12 payment periods in each year, and then press the **Enter** key.

   Note that in this text you can *enter* a cell reference in a formula or function by clicking the cell or by typing the cell reference.

5. In cell B8, enter the formula **=B6*B7** for the total number of payments in the mortgage, and then press the **Enter** key. The value 240 appears in cell B8, and cell B9 is now the active cell.

Now you will use the PMT function to calculate the required monthly payment to pay off the loan under the terms of the mortgage. You could simply type the function and its arguments into the cell, but you will often find that you have forgotten which arguments are required by the function and the correct order in which the arguments need to be entered. To assist you, Excel provides the Insert Function button on the Formula bar. Clicking this button displays a dialog box from which you can choose the function you want to enter. Once you choose a function, another dialog box opens in which you specify values for all of the function's arguments.

REFERENCE WINDOW

Inserting a Function
- Click the cell in which you will insert the function.
- Click the Insert Function button on the Formula bar.
- Select the type of function you want from the select a category list box, and then select the function category; or type information about the function in the Search for a function text box, and then click the Go button.
- Select the function in the Select a function list box.
- Click the OK button to view the arguments for the selected function.
- Enter values for each required argument in the Function Arguments dialog box.
- Click the OK button.

You will insert the PMT function in the Summary Information section of the Mortgage worksheet to determine the monthly payment required to pay off a mortgage. You will use the Insert Function button on the Formula bar to insert the PMT function.

To insert the PMT function:

1. With cell B9 as the active cell, click the **Insert Function** button fx on the Formula bar. The Insert Function dialog box opens. See Figure 2-6.

Figure 2-6   **INSERT FUNCTION DIALOG BOX**

- enter a description of the function you want to use
- click to search for a function
- select one of Excel's 10 function categories
- list of functions for each category

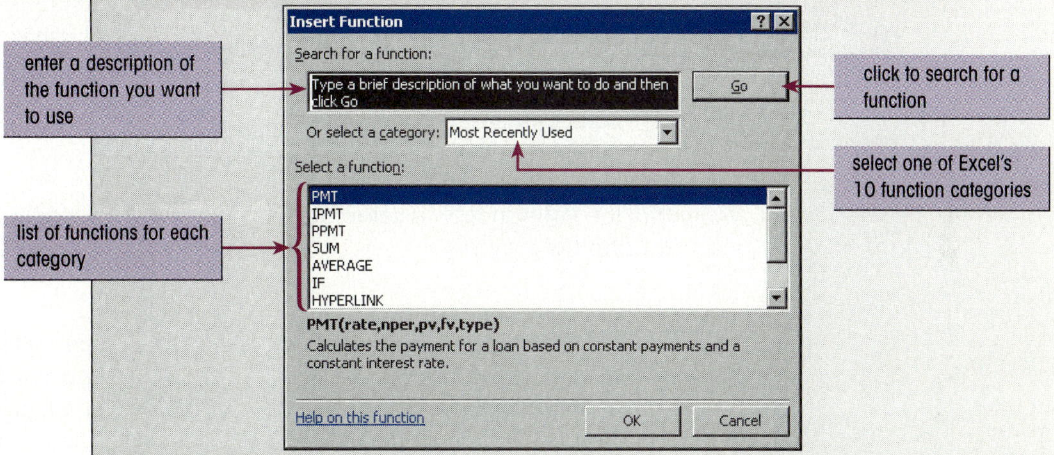

There are two ways to select a function using this dialog box. If you know something about the function but are not sure in which category the function belongs, enter a text description in the Search for a function text box and click the Go button. Excel will search for the functions that match your description. If you know the general category, select the category from the select a category list box; then Excel will list all of the functions in that category. Browse through the function list to find the function you need.

2. Type **calculate mortgage payments** in the Search for a function text box, and then click the **Go** button. Excel returns the PMT, IPMT, and NPER functions in the Select a function list box. Note that a description of the selected function and its arguments appears at the bottom of the dialog box. See Figure 2-7.

Figure 2-7 SEARCHING FOR A FUNCTION

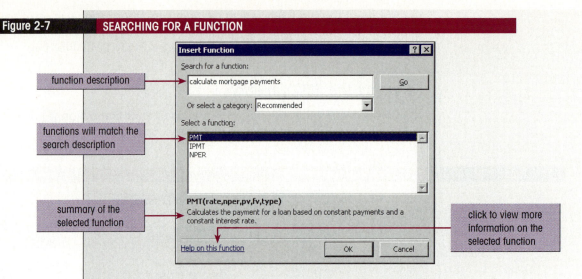

3. Verify that the PMT function is selected in the Select a function list box, and then click the **OK** button.

Excel next displays the Function Arguments dialog box, which provides all of the arguments in the selected function and the description of each argument. From this dialog box, you can select the cells in the workbook that contain the values required for each argument. Note that the expression =PMT() appears in both the Formula bar and cell B9. This display indicates that Excel is starting to insert the PMT function for you. You have to use the Function Arguments dialog box to complete the process.

You will start by entering the value for the Rate argument. Remember that rate refers to the interest rate per period. In this case, that value is 7.5% divided by 12, or if you use the cells in the worksheet, the value in cell B5 is divided by the value in cell B7. You can enter the cell references either by typing them into the appropriate argument boxes or by pointing to a cell with the mouse pointer, in which case Excel will automatically insert the cell reference into the appropriate box.

To insert values into the PMT function:

1. With the blinking insertion point in the Rate argument box, click cell **B5**, type **/**, and then click cell **B7**. The expression *B5/B7* appears in the box and the value 0.00625 appears to the right of the box.

    TROUBLE? If necessary, move the dialog box to view column B before clicking cell B5.

2. Press the **Tab** key to move to the Nper argument box.

3. Click cell **B8** for the 240 total payments needed for this loan, and then press the **Tab** key.

    The present value of the loan is $150,000, which is found in cell B4.

4. Click cell **B4** to enter the value of the loan in the Pv argument box. Figure 2-8 shows the completed Function Arguments dialog box.

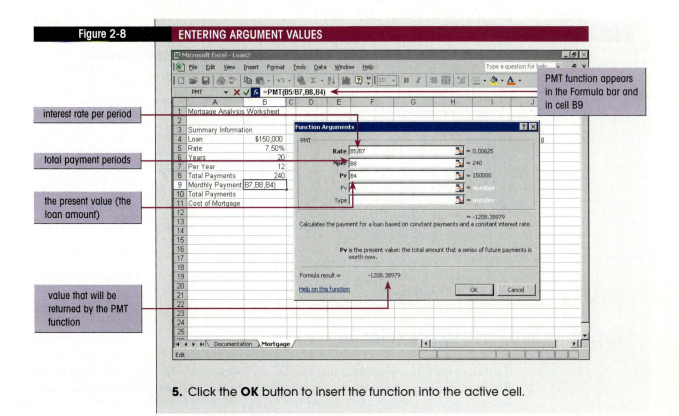

Figure 2-8 ENTERING ARGUMENT VALUES

5. Click the **OK** button to insert the function into the active cell.

Excel displays the value ($1,208.39) with a red colored font in cell B9. This is a general format that Excel uses to display negative currency values. Carol would rather have the monthly payment appear as a positive value, so you will have to insert a negative sign in front of the PMT function to switch the monthly payment to a positive value. You will also complete the rest of the Summary Information section.

To complete the Summary Information section:

1. Double-click cell **B9** to enter edit mode.

2. Click directly to the right of the = (equal sign), type **-** so that the expression changes to =-PMT(B5/B7,B8,B4), and then press the **Enter** key.

3. In cell B10, enter **=B9*B8** and then press the **Enter** key.

4. In cell B11, enter **=B10-B4** and then press the **Enter** key. Figure 2-9 shows the complete summary information for this loan.

Figure 2-9   **MORTGAGE SUMMARY**

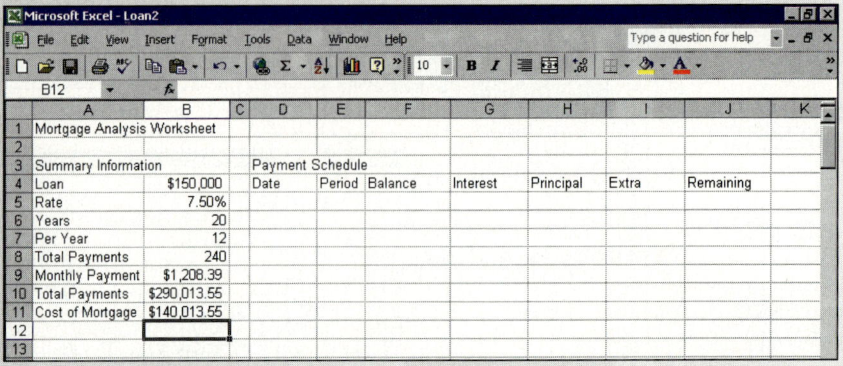

	A	B
1	Mortgage Analysis Worksheet	
2		
3	Summary Information	
4	Loan	$150,000
5	Rate	7.50%
6	Years	20
7	Per Year	12
8	Total Payments	240
9	Monthly Payment	$1,208.39
10	Total Payments	$290,013.55
11	Cost of Mortgage	$140,013.55

Payment Schedule header with columns: Date, Period, Balance, Interest, Principal, Extra, Remaining

The required monthly payment for this loan will be $1,208.39. The total interest payments will be $140,013.55.

Copying and Pasting Formulas

The next part of the worksheet that you need to work with is the payment schedule, which details the monthly payments on the mortgage. Before entering values into the payment schedule, you should consider the functions that you will use in the schedule. Each row of the payment schedule represents the condition of the loan for a single month of the mortgage.

The Date column (column D in the worksheet) will contain the date on which a payment is due. At this point you will not enter any date information (you will do that later in the tutorial). The Period column specifies the number of periods in the mortgage. The first month is period 1, the second month is period 2, and so forth. Since there are 240 payment periods, this payment schedule will extend from row 5 down to row 244 in the worksheet. The Balance column displays the balance left on the loan at the beginning of each period. The initial balance value is the amount of the loan, which is found in cell B4. After the initial period, the balance will be equal to the remaining balance from the previous period.

The Interest column is the amount of interest due on the balance, which is equal to: Balance * Interest rate per period. In this example, the interest rate per period is the annual interest rate (in cell B5) divided by the number of periods in a year (in cell B7).

Subtracting the interest due from the monthly payment (cell B9) tells you how much is paid toward reducing the principal. This value is placed in column H of the worksheet. Carol knows that sometimes clients will want to make extra payments each month in order to pay off the loan quicker (and thereby reduce the overall cost of the mortgage). The Extra column (column I in the worksheet) is used for recording these values. Finally, the remaining balance will be equal to the balance at the beginning of the month minus the payment toward the principal and any extra payments.

Now that you have reviewed what values and functions will go into each column of the payment schedule, you are ready to insert the first row of the schedule.

TUTORIAL 2 WORKING WITH FORMULAS AND FUNCTIONS

To insert the first row of values in the payment schedule:

1. Click cell **E5**, type **1** and then press the **Tab** key.

   Now you will enter the initial balance, which is equal to the amount of the loan found in cell B4. Rather than typing in the value itself, you will enter a reference to the cell. If you change the amount of the loan, this change will be automatically reflected in the payment schedule.

2. In cell F5, enter **=B4** and then press the **Tab** key.

   Next you will enter the interest due in this period, which is equal to the balance multiplied by the interest rate per period (cell B5 divided by cell B7).

3. In cell G5, enter **=F5*B5/B7** and then press the **Tab** key.

   TROUBLE? Note that if the values in cells F5 and G5 are displayed with a different number of decimal places, do not worry. You will learn more about formatting cells in Tutorial 3.

   The payment toward the principal is equal to the monthly payment (cell B9) minus the interest payment (cell G5).

4. In cell H5, enter **=B9-G5** and then press the **Tab** key.

   At this point there are no extra payments toward the mortgage so you will enter $0 in the Extra column. The balance remaining is equal to the present balance minus the payment towards the principal and any extra payments.

5. In cell I5, type **$0** and then press the **Tab** key.

6. In cell J5, enter **=F5-(H5+I5)** and then press the **Enter** key. Figure 2-10 shows the first period values in the payment schedule.

Figure 2-10   FIRST PERIOD VALUES IN THE PAYMENT SCHEDULE

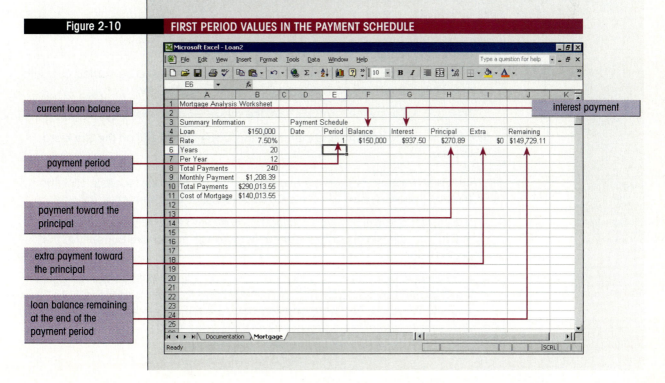

You could have also calculated the monthly interest payment using Excel's IPMT function and the monthly payment toward the principal using the PPMT function. However, both of these functions assume that there will be no extra payments toward the principal. This assumption is something that Carol does not want to omit in her payment schedule.

The second row of the payment schedule is similar to the first. The only difference is that the balance (to be displayed in cell F6) will be carried over from the remaining balance (displayed in cell J5) in the previous row. At this point, you could retype the formulas that you used in the first row of the payment schedule. However, it is much easier and more efficient to copy and paste the formulas. When you **copy** the contents of a range, Excel places the formulas and values in those cells in a memory location called the **Clipboard**. The contents remain on the Clipboard until you **paste** them. You can paste the contents of the selected cells into another location on your worksheet, into a different worksheet or workbook, or even into another Windows application.

REFERENCE WINDOW

Copying and Pasting a Cell or Range
- Select the cell or range to be copied.
- Click the Copy button on the Standard toolbar.
- Select the cell or range into which you want to copy the selection.
- Click the Paste button on the Standard toolbar.
- If necessary, click the Paste Options button to apply a paste-related option to the pasted selection.
- Press the Esc key to deselect the selection.

Next you will copy and paste a range of values in the worksheet.

To insert the second row of values in the payment schedule:

1. Click cell **E6**, type **2** and then press the **Tab** key.

2. In cell F6, enter **=J5** (since the remaining balance needs to be carried over into the second payment period), and then press the **Enter** key.

   Now you will copy the formulas from the range G5:J5 to the range G6:J6.

3. Select the range **G5:J5** and then click the **Copy** button 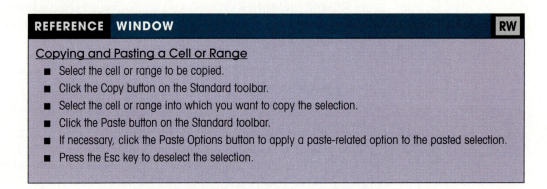 on the Standard toolbar.

   TROUBLE? If you do not see the Copy button on the Standard toolbar, click the Toolbar Options button on the Standard toolbar, and then click .

   Note that the range that you copied has a moving border surrounding it. This moving border is a visual reminder of what range values are currently in the paste buffer.

4. Click cell **G6** to make it the active cell, and then click the **Paste** button on the Standard toolbar. Note that you did not have to select a range of cells equal to the range you were copying because the cells adjacent to cell G6 were empty and could accommodate the pasted range.

The formulas from the G5:J5 range are pasted into the G6:J6 range. See Figure 2-11.

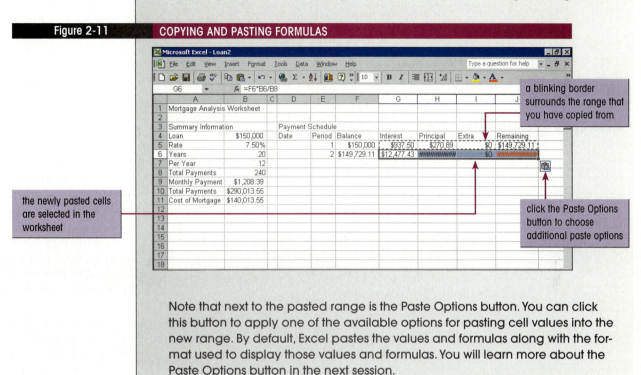

Figure 2-11   COPYING AND PASTING FORMULAS

- the newly pasted cells are selected in the worksheet
- a blinking border surrounds the range that you have copied from
- click the Paste Options button to choose additional paste options

Note that next to the pasted range is the Paste Options button. You can click this button to apply one of the available options for pasting cell values into the new range. By default, Excel pastes the values and formulas along with the format used to display those values and formulas. You will learn more about the Paste Options button in the next session.

5. Press the **Esc** key to remove the moving border.

Apparently something is wrong. Note that the interest payment in cell G6 has jumped to $12,477.43, and the principal payment in cell H6 and the remaining balance are represented with ########. Excel uses this string of symbols to represent a value that is so large that it cannot be displayed within the width of the cell. To view the value in the cell, you must either increase the width of the column or hover your mouse pointer over the cell.

To view the value in cell H6:

1. Hover your mouse pointer over cell H6. After a brief interval, the value $277,536.12 appears in a ScreenTip.

2. Click cell **G6** to make it the active cell. The Formula bar displays the formula =F6*B6/B8.

The interest payment value jumped to $12,477.43 and the payment on the principal became $277,536.12. The absurdity of these values results from the way in which Excel copies formulas. When Excel copies formulas to a new location, Excel automatically adjusts the cell references in those formulas. For example, to calculate the remaining balance for the first payment period in cell J5, the formula is =F5-(H5+I5). For the second payment period, the remaining balance in cell J6 uses the formula =F6-(H6+I6). The cell references are shifted down one row.

This automatic update of the cell references works fine for this formula, but the updating does not work for the calculation of the interest payment. The interest payment should be the balance multiplied by the interest rate per period; therefore, for the first three rows of the payment schedule, the formulas should be =F5*B5/B7, =F6*B5/B7, and =F7*B5/B7.

However, when you copied the first formula to the second row, *all* of the cell references shifted down one row and the formula automatically became =F6*B6/B8. You have a different formula; therefore, the result is a nonsensical value. Note that this is an issue only when copying a cell, not moving a cell. When you move a cell, Excel does *not* modify the cell references.

You need to be able to control how Excel adjusts cell references, so that Excel adjusts some of the cell references in the interest due formula, but not others. You can control this automatic adjusting of cell references through the use of relative and absolute references.

Relative and Absolute References

A **relative reference** is a cell reference that shifts when you copy it to a new location on the worksheet. As you saw in the preceding set of steps, a relative reference changes in relation to the change of location. If you copy a formula to a cell three rows down and five columns to the right, the relative cell reference shifts three rows down and five columns to the right. For example, the relative reference B5 becomes G8.

An **absolute reference** is a cell reference that does not change when you copy the formula to a new location on the workbook. To create an absolute reference, you preface the column and row designations with a dollar sign ($). For example, the absolute reference for B5 would be $B$5. No matter where you copy the formula, this cell reference would stay the same. (Relative references do not include dollars signs.)

A **mixed reference** combines both relative and absolute cell references. A mixed reference for B5 would be either $B5 or B$5. In the case of $B5, the row reference would shift, but the column reference would not. In the case of B$5, only the column reference shifts.

You can switch between absolute, relative, and mixed references by selecting the cell reference in the formula (either using edit mode or the Formula bar) and then pressing the F4 key on your keyboard repeatedly.

The problem you have encountered with the payment schedule formulas is that you need a relative reference for the remaining balance but an absolute reference for the interest rate divided by the payment periods per year (since those values are always located in the same place in the worksheet). So instead of the formula =F5*B5/B7, you need to use the formula =F5*$B$5/$B$7.

Next you will revise the formulas in the payment schedule to use relative and absolute references, and then copy the revised formulas.

To use relative and absolute references in the payment schedule:

1. Double-click cell **G5** to enter edit mode, use an arrow key to position the insertion point to the left of the column heading B if necessary, and then type **$**. Continue to use the arrow keys to position the insertion point in the formula before typing three more $ to change the formula to =F5*$B$5/$B$7. Press the **Enter** key.

   You also have to change the formula in cell H5, so that the formula subtracts the interest payment from the required monthly payment to calculate the payment toward the principal. Instead of typing the dollar signs to change a relative reference to an absolute reference, you will use the F4 key.

2. Double-click cell **H5**, make sure the insertion point is positioned in the B9 cell reference, and then press the **F4** key to change the formula to =$B$9-G5. Press the **Enter** key.

   Now copy these new formulas into the second row of the payment schedule. Note that you do not have to delete the contents of the range into which you are copying the updated formulas.

3. Select the range **G5:H5**, and then click the **Copy** button on the Standard toolbar.

4. Click cell **G6** and then click the **Paste** button on the Standard toolbar.

The new values are much more reasonable. The interest payment has decreased to $935.81, and the payment toward the principal has increased to $272.58. You will now add one more row to the payment schedule and copy the formulas.

To add a third row to the payment schedule:

1. Click cell **E7**, type **3** and then press the **Tab** key.

2. Select the range **F6:J6**, and then click the **Copy** button on the Standard toolbar.

3. Click cell **F7** and then click the **Paste** button on the Standard toolbar.

Figure 2-12 shows the first three rows of the payment schedule.

Figure 2-12   PASTING THE THIRD ROW OF THE PAYMENT SCHEDULE

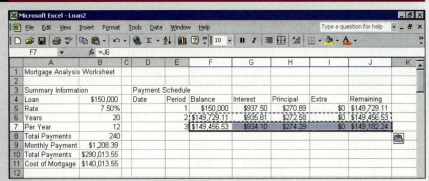

4. Examine the formulas in cells G5, G6, and G7. Note that the relative reference to the balance remaining on the loan changes from F5 to F6 to F7 as you proceed down the schedule, but the interest rate per period keeps the same absolute reference, $B$5/$B$7.

As you would expect, the interest payment schedule decreases as the remaining balance decreases, and the monthly payment that goes to the principal steadily increases. Carol would like you to complete the rest of the payment schedule for all 240 payment periods. You will explore how to complete the rest of the payment schedule in a quick and efficient way in the next session.

To close the Loan2 workbook:

1. Click **File** on the menu bar, and then click **Exit**.

2. When prompted to save your changes to Loan2.xls, click the **Yes** button.

Session 2.1 Quick Check

1. Which function would you enter to calculate the minimum value in the range B1:B50?
2. What function would you enter to calculate the ratio between the maximum value in the range B1:B50 and the minimum value?
3. A 5-year loan for $10,000 has been taken out at 7% interest compounded quarterly. What function would you enter to calculate the quarterly payment on the loan?
4. Which function would you use to determine the amount of interest due in the second quarter of the first year of the loan discussed in question 3?
5. In the formula *A8+$C$1*, *$C$1* is an example of a(n) _____ reference.
6. Cell A10 contains the formula *=A1+B1*. If the contents of this cell were copied to cell B11, what formula would be inserted into that cell?
7. Cell A10 contains the formula *=$A1+B$1*. If this cell were copied to cell B11, what formula would be inserted into that cell? What would the formula be if you moved cell A10 to B11?

SESSION 2.2

In this session you will use Excel's Auto Fill feature to automatically fill in formulas, series, and dates. You will use Excel's logical functions to create functions that return different values based on different conditions. Finally, you will learn how Excel stores dates, and then you will work with dates using Excel's library of date and time functions.

Filling in Formulas and Values

So far you have entered only three periods of the 240 total payment periods into the payment schedule. You used the copy and paste technique to enter the values for the second and third rows. You could continue to copy and paste the remaining rows of the payment schedule, but you can use a more efficient technique—the fill handle. The **fill handle** is a small black square located in the lower-right corner of a selected cell or range. When you drag the fill handle, Excel automatically fills in the formulas or formats used in the selected cells. This technique is also referred to as **Auto Fill**.

REFERENCE WINDOW

Copying Formulas Using Auto Fill

- Select the range that contains the formulas you want to copy.
- Click and drag the fill handle in the direction you want to copy the formulas.
- Release the mouse button.
- If necessary, click the Auto Fill Options button, and then select the Auto Fill option you want to apply to the selected range.

Copying Formulas

Carol wants you to copy the formulas from the range F6:J7 into the larger range F7:J244. Copying the formulas into the larger range will, in effect, calculate the monthly payments for all 240 periods of the loan—all 20 years of the mortgage.

To copy the formulas using the fill handle:

1. If you took a break after the previous session, make sure Excel is running and the Loan2 workbook is open.

2. Verify that the Mortgage sheet is the active worksheet.

3. Select the range **F6:J7**.

4. Position the pointer over the fill handle (the square box in the lower-right corner of cell J7) until the pointer changes to ✚.

5. Click and drag the fill handle down the worksheet to cell **J244**. As you drag the fill handle, an outline appears displaying the selected cells, and the worksheet automatically scrolls down.

6. Release the mouse button. By default, Excel copies the values and formulas found in the original range F6:J7 into the new range F7:J244. See Figure 2-13.

Figure 2-13   FILLING IN THE REST OF THE PAYMENT SCHEDULE VALUES

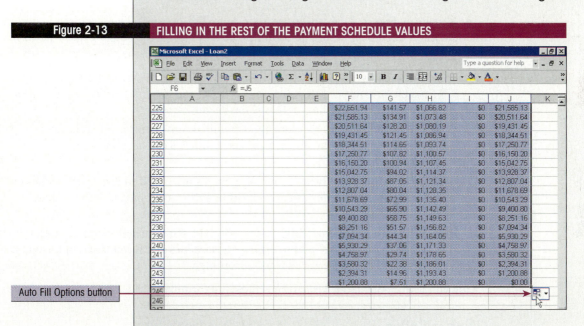

Auto Fill Options button

TROUBLE? It is very easy to "overshoot the mark" when dragging the fill handle down. If this happens, you can either click the Undo button on the Standard toolbar and try again, or simply select the extras formulas you created and delete them.

Excel has copied the formulas from the first few rows of the payment schedule into the rest of the rows and has also automatically adjusted any relative references in the formulas. For example, the formula in cell G244 is =F244*$B$5/$B$7, which is the interest due on the last loan payment, an amount of $7.51. The last row in the payment schedule shows a remaining balance of $0.00 in cell J244. The loan is paid off.

Note that to the right of the filled values is the Auto Fill Options button. Clicking this button displays the available options that you can choose from to specify how Excel should perform the Auto Fill. Click this button now to view the options.

To view the Auto Fill options:

1. Click the **Auto Fill Options** button to the right of cell J244. Excel displays the Auto Fill Options menu, as shown in Figure 2-14.

Figure 2-14   **AUTO FILL OPTIONS**

2. Click anywhere outside of the menu to hide it.

As shown in Figure 2-14, there are four Auto Fill options. These options determine whether Excel copies the values or formulas, or whether Excel simply copies the formats used to display those values and formulas. The four options and their descriptions are:

- **Copy Cells**: Copies the values and formulas into the selected range, as well as the formats used to display those values and formulas. Relative references are adjusted accordingly. This is the default option.
- **Fill Series**: Copies the values and formulas into the selected range, and completes any arithmetic or geometric series. Relative references are adjusted accordingly.
- **Fill Formatting Only**: Copies only the formats used to display the values or formulas in the cells. Values and formulas are not copied into the selected range.
- **Fill Without Formatting**: Copies the values and formulas into the selected range. The formats used to display those values and formulas are not copied. Relative references are adjusted accordingly.

You will learn more about formatting values and formulas in the next tutorial.

Filling a Series

Missing from the payment schedule are the numbers in column E. There should be a sequence of numbers starting with the value 1 in cell E5 and ending with the value 240 in cell E244. Since these numbers are all different, you cannot simply copy and paste the values. You can, however, use the fill handle to complete a series of numbers, as long as you include the first few numbers of the series. If the numbers increase by a constant value in an arithmetic series, dragging the fill handle will continue that same increase over the length of the newly selected cells.

Use the fill handle to enter the numbers for the Period column in the payment schedule.

To fill in the payment period values:

1. Press **Ctrl + Home** to return to the top of the worksheet.
2. Select the range **E5:E7**.

3. Click and drag the fill handle down to cell **E244**. Note that as you drag the fill handle a label appears indicating the current value in the series. When you reach cell E244, the label displays the value *240*.

4. Release the mouse button. Figure 2-15 shows the values in the payment schedule through the 240th payment.

Figure 2-15   **FILLING IN THE PAYMENT PERIOD NUMBERS**

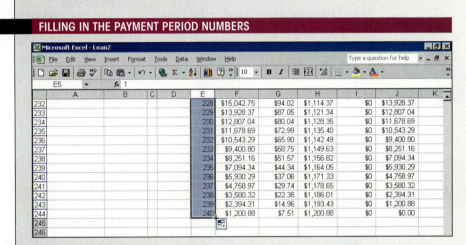

Filling In Dates

You can also use the fill handle to fill in dates—the one part of the payment schedule you have not entered yet. As with filling in a series, if you specify the initial date or dates, Excel will automatically insert the rest of the dates. The series of dates that Excel fills in depends on the dates you start with. If you start with dates that are separated by a single day, Excel will fill in a series of days. If you start with dates separated by a single month, Excel will fill in a series of months and so forth. You can also specify how to fill in the date values using the Auto Fill Options button.

Next you will insert an initial date for the loan as August 1, 2003, and then specify that each payment period is due at the beginning of the next month.

To insert the payment dates:

1. Type **8/1/2003** in cell D5, and then click the **Enter** button on the Formula bar. Note that clicking the Enter button on the Formula bar inserts the value in the cell and keeps it the active cell.

2. Drag the fill handle down to cell **D244**, and then release the mouse button. Note that as you drag the fill handle down, the date appears in the pop-up label; the date *3/27/2004* appears when you reach cell D244.

   TROUBLE? Don't worry if your computer is set up to display dates in a different format. The format doesn't affect the date value.

   By default, Excel created a series of consecutive days. You need to change the consecutive days to consecutive months.

3. Click the **Auto Fill Options** button located to the lower-right corner of cell D244.

4. Click the **Fill Months** option button. Excel fills in consecutive months in the payment schedule. The last payment date is 7/1/2023. See Figure 2-16.

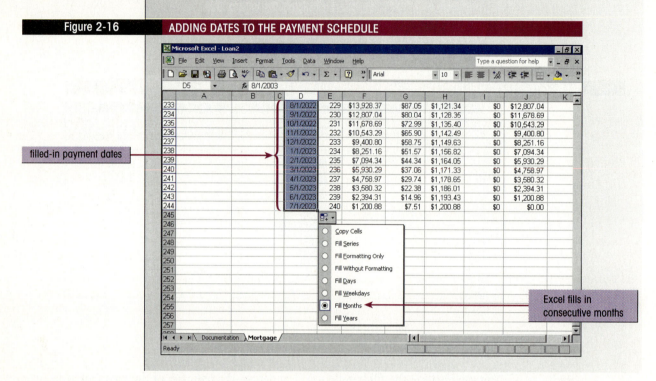

Figure 2-16   ADDING DATES TO THE PAYMENT SCHEDULE

filled-in payment dates

Excel fills in consecutive months

Excel provides other techniques for automatically inserting series of numbers into your worksheets. You can even create your own customized fill series. You can use the online Help to learn how to use the other Auto Fill options. For now though, you have completed the payment schedule.

Carol wants to verify that the numbers you have inserted into the payment schedule are correct. She suggests that, as a check, you add up the interest payments in column G. The total should match the cost of the mortgage that you calculated in cell B11.

To calculate the total interest payments:

1. Click cell **A13**, and type **Observed Payments**, and then press the **Enter** key.

2. In cell A14, type **Cost of Mortgage**, and then press the **Tab** key. The observed cost of the mortgage is the sum of interest payments in the range G5:G244.

3. In cell B14, type **=SUM(G5:G244)**, and then press the **Enter** key. As shown in Figure 2-17, the total cost of the interest payments in the payment schedule, $140,013.55, matches what was calculated in cell B11.

Figure 2-17 TOTAL INTEREST PAYMENTS FROM THE PAYMENT SCHEDULE

	A	B	C	D	E	F	G	H	I	J
1	Mortgage Analysis Worksheet									
2										
3	Summary Information			Payment Schedule						
4	Loan	$150,000		Date	Period	Balance	Interest	Principal	Extra	Remaining
5	Rate	7.50%		8/1/2003	1	$150,000	$937.50	$270.89	$0	$149,729.11
6	Years	20		9/1/2003	2	$149,729.11	$935.81	$272.58	$0	$149,456.53
7	Per Year	12		10/1/2003	3	$149,456.53	$934.10	$274.29	$0	$149,182.24
8	Total Payments	240		11/1/2003	4	$149,182.24	$932.39	$276.00	$0	$148,906.24
9	Monthly Payment	$1,208.39		12/1/2003	5	$148,906.24	$930.66	$277.73	$0	$148,628.51
10	Total Payments	$290,013.55		1/1/2004	6	$148,628.51	$928.93	$279.46	$0	$148,349.05
11	Cost of Mortgage	$140,013.55		2/1/2004	7	$148,349.05	$927.18	$281.21	$0	$148,067.84
12				3/1/2004	8	$148,067.84	$925.42	$282.97	$0	$147,784.88
13	Observed Payments			4/1/2004	9	$147,784.88	$923.66	$284.73	$0	$147,500.14
14	Cost of Mortgage	$140,013.55		5/1/2004	10	$147,500.14	$921.88	$286.51	$0	$147,213.63
15				6/1/2004	11	$147,213.63	$920.09	$288.30	$0	$146,925.33
16				7/1/2004	12	$146,925.33	$918.28	$290.11	$0	$146,635.22

Using Excel's Logical Functions

So far you have assumed that there are no extra payments toward the principal. In fact, the PMT function assumes constant periodic deposits with no additional payments. If extra payments were made, they would reduce the cost of the mortgage and speed up the payment of the loan. Carol would like to see what the effect would be on the payment schedule and the cost of the mortgage if an extra payment were made.

To add an extra payment to the schedule:

1. Click cell **I22**, which corresponds to the payment period for 1/1/2005.

   Now assume that a client makes an extra payment of $20,000 toward the principal on this date.

2. Type **$20,000** in cell I22, and then press the **Enter** key. The observed cost of the mortgage shown in cell B14 drops to $80,262.15.

3. Scroll down the worksheet until row **190** comes into view (corresponding to the date of 1/1/2019). See Figure 2-18.

Figure 2-18 NEGATIVE INTEREST PAYMENTS

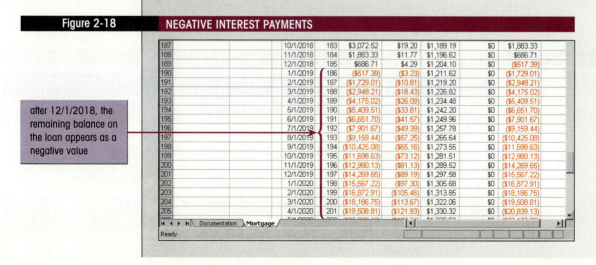

after 12/1/2018, the remaining balance on the loan appears as a negative value

Something is wrong. With the extra payment, the loan is paid off early, at the end of the 185th payment period; but starting with 12/1/2018, the payment schedule no longer makes sense. It appears that the client is still making payments on a loan that is already paid off.

The effect of this error is that the remaining balance and the interest payments appear as negative values after the loan is paid off. But remember, in cell B14, you calculated the sum of the interest payments to determine the observed cost of the mortgage. With those negative interest payment values included, that total will be wrong.

To correct this problem, you need to revise the PMT function that determines the monthly payment directed toward the principal. Currently, this function subtracts the interest due from the monthly mortgage payment to arrive at the amount of the principal payment. You need to use a function that decides which of the two following situations is true:

- The remaining balance is greater than the payment toward the principal.
- The remaining balance is less than the payment toward the principal.

A function that determines whether a condition is true or false is called a **logical function**. Excel supports several logical functions, which are described in Figure 2-19.

Figure 2-19 EXCEL'S LOGICAL FUNCTIONS

FUNCTION	DESCRIPTION
AND(*logical1*,[*logical2*], …)	Returns the value TRUE if all arguments are true; returns FALSE if one or more arguments is false
FALSE()	Returns the value FALSE
IF(*logical_test*,*value_if_true*,*value_if_false*)	Returns *value_if_true* if the *logical_test* argument is true; returns the *value_if_false* if the *logical_test* argument is false
NOT(*logical*)	Returns the value TRUE if *logical* is false; returns the value FALSE if *logical* is true
OR(*logical1*,[*logical2*], …)	Returns the value TRUE if at least one argument is true; returns FALSE if all arguments are false
TRUE()	Returns the value TRUE

In this loan workbook, you will be using an IF function. The syntax of the IF function is =IF(*logical_test*,*value_if_true*,*value_if_false*) where *logical_test* is an expression that is either true or false, *value_if_true* is an expression that Excel will run if the *logical_test* is true, and *value_if_false* is an expression that runs when the *logical_test* is false. The logical test is constructed using a comparison operator. A **comparison operator** checks whether two expressions are equal, whether one is greater than the other, and so forth. Figure 2-20 describes the six comparison operators supported by Excel.

Figure 2-20 COMPARISON OPERATORS

OPERATOR	EXAMPLE	DESCRIPTION
=	A1=B1	Checks if the value in cell A1 equals the value in cell B1
>	A1>B1	Checks if the value in cell A1 is greater than B1
<	A1<B1	Checks if the value in cell A1 is less than B1
>=	A1>=B1	Checks if the value in cell A1 is greater than or equal to B1
<=	A1<=B1	Checks if the value in cell A1 is less than or equal to B1
<>	A1<>B1	Checks if the value in cell A1 is not equal to the value in cell B1

For example, the function =IF(A1=10,20,30) tests whether the value in cell A1 is equal to 10. If so, the function returns the value 20, otherwise the function returns the value 30. You can also use cell references in place of values.

The function =IF(A1=10,B1,B2) returns the value from cell B1 if A1 equals 10, otherwise the function returns the value stored in cell B2.

You can also make comparisons with text strings. When you do, the text strings must be enclosed in quotation marks. For example, the function =IF(A1="RETAIL",B1,B2) tests whether the text RETAIL has been entered into cell A1. If so, the function returns the value from cell B1, otherwise it returns the value from cell B2.

Because some functions are very complex, you might find it easier to enter a logical function, such as the IF function, using Excel's Insert Function option. You will use the Insert Function option to enter an IF function in the first row of the payment schedule.

To enter the IF function in the first row of the payment schedule:

1. Click cell **H5** in the payment schedule, and then press the **Delete** key to clear the cell contents.

2. Click the **Insert Function** button f_x on the Formula bar.

3. Click the **Or select a category** list arrow, and then click **Logical** in the list of categories displayed.

4. Click **IF** in the Select a Function list box, and then click the **OK** button to open the Function Arguments dialog box.

   First, you need to enter the logical test. The test is whether the remaining balance in cell F5 is greater than the usual amount of payment toward the principal, which is equal to the monthly loan payment ($B$9) minus the interest payment (G5). The logical test is therefore F5>($B$9–G5).

5. In the Logical_test argument box, enter **F5>($B$9–G5)**, and then press the **Tab** key.

   If the logical test is true (in other words, if the remaining balance is greater than the principal payment), Excel should return the usual principal payment. In this case, that value is the expression $B$9–G5.

6. In the Value_if_true argument box, enter **$B$9–G5**, and then press the **Tab** key.

   If the logical test is false (which means that the balance remaining is *less* than the usual principal payment), the payment should be set equal to the remaining balance—which has the effect of paying off the loan. In this case, Excel should return the value in cell F5.

7. In the Value_if_false argument box, enter **F5**. Figure 2-21 shows the completed dialog box.

Figure 2-21   INSERTING THE IF FUNCTION

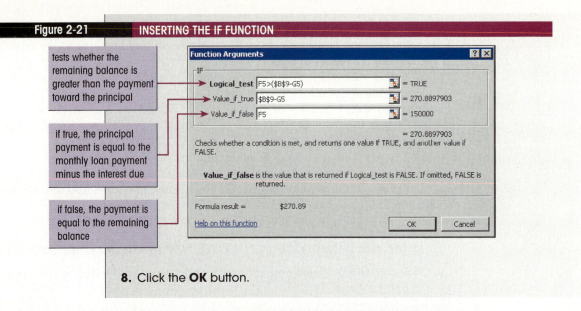

- tests whether the remaining balance is greater than the payment toward the principal
- if true, the principal payment is equal to the monthly loan payment minus the interest due
- if false, the payment is equal to the remaining balance

8. Click the **OK** button.

Now copy this new formula into the rest of the payment schedule.

To fill in the rest of the payment schedule:

1. With cell H5 the active cell, click the fill handle and drag it down to cell **H244**.

2. Scroll up to row **190**. As shown in Figure 2-22, the payment schedule now accurately shows that once the remaining balance reaches $0, the interest payments and the payments toward the principal also become $0.

Figure 2-22   NEW PAYMENT VALUES

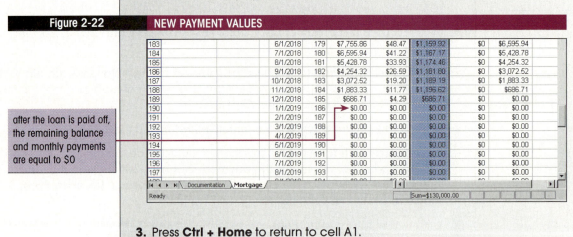

after the loan is paid off, the remaining balance and monthly payments are equal to $0

3. Press **Ctrl + Home** to return to cell A1.

Note that with the extra payment, the observed cost of the mortgage is $93,034.73. Thus, if a client were to make an extra payment of $20,000 on 1/1/2005, Carol could tell the client that there would be a savings of almost $47,000 over the history of the loan.

Making an extra payment or payments will greatly affect the number of payment periods. From the payment schedule, you can tell that the number of payment periods would be 185. The question is how can you include this information in the summary section at the top of the worksheet. To include the information, you will have to make the following change to the payment period values in column E of the payment schedule:

- If the balance is greater than 0, the period number should be one higher than the previous period number.
- If the balance is 0, set the period number to 0.

You'll make this change to the payment schedule now.

To add an IF function that adjusts the period numbers in case of extra payments:

1. Click cell **E6** to make it the active cell, and then press the **Delete** key.
2. Click the **Insert Function** button f_x on the Formula toolbar.
3. Click **IF** in the Select a function list box, and then click the **OK** button.

   The logical test is whether the balance (in cell F6) is greater than $0 or not.

4. In the Logical_test argument box, enter **F6>0**, and then press the **Tab** key.

   If the logical test is true, the period number should be equal to the previous period number (E5) plus 1.

5. In the Value_if_true argument box, enter **E5+1**, and then press the **Tab** key.

   If the logical test is false, the balance is 0. Set the period number to 0.

6. In the Value_if_false argument box, type **0**, and then click the **OK** button.
7. Verify that E6 is still the active cell, and then click and drag the fill handle down to cell **E244**.
8. Scroll up the worksheet to row **190**. Note that once the loan is paid off, the period number is equal to 0. See Figure 2-23.

Figure 2-23 **NEW PAYMENT PERIOD NUMBERS**

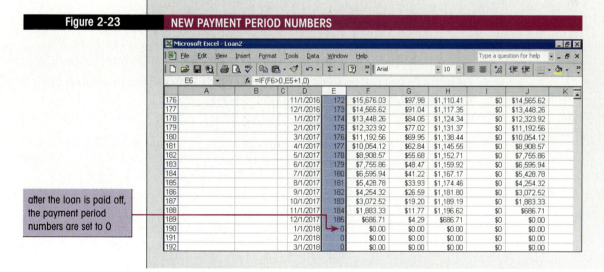

after the loan is paid off, the payment period numbers are set to 0

Using the AutoSum Button

Since the period numbers are all equal to zero after the loan is paid off, the last period number in the payment schedule will also be the largest. You can, therefore, use the MAX function to calculate the maximum, or last, payment period in the schedule. You can enter the MAX function either by typing the function directly into the active cell or by using the

Insert Function button on the Formula bar. However, Excel also provides the AutoSum button on the Standard toolbar to give you quick access to the SUM, AVERAGE, COUNT, MIN, and MAX functions. The AutoSum button can be a real timesaver, so you will use it in this situation.

To use the AutoSum button to calculate the maximum payment period:

1. Scroll to the top of the worksheet.

2. Click cell **A15**, type **Total Payments** and then press the **Tab** key.

3. Click the **list arrow** for the AutoSum button ∑ ▾ on the Standard toolbar to display a list of summary functions. See Figure 2-24.

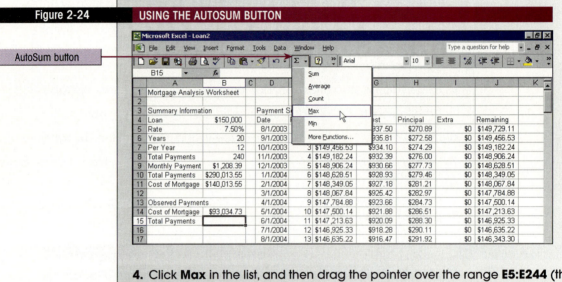

Figure 2-24   USING THE AUTOSUM BUTTON

AutoSum button

4. Click **Max** in the list, and then drag the pointer over the range **E5:E244** (the range containing the payment period numbers from the payment schedule).

5. Press the **Enter** key. The formula =MAX(E5:E244) is automatically entered into cell B15, and the value 185 appears in the cell.

Carol suggests you test the new payment schedule one more time. She asks what the effect would be if the extra payment on 1/1/2005 was increased from $20,000 to $25,000.

> **To test the new payment figures:**
>
> 1. Click cell **I22**.
> 2. Type **$25,000** and then press the **Enter** key.

The cost of the mortgage decreases to $84,368.07 and the number of payments decreases to 174.

Using Excel's Date Functions

Excel stores dates as integers, where the integer values represent the number of days since January 1, 1900. For example, the integer value for the date January 1, 2008 is 39448 because that date is 39,448 days after January 1, 1900. Most of the time you do not see these values because Excel automatically formats the integers to appear as dates, such as 1/1/2008. This method of storing the dates allows you to work with dates in the same way you work with numbers. For example, if you subtract one date from another, the answer will be the number of days separating the two dates.

In addition to creating simple formulas with date values, you can use Excel's date functions to create dates or to extract information about date values. To insert the current date into your workbook, you could use the TODAY function, for example. To determine which day of the week a particular date falls on, you could use the WEEKDAY function. Note that the date functions use your computer's system clock to return a value. Figure 2-25 describes some of Excel's more commonly used date functions.

Figure 2-25   EXCEL'S DATE FUNCTIONS

FUNCTION	DESCRIPTION
DATE(year, month, day)	Returns the integer for the date represented by the *year*, *month*, and *day* arguments
DAY(date)	Extracts the day of the month from the *date* value
MONTH(date)	Extracts the month number from the *date* value, where January=1, February=2, and so forth
NOW(), TODAY()	Returns the integer for the current date and time
WEEKDAY(date)	Calculates the day of the week using the *date* value, where Sunday=1, Monday=2, and so forth
YEAR(date)	Extracts the year number from the *date* value

On the Documentation sheet, there is a cell for entering the current date. Rather than typing the date in manually, you will enter it using the TODAY function.

To use the TODAY function:

1. Click the **Documentation** tab to make it the active worksheet, and then click cell **B4**.

2. Click the **Insert Function** button on the Formula bar.

3. Select **Date & Time** from the function category list.

4. Scroll down the list, click **TODAY**, and then click the **OK** button twice. Note that the second dialog box indicated that there are no arguments for the TODAY function. The current date is entered into cell B4 (your date will most likely be different). See Figure 2-26.

Figure 2-26   **INSERTING THE CURRENT DATE**

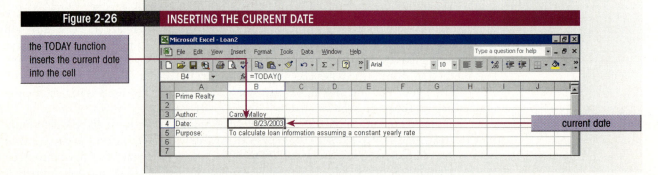

the TODAY function inserts the current date into the cell

current date

The TODAY and NOW functions will always display the current date and time. Thus, if you reopen this workbook on a different date, the date in cell B4 will be updated to reflect that change. If you want a permanent date (that might reflect when the workbook was initially developed), you enter the date directly into the cell without using a function.

You have completed your work on the Loan workbook. Carol will examine the workbook and get back to you with more assignments. For now, you can close Excel and save your work.

To save your work:

1. Click **File** on the menu bar, and then click **Exit**.

2. Click the **Yes** button when prompted to save your changes.

Session 2.2 Quick Check

1. Describe how you would create a series of odd numbers from 1 to 99 in column A of your worksheet.

2. Describe how you would create a series of yearly dates, ranging from 1/1/2003 to 1/1/2030, in column A of your worksheet.

3. What function would you enter to return the text string "Yes" if cell A1 is greater than cell B1 and "No" if cell A1 is not greater than cell B1?

4. Describe three ways of entering the SUM function into a worksheet cell.

5. Which function would you enter to extract the year value from the date entered into cell A1?

6. Which function would you enter to display the current date in the worksheet?

7. Which function would you enter to determine which day of the week a date entered into cell A1 falls on?

Review Assignments

Carol has another workbook for you to examine. Although the loan workbook was helpful, Carol realizes that most of the time she will be working with clients who can make only a specified monthly payment. She wants to have a workbook in which she enters a specific monthly payment and from that amount determine how large a mortgage her client can afford.

To determine this information, you will use the PV function: PV(*rate,nper,pmt,[fv=0],[type=0]*) where *rate* is the interest per period, *nper* is the number of payment periods, *pmt* is the monthly payment, *fv* is the future value of the loan (assumed to be 0), and *type* specifies when the loan will be paid (assumed to be 0 at the beginning of each payment period). For a loan, the *pmt* argument must be a negative number since it represents an expense and not income. The PV function then returns the present value of the loan or annuity. In Carol's workbook, the return would be the largest mortgage her clients can afford for a given monthly payment.

As with the previous workbook, Carol wants this new workbook to contain a payment schedule. The current annual interest rate is 7.5% compounded monthly. Carol wants the payment schedule to assume a 20-year mortgage with a monthly payment of $950. What is the largest mortgage her clients could get under those conditions, and how much would the interest payments total?

To complete this task:

1. Start Excel and open the **Mort1** workbook located in the Tutorial.02/Review folder on your Data Disk.

2. Save the workbook as **Mort2** in the same folder.

3. Enter your name and the current date in the Documentation sheet (use a function to automatically insert the date). Switch to the Mortgage worksheet.

4. Enter "$950" for the monthly payment in cell B4, "7.5%" as the interest rate in cell B5, "20" as the number of years, and "12" as the number of periods per year.

5. Enter a formula in cell B8 to calculate the total number of payments over the history of the loan.

Explore

6. In cell B10, use the PV function to calculate the largest mortgage a client could receive under those conditions. Also, assume that the payments are made at the beginning of each month. Remember that you need to make the monthly payment, which appears in cell B4, a negative, so the return is a positive number.

7. Complete the first row of the payment schedule, with the following formulas:
   - The initial value of the payment period should be equal to 1.
   - The initial balance should be equal to the amount of the mortgage.
   - The interest due should be equal to the balance multiplied by the interest rate per period.
   - Use the IF function to test whether the balance is greater than the monthly payment minus the interest due. If so, the principal payment should be equal to the monthly payment minus the interest due. If not, the principal payment should be equal to the balance.
   - Set the extra payment value to $0.
   - The remaining balance should be equal to the initial balance minus the principal payment and any extra payment.

8. Complete the second row of the payment schedule with the following formulas:
   - Carry the remaining balance from cell J3 into the current balance in cell F4.
   - If the current balance is equal to 0, set the period number to 0, otherwise set the period number equal to cell E3 plus 1.
   - Copy the formulas in the range G3:J3 to the range G4:J4.

9. Select the range E4:J4 and then drag the fill handle down to fill range E242:J242. What happens to the values in the Extra column when you release the mouse button?

Explore

10. Click the Auto Fill Options button next to the filled in values. Which option button is selected? Does this help you understand what happened in the previous step? Click the Copy Cells option button to fix the problem.

11. In cell D3, enter the initial date of the loan as "4/1/2003".

12. Payments are due at the beginning of each month. Fill in the rest of the payment dates in the range D3:D242 using the appropriate Auto Fill option.

13. In cell B11, enter the cost of the mortgage, which is equal to the sum of the interest payments in the payment schedule.

14. In cell B12, enter the number of observed payments, which is equal to the maximum payment period number in the payment schedule.

Explore 15. If a client pays an extra $100 for each period of the first five years of the loan, what is the cost of the mortgage and how many months will it take to pay off the loan? On what date will the loan be paid?

16. Print the entire Mort2 workbook.

17. Save and close the workbook, and then exit Excel.

CASE PROBLEMS

Case 1. Setting Up a College Fund Lynn and Peter Chao have recently celebrated the birth of their first daughter. The couple is acutely aware of how expensive a college education is. Although the couple does not have much money, they realize that if they start saving now, they can hopefully save a nice sum for their daughter's education. They have asked you for help in setting up a college fund for their daughter.

The couple has set a goal of saving $75,000 that they will use in 18 years for college. Current annual interest rates for such funds are 6.5% compounded monthly. Lynn and Peter want you to determine how much money they would have to set aside each month to reach their goal. They would also like you to create a schedule so they can see how fast their savings will grow over the next few years.

You can calculate how fast monthly contributions to a savings account will grow using the same financial functions used to determine how fast monthly payments can pay back a loan. In this case, the present value is equal to 0 (since the couple is starting out with no savings in the college fund) and the future value is $75,000 (the amount that the couple wants to have saved after 18 years.)

To complete this task:

1. Open the **School1** workbook located in the Tutorial.02/Cases folder on your Data Disk, and then save the workbook as **School2** in the same folder.

2. Enter your name and the current date in the Documentation sheet. Switch to the College Fund worksheet.

3. Enter the Chaos' saving goal in cell B3 and the assumed annual interest rate in cell B4. Enter the number of years they plan to save in cell B5 and the number of payments per year in cell B6.

4. Enter a formula to calculate the total number of payments in cell B7.

Explore 5. In cell B9, use the PMT function to calculate the monthly payment required for the Chaos to meet their savings goal. Express your answer as a positive value rather than a negative value.

6. Begin filling out the savings schedule. In the first row, enter the following information:
   - The initial date is 1/1/2003.
   - The payment period is 1.
   - The starting balance is equal to the first monthly payment.
   - Calculate the accrued interest using the IPMT function, assuming that payments are made at the end of each month. (*Hint*: Scroll the IPMT arguments list to display all the necessary arguments.)
   - Calculate the ending balance, which is equal to the starting balance plus the interest accrued in the current month.

7. Enter the second row of the table, using the following guidelines:
   - The date is one month later than the previous date.
   - The payment period is 2.
   - The starting balance is equal to the previous month's ending balance plus the monthly payment.
   - Use the IPMT function to calculate the interest for the second payment period.
   - The ending balance is once again equal to the starting balance plus the accrued interest.

8. Use the fill handle to fill in the remaining 214 months of the savings schedule. Choose the appropriate fill options to ensure that the values in the dates and the period and interest values fill in correctly.

9. Save your changes.

10. Print a copy of the College Fund worksheet, and then indicate on the printout how much the couple will have to save each month to reach their savings goal.

11. Save and close the workbook, and then exit Excel.

Case 2. Payroll Information at Sonic Sounds Jeff Gwydion manages the payroll at Sonic Sounds. He has asked you for help in setting up a worksheet to store payroll values. The payroll contains three elements: the employee's salary, the 401(k) contribution, and the employee's health insurance cost. The company's 401(k) contribution is 3% of the employee's salary for employees who have worked for the company at least one year; otherwise the company's contribution is zero. Sonic Sounds also supports two health insurance plans: Premier and Standard. The cost of the Premier plan is $6,500, and the cost of the Standard plan is $5,500.

The workbook has already been set up for you. Your job is to enter the functions and formulas to calculate the 401(k) contributions and health insurance costs for each employee.

To complete this task:

1. Open the **Sonic1** workbook located in the Tutorial.02/Cases folder on your Data Disk, and save the workbook as **Sonic2** in the same folder.

2. Enter your name and the current date (calculated using a function) in the Documentation sheet. Switch to the Payroll worksheet.

3. In cell C13, determine the number of years the employee Abbot has been employed by subtracting the date Abbot was hired from the current date and then dividing the difference by 365.

4. Use the fill handle to compute the years employed for the rest of the employees.

Explore

5. Use an IF function to compute the 401(k) contribution for each employee (*Note*: Remember that an employee must have worked at Sonic for at least one year to be eligible for the 401(k) contribution.)

Explore

6. Use an IF function to calculate the health insurance cost for each employee at the company. (*Hint*: Test whether the employee's health plan listed in column E is equal to the value in cell B4. If so, the employee is using the Premier plan, and the health cost is equal to the value in cell C4. If not, the employee is using the Standard plan, and the health cost is equal to the value in cell C5.)

7. Calculate the total salaries, total 401(k) contributions, and total health insurance expenses for all of the employees at Sonic Sounds. Place the functions in the range B7:B9.

8. Print the contents of the **Sonic2** workbook.

9. Redo the analysis, assuming that the cost of the Premier plan has risen to $7,000 and the cost of the Standard plan has risen to $6,100. What is the total health insurance cost to the company's employees?

10. Print just the Payroll sheet.

11. Save and close the workbook, and then exit Excel.

Case 3. Depreciation at Leland Hospital Leland Hospital in Leland, Ohio, has purchased a new x-ray machine for its operating room. Debra Sanchez in purchasing wants your assistance in calculating the yearly depreciation of the machine. **Depreciation** is the declining value of an asset over its lifetime. To calculate the depreciation, you need the initial cost of the asset, the number of years or periods that the asset will be used, and the final or salvage value of the asset. The new x-ray machine costs $450,000. The hospital expects that the x-ray machine will be used for 10 years and that at the end of the 10-year period the salvage value will be $50,000. Debra wants you to calculate the depreciation of the machine for each year in that 10-year period.

Accountants use several different methods to calculate depreciation. The difference between each method lies in how fast the asset declines in value. Figure 2-27 describes four Excel functions that you can use to calculate depreciation.

Figure 2-27 EXCEL'S DEPRECIATION FUNCTIONS

METHOD	FUNCTION	DESCRIPTION
Straight-line	SLN(*cost, salvage, life*)	The straight-line method distributes the depreciation evenly over the life of the asset, so that the depreciation is the same in each period. The argument *cost* is the cost of the asset, *salvage* is the salvage value at the end of the life of the asset, and *life* is the number of periods that the asset is being depreciated.
Sum-of-years	SYD(*cost, salvage, life, per*)	The sum-of-years method concentrates the most depreciation in the earliest periods of the lifetime of the asset. The argument *per* is the period that you want to calculate the depreciation for.
Fixed-declining balance	DB(*cost, salvage, life, period, [month=12]*)	The fixed-declining balance method is an accelerated depreciation method in which the highest depreciation occurs in the earliest periods. The argument *month* is an optional argument that specifies the number of months in the first year (assumed to be 12).
Double-declining balance	DDB(*cost, salvage, life, period, [factor=2]*)	The double-declining balance method is an accelerated method in which the highest depreciation occurs in the earliest periods. The optional *factor* argument controls that rate at which the balance declines.

Debra wants you to calculate the depreciation using all four methods so that she can see the impact on each method on the asset's value. She has already created the workbook containing the basic figures; she needs you to add the formulas.

To complete this task:

1. Open the **Leland1** workbook located in the Tutorial.02/Cases folder on your Data Disk and save the workbook as **Leland2** in the same folder.

2. Enter your name and the current date (calculated using a function) in the Documentation sheet. Switch to the Depreciation worksheet.

3. Enter the cost of the x-ray machine in cell B3, the lifetime of the machine in cell B4, and the salvage value in B5.

Explore 4. In the range B9:B18, enter the depreciation of the x-ray machine using the straight-line method.

5. In the range C9:C18, enter the yearly value of the machine after the depreciation is applied (*Hint*: After the first year, you must subtract the yearly depreciation from the previous year's value).

Explore 6. In the range F9:F18, enter the depreciation using the sum-of-years method.

7. In the range G9:G18, calculate the yearly value of the machine after the sum-of-years depreciation.

Explore 8. In the range B22:B31, calculate the fixed-declining depreciation for each year.

9. In the range C22:C31, calculate the value of the x-ray machine after applying the fixed-declining depreciation.

Explore

10. In the range F22:F31, calculate the double-declining depreciation for each year.

11. In the range G22:G31, calculate the yearly value of the x-ray machine after applying the double-declining depreciation.

12. Print the entire workbook.

13. Save and close the workbook, and then exit Excel.

Case 4. Analyzing Faculty Salaries at Glenmore Junior College
A complaint has been raised at Glenmore Junior College, a liberal arts college in upstate New York, that female faculty members are being paid less than their male counterparts. Professor Lawton, a member of the faculty senate, has asked you to compile basic statistics on faculty salaries, broken down by gender. The current salary figures are shown in Figure 2-28.

Figure 2-28 FACULTY SALARIES

MALE FACULTY	MALE FACULTY	MALE FACULTY	FEMALE FACULTY	FEMALE FACULTY
$40,000	$55,000	$75,000	$25,000	$60,000
$45,000	$55,000	$75,000	$30,000	$60,000
$45,000	$60,000	$75,000	$35,000	$60,000
$45,000	$60,000	$75,000	$40,000	$60,000
$45,000	$60,000	$80,000	$42,000	$62,000
$45,000	$62,000	$85,000	$45,000	$62,000
$45,000	$62,000	$95,000	$47,000	$65,000
$50,000	$65,000	$115,000	$50,000	$65,000
$50,000	$65,000		$55,000	$67,000
$52,000	$65,000		$55,000	$70,000
$55,000	$70,000		$57,000	$75,000

To complete this task:

1. Create a new workbook named **JrCol** and store it in the Tutorial.02/Cases folder on your Data Disk.

2. Insert a Documentation sheet into the workbook containing your name, the current date (calculated using a function), and the purpose of the workbook.

3. Rename Sheet1 as "Statistical Analysis" and delete any unused worksheets.

4. In the Statistical Analysis worksheet, enter the male and female faculty salaries in two separate columns labeled "Male Faculty" and "Female Faculty."

Explore

5. Use Excel's statistical functions to create a table of the following statistics for all faculty members, male faculty members, and female faculty members:
   - the count
   - the sum of the salaries
   - the average salary
   - the median salary
   - the minimum salary
   - the maximum salary
   - the range of salary values (maximum minus minimum)
   - the standard deviation of the salary values
   - the standard error of the salary values (the standard deviation divided by the square root of the number of salaries)

6. Compare the average male salary to the average female salary. Is there evidence that the female faculty members are paid significantly less?

7. Average values can sometimes be skewed by high values. Compare the median male salary to the median female salary. Is the evidence supporting the complaint stronger or weaker using the median salary figures?

Explore

8. Select the cell range containing the statistics you calculated, and then print only that selected range.

9. Save and close the workbook, and then exit Excel.

INTERNET ASSIGNMENTS

Student Union

The purpose of the Internet Assignments is to challenge you to find information on the Internet that you can use to create effective spreadsheets. The actual assignments are updated and maintained on the Course Technology Web site. Log on to the Internet and use your Web browser to go to the Student Union on the New Perspectives Series site at **www.course.com/NewPerspectives/studentunion**. Click the Online Companions link, and then click the link for this text.

QUICK CHECK ANSWERS

Session 2.1

1. =MIN(B1:B50)
2. =MAX(B1:50)/MIN(B1:B50)
3. =PMT(0.07/4,20,10000)
4. =IPMT(0.07/4,2,20,10000)
5. absolute reference
6. =B2+C2
7. =$A2+C$1; if moved, the formula would stay the same, =$A1+B$1

Session 2.2

1. Enter the values *1* and *3* in the first two rows of column A. Select the two cells and then drag the fill handle down to complete the rest of the series.

2. Enter *1/1/2003* in the first cell. Select the first cell and then drag the fill handle down 27 rows. Click the Auto Fill Options button, and then click the Fill Years option button.

3. =IF(A1>B1,"Yes","No")

4. Type the SUM function directly into the cell while in edit mode, using the Insert Function button on the Formula bar or using the AutoSum button on the Standard toolbar.

5. =YEAR(A1)

6. =TODAY()

7. =WEEKDAY(A1)

TUTORIAL 3

OBJECTIVES

In this tutorial you will:

- Format data using different fonts, sizes, and font styles
- Align cell contents
- Add cell borders and backgrounds
- Merge cells and hide rows and columns
- Format the worksheet background and sheet tabs
- Find and replace formats within a worksheet
- Create and apply styles
- Apply an AutoFormat to a table
- Format a printout using Print Preview
- Create a header and footer for a printed worksheet
- Define a print area and add a page break to a printed worksheet

DEVELOPING A PROFESSIONAL-LOOKING WORKSHEET

Formatting a Sales Report

CASE

NewGeneration Monitors

NewGeneration Monitors is a computer equipment company that specializes in computer monitors. Joan Sanchez has been entering sales data on three of the company's monitors into an Excel workbook. She plans on including the sales data in a report to be presented later in the week. Joan has made no attempt to make this data presentable to her coworkers. She has simply entered the numbers. She needs you to transform her raw figures into a presentable report.

To create a professional-looking document, you will learn how to work with Excel's formatting tools to modify the appearance of the data in each cell, the cell itself, and the entire worksheet. You will also learn how to format printouts that Joan wants to generate based on her workbook. You will learn how to create headers and footers, and control which parts of the worksheet are printed on which pages.

SESSION 3.1

In this session, you will format the contents of individual cells in your worksheet by modifying the font used in the cell or by changing the font size or style. You will also use color in your worksheet, modifying the background color of worksheet cells as well as the color of the text in a cell. You will also have an opportunity to examine various Excel commands that you can use to control text alignment and to wrap a line of text within a single cell. Finally, you will create borders around individual cells and cell ranges.

Formatting Worksheet Data

The data for Joan's sales report has already been stored in an Excel workbook. Before going further, open the workbook and save it with a new filename.

To open the Sales report workbook:

1. Start Excel, and open the **Sales1** workbook located in the Tutorial.03/Tutorial folder on your Data Disk.

2. On the Documentation worksheet, enter your name in cell B3, and enter the current date in cell B4.

3. Save the workbook as **Sales2** in the Tutorial.03/Tutorial folder on your Data Disk.

4. Click the **Sales** tab. Figure 3-1 shows the current appearance of the sales report, which is unformatted.

Figure 3-1   THE UNFORMATTED SALES WORKSHEET

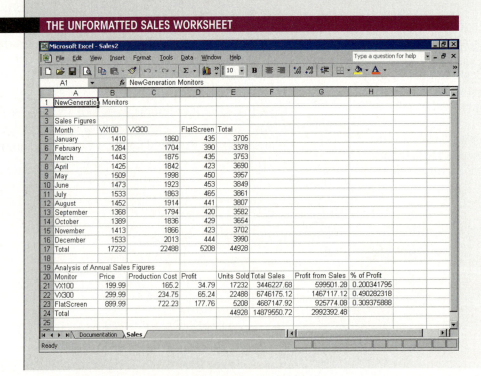

The Sales worksheet contains two tables. The first table displays the monthly sales for three of NewGeneration's monitors: the VX100, VX300, and the FlatScreen. The second table presents an analysis of these sales figures, showing the profit from the monitor sales and the percentage that each monitor contributes to the overall profit. In its current state, the worksheet is difficult to read and interpret. This is a problem that Joan wants you to solve by using Excel's formatting tools.

Formatting is the process of changing the appearance of your workbook. A properly formatted workbook can be easier to read, appear more professional, and help draw attention to important points you want to make. Formatting changes only the appearance of the data; formatting does not affect the data itself. For example, if a cell contains the value 0.124168, and you format the cell to display only up to the thousandths place (for example, 0.124), the cell still contains the precise value, even though you cannot see it displayed in the worksheet.

Up to now, Excel has been automatically formatting your cell entries using a formatting style called the General format. The **General format** aligns numbers with the right edge of the cell without dollar signs or commas, uses the minus sign for negative values, and truncates any trailing zeros to the right of the decimal point. For more control over your data's appearance, you can choose from a wide variety of other number formats. Formats can be applied using either the Formatting toolbar or the Format menu from Excel's menu bar. Formats can also be copied from one cell to another, giving you the ability to apply a common format to different cells in your worksheet.

Using the Formatting Toolbar

The Formatting toolbar is the fastest way to format your worksheet. By clicking a single button on the Formatting toolbar you can increase or decrease the number of decimal places displayed in a selected range of cells, display a value as a currency or percentage, or change the color or size of the font used in a cell.

When Joan typed in the monthly sales figures for the three monitors, she neglected to include a comma to separate the thousands from the hundreds and so forth. Rather than retype these values, you can use the Comma Style button on the Formatting toolbar to format the values with a comma. You can use the Increase Decimal or Decrease Decimal button on the Formatting toolbar to change the number of decimal places displayed in a number.

To apply the Comma format and adjust the number of decimal places displayed:

1. Select the range **B5:E17** in the Sales worksheet.

2. Click the **Comma Style** button on the Formatting toolbar. Excel adds the comma separator to each of the values in the table and displays the values with two digits to the right of the decimal point.

   TROUBLE? If you do not see the Comma Style button on the Formatting toolbar, click the Toolbar Options button on the Formatting toolbar, and then click .

   TROUBLE? If the Standard and Formatting toolbars appear on separate rows on your computer, then the Toolbar Options button might look slightly different from the Toolbar Options button used throughout this text. If you are unsure about the function of a toolbar button, hover the pointer over the button to display its name.

   Because all of the sales figures are whole numbers, you will remove the zeros.

3. Click the **Decrease Decimal** button on the Formatting toolbar twice to remove the zeros. See Figure 3-2.

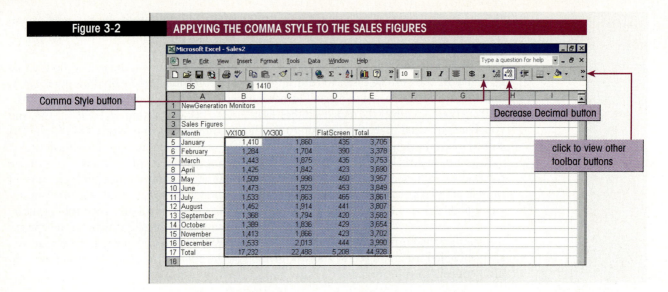

Figure 3-2   APPLYING THE COMMA STYLE TO THE SALES FIGURES

Joan's worksheet also displays the price and production cost of each monitor as well as last year's total sales and profit. She wants this information displayed using dollar signs, commas, and two decimal places. To format the values with these attributes, you can apply the Currency style.

To apply the Currency format:

1. Select the nonadjacent range **B21:D23;F21:G24**.

   TROUBLE? To select a nonadjacent range, select the first range, press and hold the Ctrl key, and then select the next range.

2. Click the **Currency Style** button $ on the Formatting toolbar. Excel adds the dollar signs and commas to the currency values and displays each value (price) to two decimal places. See Figure 3-3.

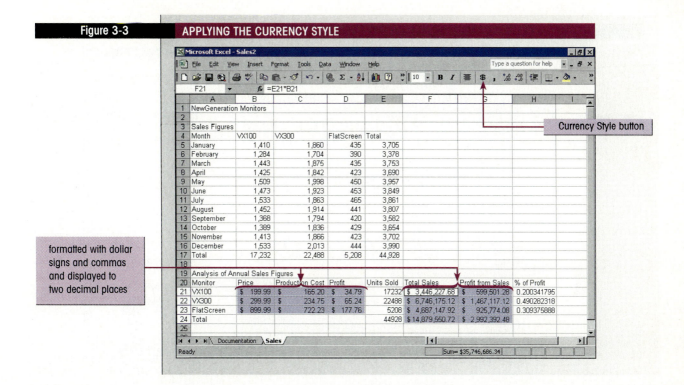

Figure 3-3 APPLYING THE CURRENCY STYLE

Finally, the range H21:H23 displays the percentage that each monitor contributes to the overall profit from sales. Joan wants these values displayed with a percent sign and to two decimal places. You will apply the Percent format; however, Excel, by default, does not display any decimal places with the Percent format. You need to increase the number of decimal places displayed.

To apply the Percent format and increase the number of decimal places:

1. Select the range **H21:H23**.

2. Click the **Percent Style** button % on the Formatting toolbar.

3. Click the **Increase Decimal** button on the Formatting toolbar twice to display the percentages to two decimal places. See Figure 3-4.

Figure 3-4 **APPLYING THE PERCENT STYLE**

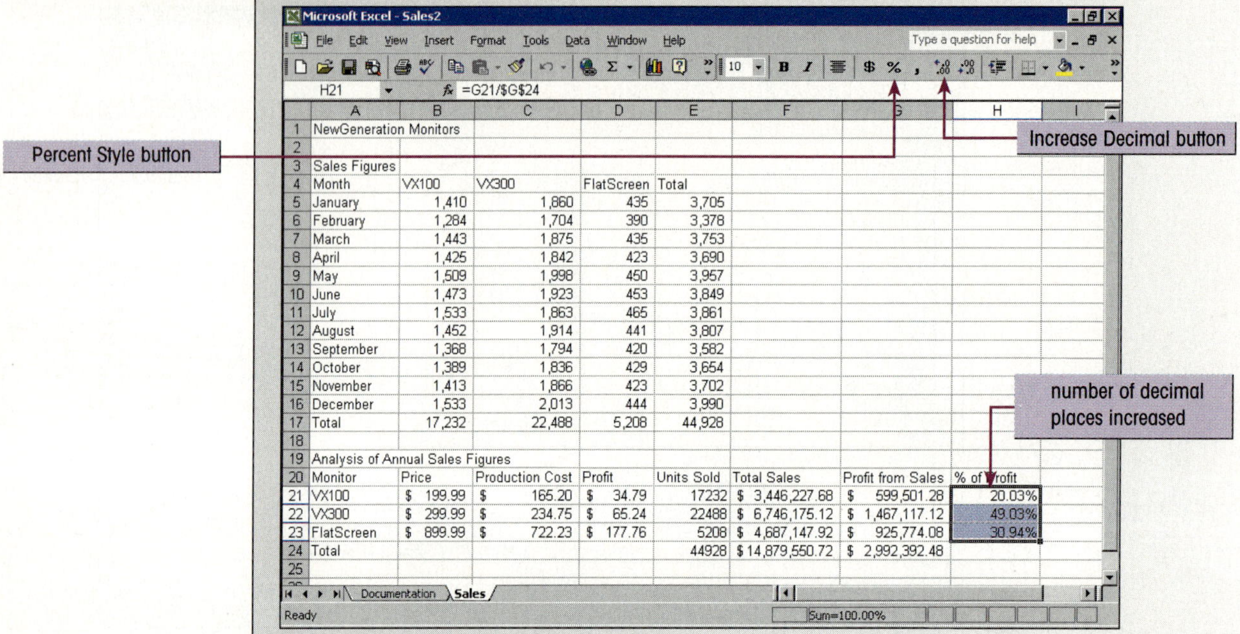

Percent Style button — (pointing to % button on toolbar)
Increase Decimal button — (pointing to toolbar)
number of decimal places increased — (pointing to H21:H23)

	A	B	C	D	E	F	G	H
1	NewGeneration Monitors							
2								
3	Sales Figures							
4	Month	VX100	VX300		FlatScreen	Total		
5	January	1,410	1,860		435	3,705		
6	February	1,284	1,704		390	3,378		
7	March	1,443	1,875		435	3,753		
8	April	1,425	1,842		423	3,690		
9	May	1,509	1,998		450	3,957		
10	June	1,473	1,923		453	3,849		
11	July	1,533	1,863		465	3,861		
12	August	1,452	1,914		441	3,807		
13	September	1,368	1,794		420	3,582		
14	October	1,389	1,836		429	3,654		
15	November	1,413	1,866		423	3,702		
16	December	1,533	2,013		444	3,990		
17	Total	17,232	22,488		5,208	44,928		
18								
19	Analysis of Annual Sales Figures							
20	Monitor	Price		Production Cost	Profit	Units Sold	Total Sales	Profit from Sales	% of Profit
21	VX100	$ 199.99	$ 165.20	$ 34.79	17232	$ 3,446,227.68	$ 599,501.28	20.03%
22	VX300	$ 299.99	$ 234.75	$ 65.24	22488	$ 6,746,175.12	$ 1,467,117.12	49.03%
23	FlatScreen	$ 899.99	$ 722.23	$ 177.76	5208	$ 4,687,147.92	$ 925,774.08	30.94%
24	Total				44928	$ 14,879,550.72	$ 2,992,392.48	

By displaying the percent values using the Percent format, you can quickly see that one monitor, the VX300, accounts for almost half of the profit from monitor sales.

Copying Formats

As you look over the sales figures, you see that one area of the worksheet still needs to be formatted. The Units Sold column in the range E21:E24 still does not display the comma separator you used in the sales figures table. To fix a formatting problem like this one, you can use one of the methods that Excel provides for copying a format from one location to another.

One of these methods is the Format Painter button located on the Standard toolbar. When you use the Format Painter option, you "paint" a format from one cell to another cell or to a range of cells. You can also use the fill handle and its Auto Fill options to copy a format from one cell to another. Another method for copying a format is using the Copy and Paste commands, which are available on both the Standard toolbar and the Edit menu. The Copy and Paste method requires you to click the Formatting Only option button that appears when you paste the selected cell, so that only the formatting of the pasted cell, not its content, is applied. Using the Format Painter button does all of this in fewer steps.

You will use the Format Painter button to copy the format used in the sales figures table and to paste that format into the range E21:E24.

To copy the format using the Format Painter button:

1. Select cell **B5**, which contains the formatting that you want to copy. You do not have to copy the entire range, because the range is formatted in the same way.

2. Click the **Format Painter** button on the Standard toolbar.

   As you move the pointer over the worksheet area, the pointer changes to ✥🖌.

TUTORIAL 3 DEVELOPING A PROFESSIONAL-LOOKING WORKSHEET   EX 3.07   EXCEL

> **TROUBLE?** If you do not see the Format Painter button, click the Toolbar Options button on the Standard toolbar, and then click.
>
> 3. Select the range **E21:E23**. The format that you used in the sales figures table is applied to the cells in the range E21:E23.

You have not applied the format to cell E24 yet. Rather than using the Format Painter button again, you can drag the fill handle down over the cell. Recall that you can use the fill handle to copy formulas and values from one range into another. You can also use the fill handle to copy formats.

To copy the format using the fill handle:

> 1. Click and drag the fill handle down to the range **E21:E24**.
>
>   When you release the mouse button, the word "Price" appears. This occurs because the default action of the fill handle in this case is to fill the values in the range E21:E23 into cell E24. You'll override this default behavior by choosing a different option from the list of Auto Fill options.
>
> 2. Click the **Auto Fill Options** button located at the lower-right corner of the selected range.
>
> 3. Click the **Fill Formatting Only** option button. Excel extends the format from the range E21:E23 into cell E24.

The Formatting toolbar is a fast and easy way to copy and apply cell formats, but there are other ways of formatting your data.

Using the Format Cells Dialog Box

Joan stops by to view your progress. She agrees that formatting the values has made the worksheet easier to read, but she has a few suggestions. She does not like the way the currency values are displayed with the dollar signs ($) placed at the left edge of the cell, leaving a large blank space between the dollar sign and the numbers. She would like to have the dollar sign placed directly to the left of the dollar amounts, leaving no blank spaces.

The convenience of the Formatting toolbar's one-click access to many of the formatting tasks you will want to perform does have its limits. As you can see in the worksheet, when you use the Formatting toolbar, you cannot specify how the format is applied. To make the change that Joan suggests, you need to open the Format Cells dialog box, which gives you more control over the formatting.

To open the Format Cells dialog box:

> 1. Select the nonadjacent range **B21:D23;F21:G24**.
>
> 2. Click **Format** on the menu bar, and then click **Cells**. The Format Cells dialog box opens. See Figure 3-5.

Figure 3-5 — FORMAT CELLS DIALOG BOX

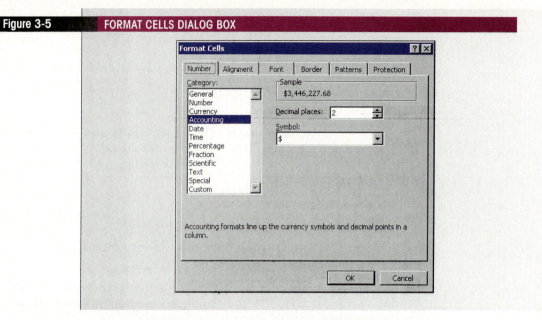

The Format Cells dialog box contains the following six tabs, each dedicated to a different set of format properties:

- **Number**—used to format the appearance of text and values within selected cells
- **Alignment**—used to control how text and values are aligned within a cell
- **Font**—used to choose the font type, size, and style
- **Border**—used to create borders around selected cells
- **Patterns**—used to create and apply background colors and patterns for selected cells
- **Protection**—used to lock or hide selected cells, preventing other users from modifying the cells' contents

So far, you have worked with number formats only. Excel supports several categories of number formats, ranging from Accounting and Currency formats to Scientific formats that might be used for recording engineering data. Figure 3-6 describes some of the number format categories.

Figure 3-6 — NUMBER FORMAT CATEGORIES

CATEGORY	DESCRIPTION
General	Default format; numbers are displayed without dollar signs, commas, or trailing decimal places
Number	Used for a general display of numbers
Currency, Accounting	Used for displaying monetary values; use Accounting formats to align decimal points within a column
Date, Time	Used for displaying date and time values
Percentage	Used for displaying decimal values as percentages
Fraction, Scientific	Used for displaying values as fractions or in scientific notation
Text	Used for displaying values as text strings
Special	Used for displaying zip codes, phone numbers, and social security numbers

As shown in Figure 3-5, Excel applied an Accounting format, displaying the dollar sign and two decimal places, to the sales figures. The Accounting format differs from the Currency format; the Accounting format lines up the decimal points and the dollar signs for values within a column so that all the dollar signs appear at the left edge of the cell border. To align the dollar signs closer to the numbers, you can change the format to the Currency format.

To apply the Currency format:

1. On the Number tab, click **Currency** in the Category list box.

   As shown in the Negative numbers list box, Excel displays negative currency values either with a minus sign (-) or with a combination of a red font and parentheses. Joan wants any negative currency values to be displayed with a minus sign.

2. Click the first entry in the Negative numbers list box.

3. Click the **OK** button. Excel changes the format of the currency values, removing the blank spaces between the dollar signs and the currency values, rather than having the dollar signs lined up within each column.

By using the Format Cells dialog box, you can control the formatting to ensure that text and values are displayed the way you want them to be.

Working with Fonts and Colors

A **font** is the design applied to characters, letters, and punctuation marks. Each font is identified by a **font name** (or **typeface**). Some of the more commonly used fonts are Arial, Times Roman, and Courier. Each font can be displayed using one of the following styles: regular, italic, bold, or bold italic. Fonts can also be displayed with special effects, such as strikeout, underline, and color.

Fonts can also be rendered in different sizes. Sizes are measured using "points." By default, Excel displays characters using a 10-point Arial font in a regular style. To change the font used in a selected cell, you either click the appropriate buttons on the Formatting toolbar or select options in the Format Cells dialog box.

In the logo that the company uses on all its correspondence and advertising materials, the name "NewGeneration Monitors" appears in a large Times New Roman font. Joan wants you to modify the title in cell A1 to reflect this company-wide format.

To change the font and font size of the title:

1. Click cell **A1** to make it the active cell.

2. Click the **list arrow** for the Font button [Arial] on the Formatting toolbar, scroll down the list of available fonts, and then click **Times New Roman**.

   TROUBLE? If you do not have the Times New Roman font installed on your computer, choose a different Times Roman font or choose MS Serif in the list.

3. Click the **list arrow** for the Font Size button [10] on the Formatting toolbar, and then click **18**. Figure 3-7 shows the revised format for the title in cell A1.

Figure 3-7 CHANGING THE FONT AND FONT SIZE

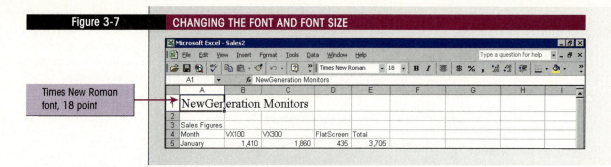

Times New Roman font, 18 point

Joan wants the column titles of both tables displayed in bold font and the word "Total" in both tables displayed in italics. To make these modifications, you will again use the Formatting toolbar.

To apply the bold and italic styles:

1. Select the nonadjacent range **A4:E4;A20:H20**.

2. Click the **Bold** button on the Formatting toolbar. The titles in the two tables now appear in a boldface font.

3. Select cell **A17**, press and hold the **Ctrl** key, and then click cell **A24**.

4. Click the **Italic** button on the Formatting toolbar. The word "Total" in cells A17 and A24 is now italicized.

Joan points out that NewGeneration's logo usually appears in a red font. Color is another one of Excel's formatting tools. Excel allows you to choose a text color from a palette of 40 different colors. If the color you want is not listed, you can modify Excel's color configuration to create a different color palette. Excel's default color settings will work for most situations, so in this case you will not modify Excel's color settings.

To change the font color of the title to red:

1. Click cell **A1** to make it the active cell.

2. Click the **list arrow** for the Font Color button on the Formatting toolbar. A color palette appears. See Figure 3-8.

Figure 3-8 CHOOSING A RED FONT COLOR

Font Color button

3. In the color palette, click the **Red** square (third row, first column). Excel changes the color of the font in cell A1 to red. See Figure 3-9.

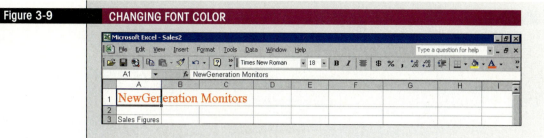

Figure 3-9 CHANGING FONT COLOR

Aligning Cell Contents

When you enter numbers and formulas into a cell, Excel automatically aligns them with the cell's right edge and bottom border. Text entries are aligned with the left edge and bottom border. The default Excel alignment does not always create the most readable worksheets. As a general rule, you should center column titles, format columns of numbers so that the decimal places are lined up within a column, and align text with the left edge of the cell. You can change alignment using the alignment tools on the Formatting toolbar or the options on the Alignment tab in the Format Cells dialog box.

Joan wants the column titles centered above the values in each column.

To center the column titles using the Formatting toolbar:

1. Select the nonadjacent range **B4:E4;B20:H20**.

2. Click the **Center** button on the Formatting toolbar. Excel centers the text in the selected cells in each column.

The Formatting toolbar also provides the Align Left button and the Align Right button so that you can left- and right-align cell contents. If you want to align the cell's contents vertically, you have to open the Format Cells dialog box and choose the vertical alignment options on the Alignment tab.

Another alignment option available in the Format Cells dialog box is the Merge and Center option, which centers the text in one cell across a range of cells. Joan wants the company logo to be centered at the top of the worksheet. In other words, she wants the contents of cell A1 to be centered across the range A1:H1.

To center the text across the range A1:H1:

1. Select the range **A1:H1**.

2. Click **Format** on the menu bar, and then click **Cells**.

3. Click the **Alignment** tab.

4. Click the **Horizontal** list arrow in the Text alignment pane, and then click **Center Across Selection**. See Figure 3-10.

Figure 3-10   **ALIGNMENT TAB**

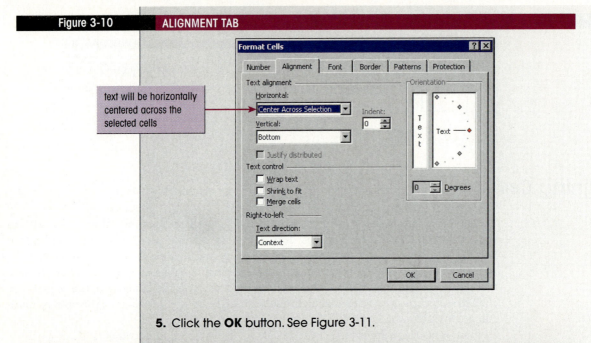

5. Click the **OK** button. See Figure 3-11.

Figure 3-11   **CENTERING TEXT WITHIN CELLS AND ACROSS COLUMNS**

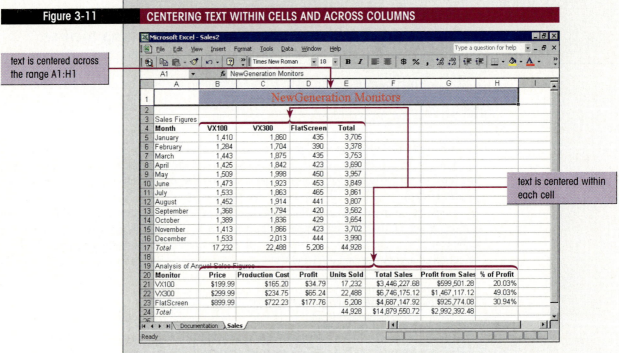

Indenting and Wrapping Text

Sometimes you will want a cell's contents offset, or indented, a few spaces from the cell's edge. This is particularly true for text entries that are aligned with the left edge of the cell. Indenting is often used for cell entries that are considered "subsections" of your worksheet. In the sales figures table, Joan wants you to indent the names of the months in the range A5:A16 and the monitor titles in the range A21:A23.

TUTORIAL 3 DEVELOPING A PROFESSIONAL-LOOKING WORKSHEET   EX 3.13   EXCEL

To indent the months and monitor titles:

1. Select the nonadjacent range **A5:A16;A21:A23**.

2. Click the **Increase Indent** button on the Formatting toolbar. Excel shifts the contents of the selected cells to the right.

   TROUBLE? You may have to click the Toolbar Options button, and then choose the Add or Remove Buttons option before you can click the Increase Indent button. As you use more buttons on the Formatting toolbar, they are added to the toolbar. If your Standard and Formatting toolbars now appear on separate rows, that is okay. The rest of the figures in this book might not look exactly like your screen, but this will not affect your work.

Clicking the Increase Indent button increases the amount of indentation by roughly one character. To decrease or remove an indentation, click the Decrease Indent button or modify the indent value using the Format Cells dialog box.

If you enter text that is too wide for a cell, Excel either extends the text into the adjoining cells (if the cells are empty) or truncates the display of the text. You can also have Excel wrap the text within the cell so that the excess text is displayed on additional lines within the cell. To wrap text, you use the Format Cells dialog box.

Joan notes that some of the column titles in the second table are long. For example, the "Production Cost" label in cell C20 is much longer than the values below it. This formatting has caused some of the columns to be wider than they need to be. Joan suggests that you wrap the text within the column titles and then reduce the width of the columns.

To wrap the title text within a cell and reduce the column widths:

1. Select the cell range **A20:H20**.

2. Click **Format** on the menu bar, and then click **Cells**.

3. Click the **Wrap text** check box in the Text control pane.

4. Click the **OK** button. The text in cells C20 and G20 now appears on two rows within the cells.

5. Reduce the width of column **C** to about **10** characters.

6. Reduce the width of column **G** to about **12** characters.

7. Reduce the width of column **H** to about **8** characters. See Figure 3-12.

Figure 3-12   WRAPPING TEXT WITHIN A CELL

long column titles wrap to a new line and the widths of the columns are reduced

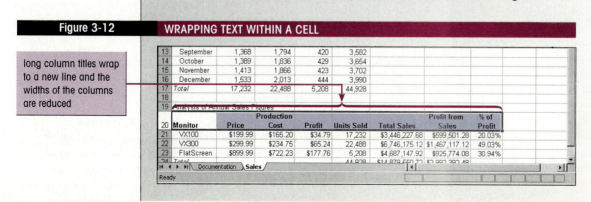

> **TROUBLE?** Different monitors have different screen resolutions and column widths. If your screen does not match Figure 3-12, resize the columns accordingly.

Other Formatting Options

Excel supports even more formatting options than have been discussed so far. For example, instead of wrapping the text, you can have Excel shrink it to fit the size of the cell. If you reduce the cell later on, Excel will automatically resize the text to match. You can also rotate the contents of the cell, displaying the cell entry at almost any angle (see Figure 3-13). Joan does not need to use either of these options in her workbook, but they might be useful later on another project.

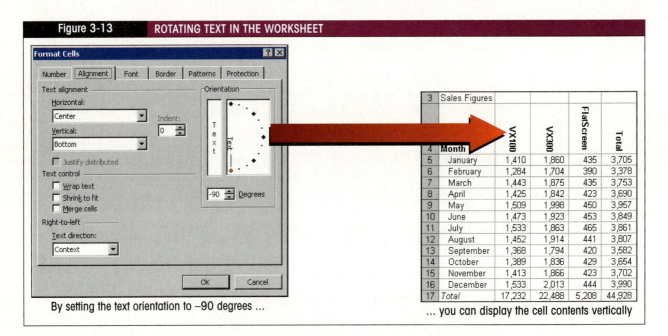

Figure 3-13 ROTATING TEXT IN THE WORKSHEET

By setting the text orientation to –90 degrees ... ... you can display the cell contents vertically

Working with Cell Borders and Backgrounds

Up to now, all the formatting you have done has been applied to the contents of a cell. Excel also provides a range of tools to format the cells themselves. Specifically, you can add borders to the cells and color the cell backgrounds.

Adding a Cell Border

As you may have noticed from the printouts of other worksheets, the gridlines that appear in the worksheet window are not displayed on the printed page. In some cases, however, you might want to display borders around individual cells in a worksheet. This would be particularly true when you have different sections or tables in a worksheet, as in Joan's Sales worksheet.

You can add a border to a cell using either the Borders button on the Formatting toolbar or the options on the Border tab in the Format Cells dialog box. The Borders button allows you to create borders quickly, whereas the Format Cells dialog box lets you further refine your choices.

Joan wants you to place a border around each cell in the two tables in the worksheet. You'll select the appropriate border style from the list of available options on the Borders palette.

To create a grid of cell borders in the two tables:

1. Select the nonadjacent range **A4:E17;A20:H24**.

2. Click the **list arrow** for the Borders button on the Formatting toolbar. See Figure 3-14.

Figure 3-14   BORDER OPTIONS

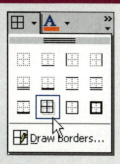

3. Click the **All Borders** option (third row, second column) in the gallery of border options. A thin border appears around each cell in the selected range.

4. Click cell **A1** to deselect the range.

You can also place a border around the entire range itself (and not the individual cells) by selecting a different border style. Try this by creating a thick border around the cell range.

To create a thick border around the selected range:

1. Select the range **A4:E17;A20:H24** again.

2. Click the **list arrow** for the Borders button on the Formatting toolbar, and then click the **Thick Box Border** option (third row, fourth column) in the border gallery.

3. Click cell **A2**. Figure 3-15 shows the two tables with their borders.

Figure 3-15 BORDERS WITHIN AND AROUND THE TWO SALES TABLES

	A	B	C	D	E	F	G	H	I
2									
3	Sales Figures								
4	Month	VX100	VX300	FlatScreen	Total				
5	January	1,410	1,860	435	3,705				
6	February	1,284	1,704	390	3,378				
7	March	1,443	1,875	435	3,753				
8	April	1,425	1,842	423	3,690				
9	May	1,509	1,998	450	3,957				
10	June	1,473	1,923	453	3,849				
11	July	1,533	1,863	465	3,861				
12	August	1,452	1,914	441	3,807				
13	September	1,368	1,794	420	3,582				
14	October	1,389	1,836	429	3,654				
15	November	1,413	1,866	423	3,702				
16	December	1,533	2,013	444	3,990				
17	Total	17,232	22,488	5,208	44,928				
18									
19	Analysis of Annual Sales Figures								
20	Monitor	Price	Production Cost	Profit	Units Sold	Total Sales	Profit from Sales	% of Profit	
21	VX100	$199.99	$165.20	$34.79	17,232	$3,446,227.68	$599,501.28	20.03%	
22	VX300	$299.99	$234.75	$65.24	22,488	$6,746,175.12	$1,467,117.12	49.03%	
23	FlatScreen	$899.99	$722.23	$177.76	5,208	$4,687,147.92	$925,774.08	30.94%	
24	Total				44,928	$14,879,550.72	$2,992,392.48		

Borders button (indicated on the Formatting toolbar)

If you want a more interactive way of drawing borders on your worksheet, you can use the Draw Border button, which is also one of the options on the Borders palette. To see how this option works, you will add a thick black line under the column titles in both of the tables.

To draw borders using the Draw Border tool:

1. Click the **list arrow** for the Borders button on the Formatting toolbar, and then click the **Draw Border** button at the bottom of the border gallery.

    The pointer changes to a pencil, and a floating Borders toolbar opens with four tools. The Draw Border button (currently selected) draws a border line on the worksheet; the Erase Border button erases border lines; the Line Style button specifies the style of the border line; and the Line Color button specifies the line color.

2. Click the **list arrow** for the Line Style button, and then click the **thick line** option (the eighth from the top) in the list.

3. Click and drag the pointer over the lower border of the range **A4:E4**.

4. Click and drag the pointer over the lower border of the range **A20:H20**.

5. Click the **Close** button on the floating Borders toolbar to close it.

Finally, you will add a double line above the Total row in each table. You will add the line using the options in the Format Cells dialog box.

TUTORIAL 3 DEVELOPING A PROFESSIONAL-LOOKING WORKSHEET   EX 3.17   EXCEL

To create the double border lines:

1. Select the nonadjacent range **A16:E16;A23:H23**.
2. Click **Format** on the menu bar, and then click **Cells**.
3. Click the **Border** tab. The Border tab displays a diagram showing what borders, if any, are currently surrounding the selected cells.

   The bottom border is currently a single thin line. You want to change this to a double line.
4. Click the **double line** style in the Line Style list box located on the right side of the tab.
5. Click the **bottom border** in the border diagram. The bottom border changes to a double line. See Figure 3-16.

Figure 3-16 **BORDER TAB**

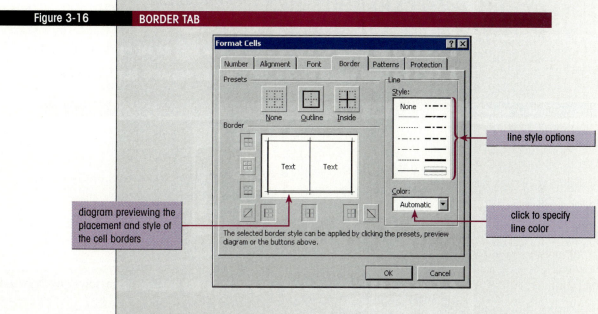

6. Click the **OK** button.
7. Click cell **A2** to deselect the ranges. See Figure 3-17.

Figure 3-17 **TOTAL ROWS SEPARATED WITH DOUBLE LINES**

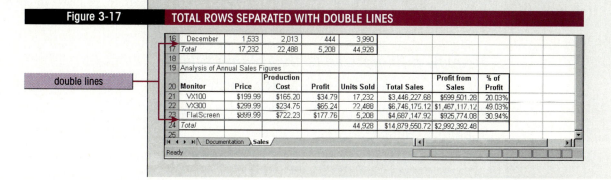

You can also specify a color for the cell borders by using the Color list box located on the Border tab (see Figure 3-16). Joan does not need to change the border colors, but she would like you to change the background color for the column title cells.

Setting the Background Color and Pattern

Patterns and color can be used to enliven a dull worksheet or provide visual emphasis to the sections of the worksheet that you want to stress. If you have a color printer or a color projection device, you might want to take advantage of Excel's color tools. By default, worksheet cells are not filled with any color (the white you see in your worksheet is not a fill color for the cells). To change the background color in a worksheet, you can use the Fill Color button on the Formatting toolbar, or you can use the Format Cells dialog box, which also provides patterns that you can apply to the background.

Joan wants to change the background color of the worksheet. When she makes her report later in the week, she will be using the company's color laser printer. So she would like you to explore using background color in the column titles for the two sales tables. She suggests that you try formatting the column titles with a light yellow background.

To apply a fill color to the column titles:

1. Select the nonadjacent range **A4:E4;A20:H20**.
2. Click the **list arrow** for the Fill Color button on the Formatting toolbar.
3. Click the **Light Yellow** square (fifth row, third column). See Figure 3-18.

Figure 3-18   **SELECTING A FILL COLOR**

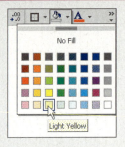

4. Click cell **A2** to deselect the column titles. The column titles now have light yellow backgrounds.

Joan would also like to investigate whether you can apply a pattern to the fill background. Excel supports 18 different fill patterns. To create and apply a fill pattern, you have to open the Format Cells dialog box.

To apply a fill pattern to the column titles:

1. Select the nonadjacent range **A4:E4;A20:H20**.
2. Click **Format** on the menu bar, and then click **Cells**.
3. Click the **Patterns** tab.
4. Click the **Pattern** list arrow. Clicking the Pattern list arrow displays a gallery of patterns and a palette of colors applied to the selected pattern. The default pattern color is black. You will choose just a pattern now.
5. Click the **50% Gray** pattern (first row, third column) in the pattern gallery. See Figure 3-19.

Figure 3-19 SELECTING A FILL PATTERN

6. Click the **OK** button.

7. Click cell **A2** to deselect the ranges and to see the pattern.

The background pattern you have chosen overwhelms the text in these column titles. You can improve the appearance by changing the color of the pattern itself from black to a light orange.

To change the pattern color:

1. Select the range **A4:E4;A20:H20** again.

2. Click **Format** on the menu bar, and then click **Cells**.

3. Click the **Pattern** list arrow. The default (or automatic) color of a selected pattern is black. You can choose a different color for the pattern using the color palette below the patterns.

4. Click the **Light Orange** square (third row, second column) in the color palette.

5. Click the **OK** button.

6. Click cell **A2** to deselect the ranges. Figure 3-20 shows the patterned background applied to the column titles. Note that the light orange pattern does not overwhelm the column titles.

Figure 3-20
COLUMN TITLES WITH FORMATTED BACKGROUND

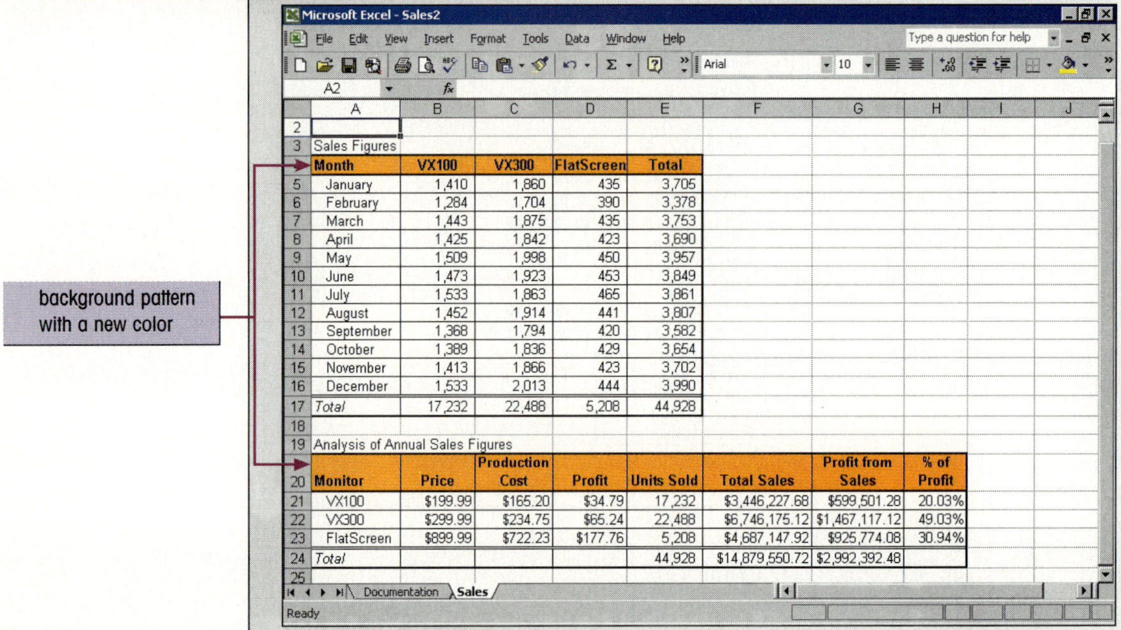

background pattern with a new color

7. Save and close the workbook.

Joan is pleased with the progress you have made. In the next session, you will explore other formatting features.

Session 3.1 QUICK CHECK

1. Describe two ways of applying a Currency format to cells in your worksheet.
2. If the number 0.05765 has been entered into a cell, what will Excel display if you:
   a. format the number using the Percent format with one decimal place?
   b. format the number using the Currency format with two decimal places and a dollar sign?
3. Which two buttons can you use to copy a format from one cell range to another?
4. A long text string in one of your worksheet cells has been truncated. List three ways to correct this problem.
5. How do you center the contents of a single cell across a range of cells?
6. Describe three ways of creating a cell border.
7. How would you apply a background pattern to a selected cell range?

SESSION 3.2

In this session, you will format a worksheet by merging cells, hiding rows and columns, inserting a background image, and finding and replacing formats. You will also be introduced to styles. You will see how to create and apply styles, and you will learn how styles can be used to make formatting more efficient. You will also learn about Excel's gallery of AutoFormats. Finally, you will work with the Print Preview window to control the formatting applied to your printed worksheets.

Formatting the Worksheet

In the previous session you formatted individual cells within the worksheet. Excel also provides tools for formatting the entire worksheet or the entire workbook. You will explore some of these tools as you continue to work on Joan's Sales report.

Merging Cells into One Cell

Joan has reviewed the Sales worksheet and has a few suggestions. She would like you to format the titles for the two tables in her report so that they are centered in a bold font above the tables. You could do this by centering the cell title across a cell range, as you did for the title in the last session. Another way is to merge several cells into one cell and then center the contents of that single cell. Merging a range of cells into a single cell removes all of the cells from the worksheet, except the cell in the upper-left corner of the range. Any content in the other cells of the range is deleted. To merge a range of cells into a single cell, you can use the Merge option on the Alignment tab in the Format Cells dialog box or click the Merge and Center button on the Formatting toolbar.

To merge and center the cell ranges containing the table titles:

1. If you took a break after the previous session, start Excel and open the Sales2 workbook.

2. In the Sales worksheet, select the range **A3:E3**.

3. Click the **Merge and Center** button on the Formatting toolbar. The cells in the range A3:E3 are merged into one cell at the cell location, A3. The text in the merged cell is centered as well.

4. Click the **Bold** button on the Formatting toolbar.

5. Select the range **A19:H19**, click, and then click.

6. Click cell **A2** to deselect the range. Figure 3-21 shows the merged and centered table titles.

Figure 3-21 MERGING AND CENTERING CELLS

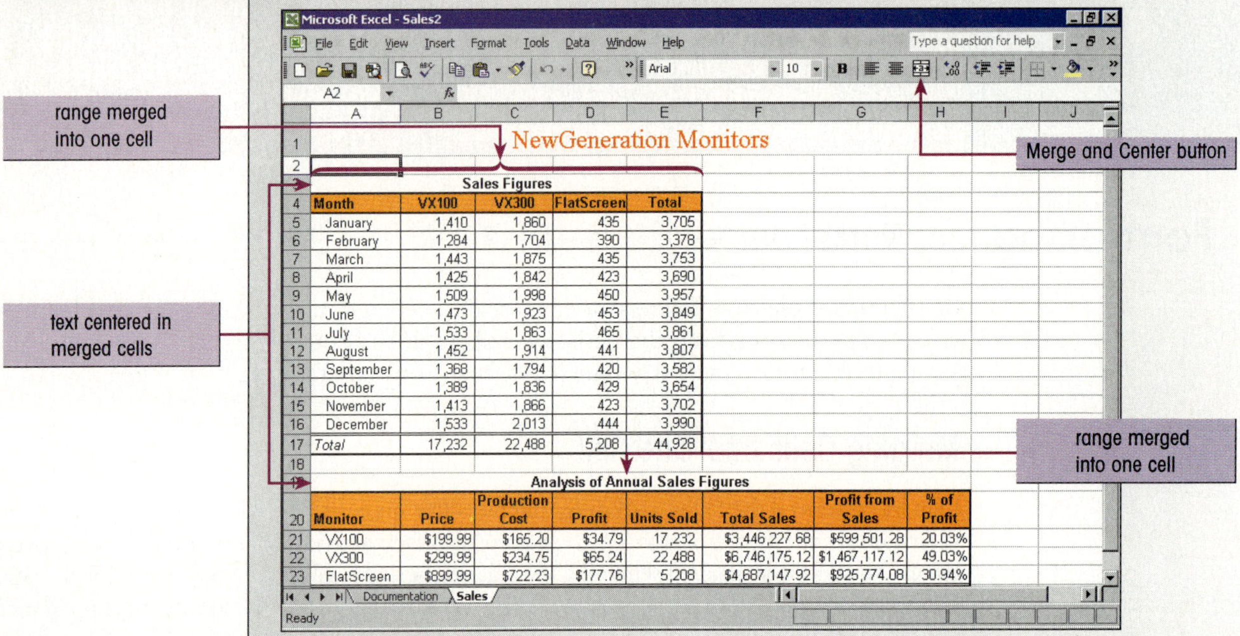

[Screenshot of Microsoft Excel - Sales2 showing merged and centered cells with "NewGeneration Monitors" as a merged title, a Sales Figures table (rows 4–17) with columns Month, VX100, VX300, FlatScreen, Total, and an Analysis of Annual Sales Figures table below with columns Monitor, Price, Production Cost, Profit, Units Sold, Total Sales, Profit from Sales, % of Profit. Callouts point to: "range merged into one cell" (A2), "text centered in merged cells", "Merge and Center button", and "range merged into one cell".]

To split a merged cell back into individual cells, regardless of the method you used to merge the cells, you select the merged cell and then click the Merge and Center button again. You can also merge and unmerge cells using the Alignment tab in the Format Cells dialog box.

Hiding Rows and Columns

Sometimes Joan does not need to view the monthly sales for the three monitors. She does not want to remove this information from the worksheet, but she would like the option of temporarily hiding that information. Excel provides this capability. Hiding a row or column does not affect the data stored there, nor does it affect any other cell that might have a formula referencing a cell in the hidden row or column. Hiding part of your worksheet is a good way of removing extraneous information, allowing you to concentrate on the more important data contained in your worksheet. To hide a row or column, first you must select the row(s) or column(s) you want to hide. You can then use the Row or Column option on the Format menu or right-click the selection to open its shortcut menu.

You will hide the monthly sales figures in the first table in the worksheet.

To hide the monthly sales figures:

1. Select the headings for rows **5** through **16**.

2. Right-click the selection, and then click **Hide** on the shortcut menu. Excel hides rows 5 through 16. Note that the total sales figures in the range B17:E17 are not affected by hiding the monthly sales figures. See Figure 3-22.

TUTORIAL 3 DEVELOPING A PROFESSIONAL-LOOKING WORKSHEET EX 3.23

Figure 3-22   HIDING WORKSHEET ROWS

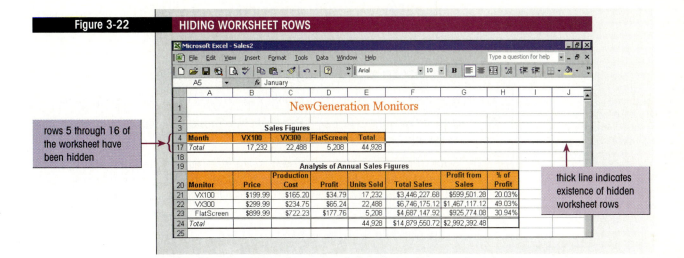

rows 5 through 16 of the worksheet have been hidden

thick line indicates existence of hidden worksheet rows

To unhide a hidden row or column, you must select the headings of the rows or columns that border the hidden area; then you can use the right-click method or the Row or Column command on the Format menu. You will let Joan know that it is easy to hide any row or column that she does not want to view. But for now you will redisplay the hidden sales figures.

To unhide the monthly sales figures:

1. Select the row headings for rows **4** and **17**.
2. Right-click the selection, and then click **Unhide** on the shortcut menu. Excel redisplays rows 5 through 16.
3. Click cell **A2** to deselect the rows.

Hiding and unhiding a column follows the same process, except that you select the worksheet column headings rather than the row headings.

Formatting the Sheet Background

In the previous session you learned how to create a background color for individual cells within the worksheet. Excel also allows you to use an image file as a background. The image from the file is tiled repeatedly until the images fill up the entire worksheet. Images can be used to give the background a textured appearance, like that of granite, wood, or fibered paper. The background image does not affect the format or content of any cell in the worksheet, and if you have already defined a background color for a cell, Excel displays the color on top, hiding that portion of the image.

REFERENCE WINDOW

Adding a Background Image to the Worksheet
- Click Format on the menu bar, point to Sheet, and then click Background.
- Locate the image file that you want tiled over the worksheet background.
- Click the Insert button.

To delete the background image:
- Click Format on the menu bar, point to Sheet, and then click Delete Background.

Joan wants you to experiment with using a background image for the Sales worksheet. She has an image file that she wants you to try.

To add a background image to the worksheet:

1. Click **Format** on the menu bar, point to **Sheet**, and then click **Background**.

2. Locate and select the **Back** image file in the Tutorial.03/Tutorial folder on your Data Disk, and then click the **Insert** button.

   The Back image file is tiled over the worksheet, creating a textured background for the Sales sheet. Notice that the tiling is hidden in the cells that already contained a background color. In order to make the sales figures easier to read, you'll change the background color of those cells to white.

3. Select the nonadjacent range **A5:E17;A21:H24**.

4. Click the **list arrow** for the Fill Color button on the Formatting toolbar, and then click the **White** square (last row, last column) in the color palette.

5. Click cell **A2**. Figure 3-23 shows the Sales worksheet with the formatted background.

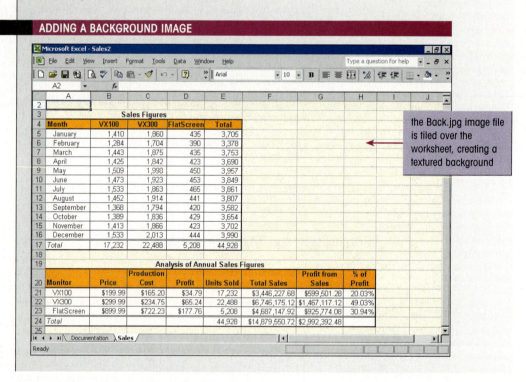

Figure 3-23 ADDING A BACKGROUND IMAGE

Note that you cannot apply a background image to all of the sheets in a workbook at the same time. If you want to apply the same background to several sheets, you must format each sheet separately.

Formatting Sheet Tabs

In addition to the sheet background, you can also format the background color of worksheet tabs. This color is only visible when the worksheet is not the active sheet in the workbook; the background color for the active sheet is always white. You can use tab colors to better organize the various sheets in your workbook. For example, worksheets that contain sales information could be formatted with blue tabs, and sheets that describe the company's cash flow or budget could be formatted with green tabs.

If Joan's workbook contained many sheets, it would be easier to locate information if the sheet tabs were different colors. To explore how to color sheet tabs, you will change the tab color of the Sales worksheet to light orange.

To change the tab color:

1. Right-click the **Sales** tab, and then click **Tab Color** on the shortcut menu.
2. Click the **Light Orange** square (third row, second column) in the color palette.
3. Click the **OK** button. A light orange horizontal stripe appears at the bottom of the tab, but because Sales is the active worksheet, the background color is still white.
4. Click the **Documentation** tab. Now that Documentation is the active sheet, you can see the light orange color of the Sales sheet tab.
5. Click the **Sales** tab to make it the active sheet again.

Clearing and Replacing Formats

Sometimes you might want to change or remove some of the formatting from your workbooks. As you experiment with different formats, you will find a lot of use for the Undo button on the Standard toolbar as you remove formatting choices that did not work out as well as you expected. Another choice is to clear the formatting from the selected cells, returning the cells to their initial, unformatted appearance. To see how this option works, you will remove the formatting from the company name in cell A1 on the Sales worksheet.

To clear the format from cell A1:

1. Click cell **A1** to select it.
2. Click **Edit** on the menu bar, point to **Clear**, and then click **Formats**. Excel removes the formatting that was applied to the cell text and removes the formatting that centered the text across the range A1:H1.
3. Click the **Undo** button on the Standard toolbar to undo your action, restoring the formats you cleared.

Sometimes you will want to make a formatting change that applies to several different cells. If those cells are scattered throughout the workbook, you may find it time-consuming to search and replace the formats for each individual cell. If the cells share a common format that you want to change, you can use the Find and Replace command to locate the formats and modify them.

REFERENCE WINDOW

Finding and Replacing a Format
- Click Edit on the menu bar, and then click Replace.
- Click the Options >> button, if necessary, to display the format choices.
- Click the top Format list arrow, and then click Format.
- Specify the format you want to find in the Find Format dialog box, and then click the OK button.
- Click the bottom Format list arrow, and then click Format.
- Enter a new format with which you want to replace the old format, and then click the OK button.
- Click the Replace All button to replace all occurrences of the old format; or click the Replace button to replace the currently selected cell containing the old format; or click the Find Next button to find the next occurrence of the old format before replacing it.
- Click the Close button.

For example, in the Sales worksheet, the table titles and column titles are displayed in a bold font. After seeing how the use of color has made the worksheet come alive, Joan wants you to change the titles to a boldface blue. Rather than selecting the cells that contain the table and column titles and formatting them, you can replace all occurrences of the boldface text with blue boldface text.

To find and replace formats:

1. Click **Edit** on the menu bar, and then click **Replace**. The Find and Replace dialog box opens. You can use this dialog box to find and replace the contents of the cells. In this case, you will use it only for finding and replacing formats, leaving the contents of the cells unchanged.

2. Click the **Options >>** button to display additional find and replace options. See Figure 3-24.

   TROUBLE? If the button on your workbook appears as Options <<, the additional options are already displayed, and you do not need to click any buttons.

Figure 3-24 FIND AND REPLACE DIALOG BOX

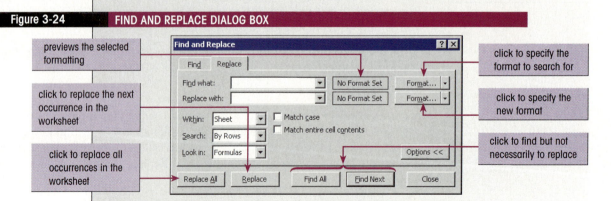

The dialog box expands to display options that allow you to find and replace cell formats. It also includes options to determine whether to search within the active sheet or the entire workbook. Currently no format options have been set.

3. Click the top **Format** list arrow, and then click **Format**.

The Find Format dialog box opens. Here is where you specify the format you want to search for. In this case, you are searching for cells that contain boldface text.

4. Click the **Font** tab, and then click **Bold** in the Font style list box. See Figure 3-25.

Figure 3-25   FIND FORMAT DIALOG BOX

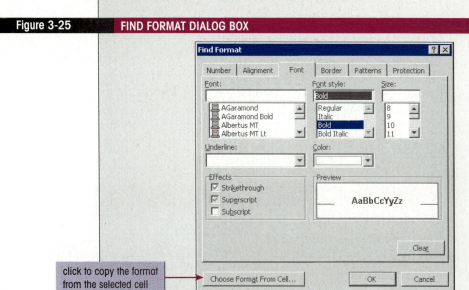

click to copy the format from the selected cell

5. Click the **OK** button.

Next, you have to specify the new format that you want to use to replace the boldface text. In this case, you need to specify a blue boldface text.

6. Click the bottom **Format** list arrow, and then click **Format**.

7. Click **Bold** in the Font style list box.

8. Click the **Color** list box, and then click the **Blue** square (second row, sixth column) in the color palette.

9. Click the **OK** button.

10. Click the **Replace All** button to replace all boldface text in the worksheet with boldface blue text. Excel indicates that it has completed its search and made 15 replacements.

11. Click the **OK** button, and then click the **Close** button. See Figure 3-26.

Figure 3-26   **SALES WORKSHEET WITH BOLDFACE BLUE TEXT**

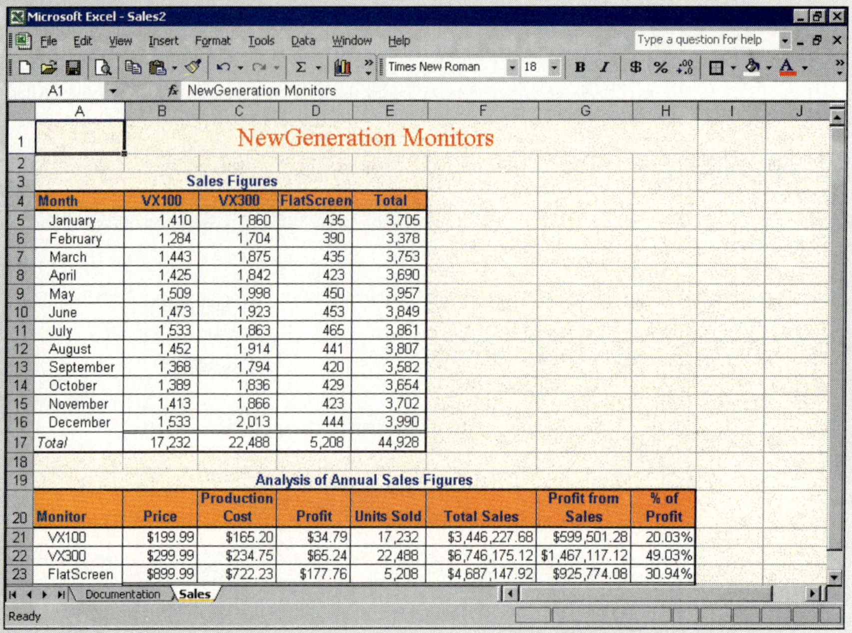

Using Styles

If you have several cells that employ the same format, you can create a style for those cells. A **style** is a saved collection of formatting options—number formats; text alignment; font sizes and colors; borders; and background fills—that can be applied to cells in the worksheet. When you apply a style, Excel remembers which styles are associated with which cells in the workbook. If you want to change the appearance of a particular type of cell, you need only modify the specifications for the style, and the appearance of any cell associated with that style would be automatically changed to reflect the new style.

You can create a style in one of two ways: by selecting a cell from the worksheet and basing the style definition on the formatting choices already defined for that cell or by manually entering the style definitions into a dialog box. Once you create and name a style, you can apply it to cells in the workbook.

Excel has eight built-in styles named Comma, Comma [0], Currency, Currency [0], Followed Hyperlink, Hyperlink, Normal, and Percent. You have been using styles all of this time without knowing it. Most cells are formatted with the Normal style, but when you enter a percentage, Excel formats it using the Percent style. Similarly, currency values are automatically formatted using the Currency style, and so forth.

Creating a Style

Joan wants you to further modify the appearance of the worksheet by changing the background color of the months in the first table and the monitor names in the second table to yellow. Rather than applying new formatting to the cells, you decide to create a new style called "Category" that you will apply to the category columns of the tables in your workbook. You will create the style using the format already applied to cell A5 of the worksheet as a basis.

To create a style using a formatted cell:

1. Click cell **A5** to select it. The format applied to this cell becomes the basis of the new style that you want to create.

2. Click **Format** on the menu bar, and then click **Style**. The Style dialog box opens. All of the formatting options associated with the style of the active cell are listed. For example, the font is 10-point Arial.

   To create a new style for this cell, you simply type a different name into the list box.

3. Verify that Normal is highlighted in the Style name list box, and then type **Category**. See Figure 3-27.

Figure 3-27   **STYLE DIALOG BOX**

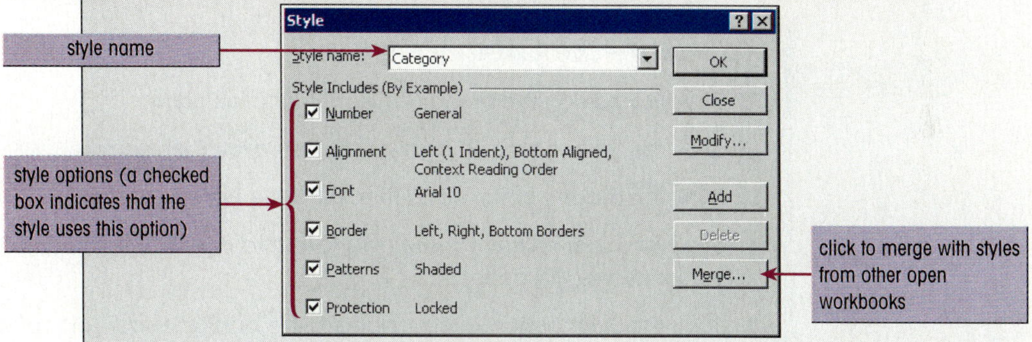

- style name
- style options (a checked box indicates that the style uses this option)
- click to merge with styles from other open workbooks

Style name: Category
Style Includes (By Example)
- Number — General
- Alignment — Left (1 Indent), Bottom Aligned, Context Reading Order
- Font — Arial 10
- Border — Left, Right, Bottom Borders
- Patterns — Shaded
- Protection — Locked

If you do not want all of these formatting options to be part of the Category style, you can deselect the options you no longer want included. You can also modify a current format option or add a new format option. You'll change the background color in the Category style to yellow.

4. Click the **Modify** button. The Format Cells dialog box opens.

5. Click the **Patterns** tab, and then click the **Yellow** square (fourth row, third column) in the color palette.

6. Click the **OK** button to close the Format Cells dialog box.

   If you click the OK button in the Style dialog box, the style definition changes and the updated style is applied to the active cell. If you click the Add button in the dialog box, the change is added, or saved, to the style definition but the updated style is not applied to the active cell.

7. Click the **OK** button. The background color of cell A5 changes to yellow.

Now you need to apply this style to other cells in the workbook.

Applying a Style

To apply a style to cells in a worksheet, you first select the cells you want associated with the style and then open the Styles dialog box.

To apply the Category style:

1. Select the nonadjacent range **A6:A16;A21:A23**.

2. Click **Format** on the menu bar, and then click **Style**.

3. Click the **Style name** list arrow, and then click **Category**.

4. Click the **OK** button, and then click cell **A2** to deselect the cells. A yellow background color is applied to all of the category cells in the two tables.

The yellow background appears a bit too strong. You decide to change it to a light yellow background. Since all the category cells are now associated with the Category style, you need only modify the definition of the Category style to make this change.

To modify the Category style:

1. Click **Format** on the menu bar, and then click **Style**.

2. Click the **Style name** list arrow, and then click **Category**.

3. Click the **Modify** button, and then click the **Patterns** tab, if necessary.

4. Click the **Light Yellow** square (fifth row, third column) in the color palette, and then click the **OK** button.

5. Click the **Add** button. Excel changes the background color of all the cells associated with the Category style.

   TROUBLE? Do not click the OK button. Clicking the OK button will apply the Category style only to the active cell.

6. Click the **Close** button. See Figure 3-28.

Figure 3-28 **CATEGORY STYLE IN THE SALES WORKSHEET**

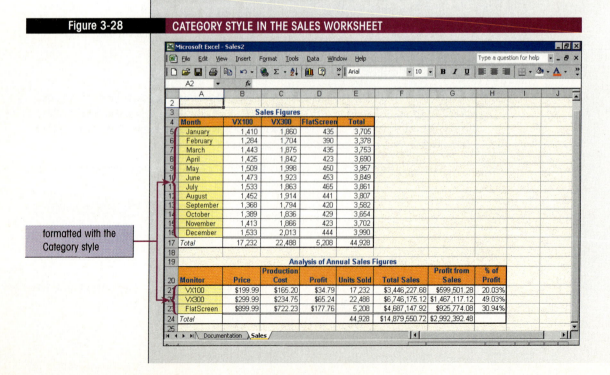

formatted with the Category style

You can also copy styles from one workbook to another. Copying styles allows you to create a collection of workbooks that share a common look and feel.

Using AutoFormat

Excel's **AutoFormat** feature lets you choose an appearance for your worksheet cells from a gallery of 17 predefined formats. Rather than spending time testing different combinations of fonts, colors, and borders, you can apply a professionally designed format to your worksheet by choosing one from the AutoFormat Gallery. You have done a lot of work already formatting the data in the Sales workbook to give it a more professional and polished look, but you decide to see how the formatting you have done compares to one of Excel's AutoFormat designs.

Apply an AutoFormat to the Sales Figures table so that you can compare the professionally designed format to the format you have worked on.

To apply an AutoFormat to the table:

1. Select the range **A3:E17**.

2. Click **Format** on the menu bar, and then click **AutoFormat**. The AutoFormat dialog box opens. See Figure 3-29.

Figure 3-29   **AUTOFORMAT GALLERY**

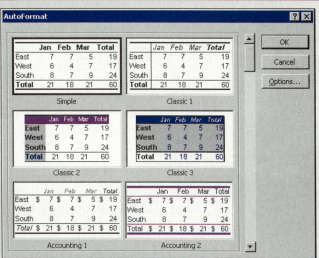

The dialog box displays a preview of how each format will appear when applied to cells in a worksheet.

3. Click **Classic 3** in the list of available designs, and then click the **OK** button.

4. Click cell **A2** to remove the highlighting from the first table. Figure 3-30 shows the appearance of the Classic 3 design in your workbook.

Figure 3-30 APPLYING AN AUTOFORMAT

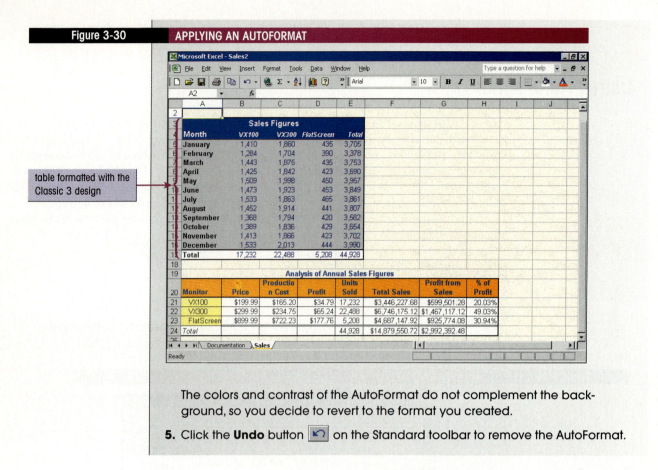

table formatted with the Classic 3 design

The colors and contrast of the AutoFormat do not complement the background, so you decide to revert to the format you created.

5. Click the **Undo** button on the Standard toolbar to remove the AutoFormat.

Although you will not use an AutoFormat in this case, you can see how an AutoFormat can be used as a starting point. You could start with Excel's professional design and then make modifications to the worksheet to fit your own needs.

Formatting the Printed Worksheet

You have settled on an appearance for the Sales worksheet—at least the appearance that is displayed on your screen. But that is only half of your job. Joan also wants you to format the appearance of this worksheet when it is printed out. You have to decide how to arrange the report on the page, the size of the page margins, the orientation of the page, and whether the page will have any headers or footers. You can make many of these choices through Excel's Print Preview.

Opening the Print Preview Window

As the name implies, the **Print Preview window** shows you how each page of your worksheet will look when it is printed. From the Print Preview window, you can make changes to the page layout before you print your worksheet.

To preview the Sales worksheet printout:

1. Click the **Print Preview** button on the Standard toolbar. The Print Preview window opens, displaying the worksheet as it will appear on the printed page. See Figure 3-31.

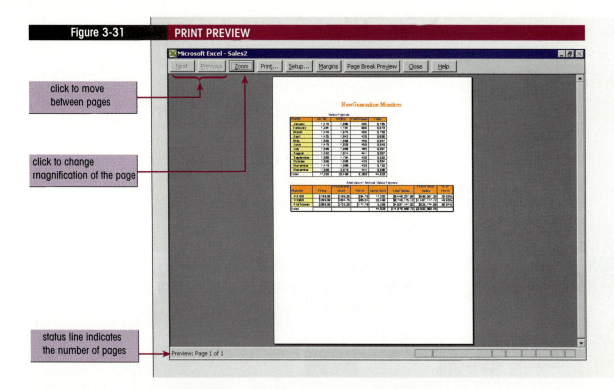

Figure 3-31 PRINT PREVIEW

Excel displays the full page in the Print Preview window. You might have difficulty reading the text because it is so small. Do not worry if the preview is not completely readable. One purpose of Print Preview is to see the overall layout of the worksheet. If you want a better view of the text, you can increase the magnification by either using the Zoom button on the Print Preview toolbar or by clicking the page with the 🔍 pointer. Clicking the Zoom button again, or clicking the page a second time with the pointer, reduces the magnification, bringing the whole page back into view.

> ### To enlarge the preview:
> 1. Click the **Zoom** button on the Print Preview toolbar.
> 2. Use the horizontal and vertical scroll bars to move around the worksheet.
> 3. Click anywhere within the page with the pointer to reduce the magnification.

You can also make changes to the layout of a worksheet page using the Setup and Margins buttons on the Print Preview toolbar.

Defining the Page Setup

You can use the Page Setup dialog box to control how a worksheet is placed on a page. You can adjust the size of the **margins**, which are the spaces between the page content and the edges of the page. You can center the worksheet text between the top and bottom margins (horizontally) or between the right and left margins (vertically). You can change the **page orientation**, which determines if the page is wider than it is tall or taller than it is wide. You can also use the Page Setup dialog box to display text that will appear at the top (a header) or bottom (a footer) of each page of a worksheet. You can open the Page Setup dialog box using the File menu or using the Print Preview toolbar.

By default, Excel places a 1-inch margin above and below the report and a ¾-inch margin to the left and right. Excel also aligns column A in a worksheet at the left margin and row 1 at the top margin. Depending on how many columns and rows there are in the worksheet, you might want to increase or decrease the page margins or center the worksheet between the left and right margins or between the top and bottom margins.

You want to increase the margin size for the Sales worksheet to 1 inch all around. You also want the worksheet to be centered between the right and left margins.

To change the margins and center the worksheet horizontally on the page:

1. Click the **Setup** button on the Print Preview toolbar.

2. Click the **Margins** tab. See Figure 3-32.

Figure 3-32 MARGINS TAB

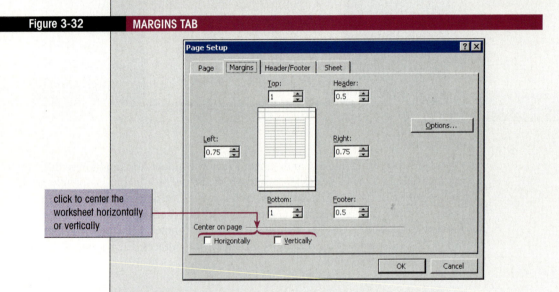

click to center the worksheet horizontally or vertically

The Margins tab provides a diagram showing the placement of the worksheet on the page. In addition to adjusting the sizes of the margins, you can also adjust the space allotted to the header and footer.

3. Click the **Left** up arrow to set the size of the left margin to **1** inch.

4. Click the **Right** up arrow to increase the size of the right margin to **1** inch.

5. Click the **Horizontally** check box, and then click the **OK** button.

The left and right margins change, but there is now less room for the worksheet. As indicated in the status line located in the lower-left corner of the Print Preview window, the worksheet now covers two pages instead of one; the last column in the Sales Analysis table has been moved to the second page. You can restore the margins to their default sizes, and the worksheet will once again fit on a single page. Another option is to change the orientation of the page from portrait to landscape. **Portrait orientation** (which is the default) displays the page taller than it is wide. **Landscape orientation** displays the page wider than it is tall.

You want to change the page orientation to landscape so the last column of the Sales Analysis table will fit on the same page as the rest of the columns in the table.

TUTORIAL 3 DEVELOPING A PROFESSIONAL-LOOKING WORKSHEET EX 3.35 EXCEL

To change the page orientation:

1. Click the **Setup** button, and then click the **Page** tab.
2. Click the **Landscape** option button. See Figure 3-33.

Figure 3-33 PAGE SETUP DIALOG BOX

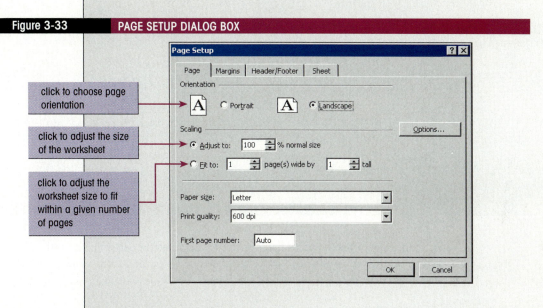

3. Click the **OK** button. Excel changes the orientation to landscape. Note that the entire report now fits on a single page.

The Page tab in the Page Setup dialog box contains other useful formatting features. You can reduce or increase the size of the worksheet on the printed page. The default size is 100%. You can also have Excel automatically reduce the size of the report to fit within a specified number of pages.

Working with Headers and Footers

Joan wants you to add a header and footer to the report. A **header** is text printed in the top margin of every worksheet page. A **footer** is text printed at the bottom of every page. Headers and footers can add important information to your printouts. For example, you can create a header that displays your name and the date the report was created. If the report covers multiple pages, you can use a footer to display the page number and the total number of pages. You use the Page Setup dialog box to add headers and footers to a worksheet.

Excel tries to anticipate headers and footers that you might want to include in your worksheet. Clicking the Header or Footer list arrow displays a list of possible headers or footers (the list is the same for both). For example, the "Page 1" entry inserts the page number of the worksheet prefaced by the word "Page" in the header; the "Page 1 of ?" displays the page number and the total number of pages. Other entries in the list include the name or the worksheet or workbook.

If you want to use a header or footer not available in the lists, you click the Custom Header or Custom Footer button and create your own header and footer. The Header dialog box and the Footer dialog box are similar. Each dialog box is divided into three sections, left, center, and right. If you want to enter information such as the filename or the day's date into the header or footer, you can either type the text or click one of the format buttons located above the three section boxes. Figure 3-34 describes the format buttons and the corresponding format codes.

Figure 3-34 HEADER/FOOTER FORMATTING BUTTONS

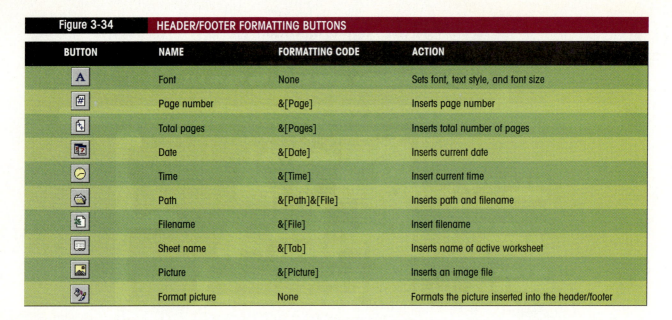

BUTTON	NAME	FORMATTING CODE	ACTION
	Font	None	Sets font, text style, and font size
	Page number	&[Page]	Inserts page number
	Total pages	&[Pages]	Inserts total number of pages
	Date	&[Date]	Inserts current date
	Time	&[Time]	Insert current time
	Path	&[Path]&[File]	Inserts path and filename
	Filename	&[File]	Insert filename
	Sheet name	&[Tab]	Inserts name of active worksheet
	Picture	&[Picture]	Inserts an image file
	Format picture	None	Formats the picture inserted into the header/footer

Joan wants a header that displays the filename at the left margin and today's date at the right margin. She wants a footer that displays the name of the workbook author, with the text aligned at the right margin of the footer. You'll create the header and footer now.

To add a custom header to the workbook:

1. Click the **Setup** button on the Print Preview toolbar, and then click the **Header/Footer** tab.

2. Click the **Custom Header** button. The Header dialog box opens. See Figure 3-35.

Figure 3-35 HEADER DIALOG BOX

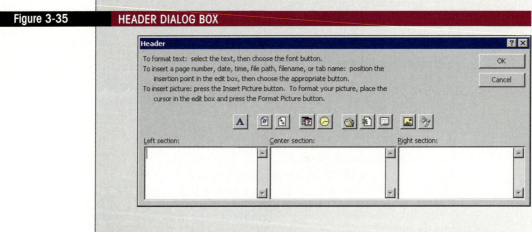

3. In the Left section box, type **Filename:** and then press the **spacebar**.

4. Click the **Filename** button to insert the format code. The formatting code for the name of the file, &(File), appears after the text string that you entered in the Left section box.

5. Click the **Right section** box, and then click the **Date** button. Excel inserts the &(DATE) format code into the section box.

6. Click the **OK** button to close the Header dialog box.

7. Click the **Custom Footer** button. The Footer dialog box opens.

8. Click the **Right section** box, type **Prepared by:** and then type your name.

9. Click the **OK** button. The Page Setup dialog box displays the custom header and footer that you created.

10. Click the **OK** button. The Print Preview window displays the worksheet with the new header and footer.

11. Click the **Close** button on the Print Preview toolbar.

Working with the Print Area and Page Breaks

When you displayed the worksheet in the Print Preview window, how did Excel know which parts of the active worksheet you were going to print? The default action is to print all parts of the active worksheet that contain text, formulas, or values, which will not always be what you want. If you want to print only a part of the worksheet, you can define a **print area** that contains the content you want to print. To define a print area, you must first select the cells you want to print, and then select the Print Area option on the File menu.

A print area can include an adjacent range or nonadjacent ranges. You can also hide rows or columns in the worksheet in order to print nonadjacent ranges. For her report, Joan might decide against printing the sales analysis information. To remove those cells from the printout, you need to define a print area that excludes the cells for the second table.

To define the print area:

1. Select the range **A1:H17**.

2. Click **File** on the menu bar, point to **Print Area**, and then click **Set Print Area**.

3. Click cell **A2**. Excel places a dotted black line around the selected cells of the print area. This is a visual indicator of what parts of the worksheet will be printed.

4. Click the **Print Preview** button on the Standard toolbar. The Print Preview window displays only the first table. The second table has been removed from the printout because it is not in the defined print area.

5. Click the **Close** button on the Print Preview toolbar.

Another approach that Joan might take is to place the two tables on separate pages. You can do this for her by creating a **page break**, which forces Excel to place a portion of a worksheet on a new page.

Before inserting a page break, you must first redefine the print area to include the second table.

To redefine the print area, and then insert a page break:

1. Select the range **A1:H24**.

2. Click **File** on the menu bar, point to **Print Area**, and then click **Set Print Area**.

   Before you insert the page break, you need to indicate where in the worksheet you want the break to occur. Because you want to print the second table on a separate page, you will set the page break at cell A18, which will force rows 18 through 24 to a new page.

3. Click cell **A18**, click **Insert** on the menu bar, and then click **Page Break**. Another blank dotted line appears—this time above cell A18, indicating there is a page break at this point in the print area. See Figure 3-36.

Figure 3-36   ADDING A PAGE BREAK TO THE PRINT AREA

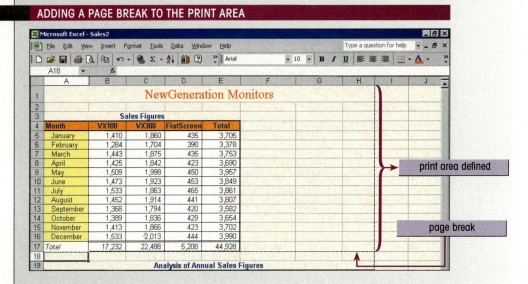

4. Click the **Print Preview** button on the Standard toolbar. Excel displays the first table on page 1 in the Print Preview window.

5. Click the **Next** button to display page 2.

6. Click the **Close** button on the Print Preview toolbar.

You show the print preview to Joan and she notices that the name of the company, "NewGeneration Monitors," appears on the first page, but not on the second. That is not surprising because the range that includes the company name is limited to the first page of the printout. However, Joan would like to have this information repeated on the second page.

You can repeat information, such as the company name, by specifying which cells in the print area should be repeated on each page. This is particularly useful in long tables which extend over many pages. In such cases, you can have the column titles repeated for each page in the printout.

To set rows or columns to repeat on each page, you have to open the Page Setup dialog box from the worksheet window.

To repeat the first row on each page:

1. Click **File** on the menu bar, and then click **Page Setup**.

2. Click the **Sheet** tab. See Figure 3-37.

Figure 3-37 ADDING A PAGE BREAK TO THE PRINT AREA

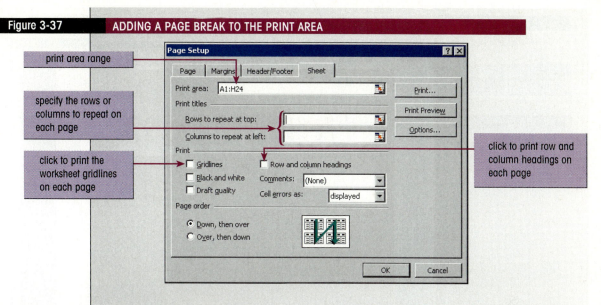

The Sheet tab displays options you can use to control how the worksheet is printed. As shown in Figure 3-37, the print area you have defined is already entered into the Print area box. Joan wants the company name to appear above the second table, so you need to have Excel repeat the first row on the second page.

3. Click the **Rows to repeat at top** box.

4. Click cell **A1**. A flashing border appears around the first row in the worksheet. This is a visual indicator that the contents of the first row will be repeated on all pages of the printout. In the Rows to repeat at top box, the format code *$1:$1* appears.

5. Click the **OK** button.

The Sheet tab also provides other options, such as the ability to print the worksheet's gridlines or row and column headings. You can also have Excel print the worksheet in black and white or draft quality. If there are multiple pages in the printout, you can indicate whether the pages should be ordered going down the worksheet first and then across, or across first and then down.

Next, you'll preview the worksheet to see how the pages look with the company name above each table, and then you'll print the worksheet.

To preview and print the worksheet:

1. Click the **Print Preview** button on the Standard toolbar. The first page of the printout appears in the Print Preview window.

2. Click the **Next** button to display the second page of the printout. Note that the title "NewGeneration Monitors" appears on the page. See Figure 3-38.

Figure 3-38 SECOND PAGE OF THE SALES PRINTOUT

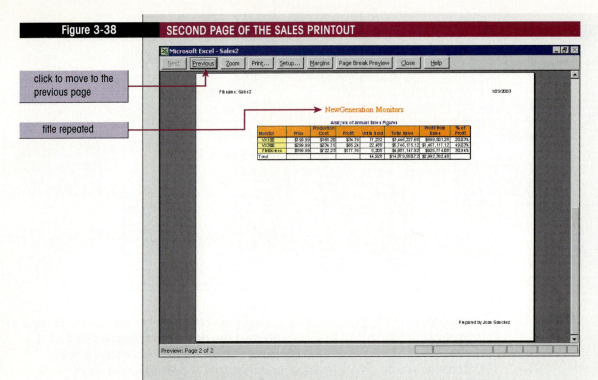

click to move to the previous page

title repeated

3. Click the **Print** button, select your printer from the Name list box, and then click the **OK** button.

   For now your work is done. When you save the workbook, your printing options are saved along with the file, so you will not have to re-create the print format in the future.

4. Save and close the workbook, and then exit Excel.

You show the final version of the workbook and the printout to Joan. She is very happy with the way in which you have formatted her report. She will spend some time going over the printout and will get back to you with any further changes she wants you to make.

Session 3.2 QUICK CHECK

1. Describe two ways of merging a range of cells into one.
2. How do you clear a format from a cell without affecting the underlying data?
3. How do you add a background image to the active worksheet?
4. To control the amount of space between the content on a page and its edges, you can adjust the page's _____.
5. By default, Excel prints what part of the active worksheet?
6. How do you define a print area? How do you remove a print area?
7. How do you insert a page break into your worksheet?

REVIEW ASSIGNMENTS

Joan Sanchez has another report that she wants to format. The report displays regional sales for the three monitor brands you worked on earlier. As before, Joan wants to work on the overall appearance of the worksheet so the printout of the report is polished and professional looking.

To format the report:

1. Start Excel and open the **Region1** workbook located in the Tutorial.03/Review folder on your Data Disk.

2. Save the workbook as **Region2** in the same folder.

Explore

3. Enter your name and the current date in the Documentation sheet. Format the date to display the day of the week and the name of the month as well as the day and year. Switch to the Regional Sales worksheet.

4. Format the text in cell A1 with a 20-point, boldfaced, italicized, red Times New Roman font. Select the cell range A1:F1, and then center the text in cell A1 across the selection (do not merge the cells).

5. Select the range A3:E14, and then apply the List 2 format from the AutoFormat Gallery.

6. Change the format of all the values in the Sales by Region table to display a comma separator, but no decimal places.

7. Change the format of the units sold values in the second table to display a comma separator, but no decimal places.

8. Indent the region names in the range A5:A13 by one character.

9. Display the text in cell A16 in bold.

10. Change the format of the values in the Total Sales and Profit from Sales columns to display a dollar sign directly to the left of the values and no decimal places.

11. Change the format of the % of Profit column as percentages with two decimal places.

12. Allow the text in the range A17:F17 to wrap to a second line of text. Change the font of the text to bold.

Explore

13. Merge the cells in the range A18:A20, and then vertically align the text with the top of the cell. Apply this format to the cells in the following ranges: A21:A23, A24:A26, and A27:A29.

14. Change the background color of the cells in the range A17:F17;A18:A29 to Sea Green (third row, fourth column of the color palette). Change the font color to white.

15. Change the background color of the cells in the range B18:F29 to white. Change the background color of the cells in the range B20:F20;B23:F23;B26:F26;B29:F29 to Light Green (fifth row, fourth column of the color palette).

16. Surround the borders of all cells in the range A17:F29 with a black line.

Explore

17. Place a double red line on the bottom border of the cells in the range B20:F20;B23:F23;B26:F26.

18. Set the print area as the range A1:F29. Insert a page break above row 16. Repeat the first row of the worksheet on every page of any printouts you produce from this worksheet.

19. Set up the page to print in portrait orientation with 1-inch margins on all sides. Center the contents of the worksheet horizontally on the page.

20. Add a footer with the following text in the Left section box of the footer (with the date on a separate line): "Filename: *the name of the file*" and "Date: *current date*," and then the following text in the Right section box of the footer: "Prepared by: *your name*."

Explore

21. Add a header with the text "Regional Sales Report" displayed in the Center section using a 14-point Times New Roman font with a double underline. (*Hint*: Select the text in the Center section, and then use the Formatting toolbar to change the appearance of the text.)

22. Print the Regional Sales worksheet.

23. Save and close the workbook, and then exit Excel.

CASE PROBLEMS

Case 1. Jenson Sports Wear Quarterly Sales Carol Roberts is the national sales manager for Jenson Sports Wear, a company that sells sportswear to major department stores. She has been using an Excel worksheet to track the results of her staff's sales incentive program. She has asked you to format the worksheet so that it looks professional. She also wants a printout before she presents the worksheet at the next sales meeting.

Complete these steps to format and print the worksheet:

1. Open the **Running1** workbook located in the Tutorial.03/Cases folder on your Data Disk, and then save the file as **Running2** in the same folder.

2. Enter your name and the current date in the Documentation sheet. Switch to the Sales worksheet.

3. Complete the following calculations:
   a. Calculate the totals for each product.
   b. Calculate the quarterly subtotals for the Shoes and Shirts departments.
   c. Calculate the totals for each quarter and an overall total.

Explore

4. Format the data in the range A1:F14 so that it resembles the table shown in Figure 3-39.

Figure 3-39

		Jenson Sports Wear			
		Quarterly Sales by Product			
Shoes	Qtr1	Qtr2	Qtr3	Qtr4	Total
Running	2,250	2,550	2,650	2,800	10,250
Tennis	2,800	1,500	2,300	2,450	9,050
Basketball	1,250	1,400	1,550	1,550	5,750
Subtotal	6,300	5,450	6,500	6,800	25,050
Shirts	Qtr1	Qtr2	Qtr3	Qtr4	Total
Tee	1,000	1,150	1,250	1,150	4,550
Polo	2,100	2,200	2,300	2,400	9,000
Sweat	250	250	275	300	1,075
Subtotal	3,350	3,600	3,825	3,850	14,625
Grand Total	9,650	9,050	10,325	10,650	39,675

Explore

5. Create a style named "Subtotal" that is based on the font, border, and pattern formats found in the cell ranges A7:F7 and A13:F13.

6. Use the Page Setup dialog box to center the table both horizontally and vertically on the printed page and to change the page orientation to landscape.

7. Add the filename, your name, and the date on separate lines in the Right section box of the footer.

8. Print the sales report.

9. Save and close the workbook, and then exit Excel.

Case 2. Wisconsin Department of Revenue Ted Crawford works for the Wisconsin Department of Revenue. Recently he compiled a list of the top 50 women-owned businesses in the state. He would like your help in formatting the report, in regard to both how it appears in the worksheet window and how it appears on the printed page.

Complete the following:

1. Open the **WBus1** workbook located in the Tutorial.03/Cases folder on your Data Disk, and then save the file as **WBus2** in the same folder.

2. Enter your name and the current date in the Documentation sheet. Switch to the Business Data worksheet.

3. Change the font in cell A1 to a boldface font that is 14 points in size. Merge and center the title across the range A1:F1.

4. Display the text in the range A2:F2 in bold, and then center the text in the range C2:F2. Place a double line on the bottom border of the range A2:F2.

5. Display the sales information in the Accounting format with no decimal places; enlarge the width of the column, if necessary.

6. Display the employees' data using a comma separator with no decimal places.

7. Change the background color of the cells in the range A3:F3 to light green. Change the background color of the cells in A4:F4 to white.

Explore 8. Select the range A3:F4 and use the Format Painter to apply the format to the cells in the range A5:F52. How is the format applied to the cells?

9. Change the page orientation of the worksheet to landscape. Set the bottom margin to 1.5 inches. Center the contents of the worksheet horizontally on the page.

10. Set the print area as the cell range A1:F52. Repeat the first two rows of the worksheet in any printouts.

11. Remove any header from the printed page. Display the following text on separate lines in the Right section box of the footer: "Compiled by *your name*," "*the current date*," "Page *the current page* of *total number of pages*."

Explore 12. Fit the worksheet on output that is 1 page wide by 2 pages tall.

13. Preview the worksheet, and then print it.

14. Save and close the workbook, and then exit Excel.

Case 3. Sales Report at Davis Blades Andrew Malki is a financial officer at Davis Blades, a leading manufacturer of roller blades. He has recently finished entering data for the yearly sales report. Andrew has asked you to help him with the design of the main table in the report. A preview of the format you will apply is shown in Figure 3-40.

Figure 3-40

Davis Blades Yearly Sales Report
Units Sold

		Northeast	East	Southeast	Midwest	Southwest	West	All Regions
Black Hawk	Qtr 1	641	748	733	676	691	783	4,272
	Qtr 2	708	826	811	748	763	866	4,722
	Qtr 3	681	795	780	719	734	833	4,542
	Qtr 4	668	779	764	705	720	816	4,452
	Total	2,698	3,148	3,088	2,848	2,908	3,298	17,988
Blademaster	Qtr 1	513	598	587	541	552	627	3,418
	Qtr 2	567	661	648	598	611	693	3,778
	Qtr 3	545	636	624	575	587	666	3,633
	Qtr 4	534	623	611	564	576	653	3,561
	Total	2,159	2,518	2,470	2,278	2,326	2,639	14,390
The Professional	Qtr 1	342	399	391	361	368	418	2,279
	Qtr 2	378	441	432	399	407	462	2,519
	Qtr 3	363	424	416	383	391	444	2,421
	Qtr 4	356	415	407	376	384	435	2,373
	Total	1,439	1,679	1,646	1,519	1,550	1,759	9,592
All Models	Qtr 1	1,496	1,745	1,711	1,578	1,611	1,828	9,969
	Qtr 2	1,653	1,928	1,891	1,745	1,781	2,021	11,019
	Qtr 3	1,589	1,855	1,820	1,677	1,712	1,943	10,596
	Qtr 4	1,558	1,817	1,782	1,645	1,680	1,904	10,386
	Total	6,296	7,345	7,204	6,645	6,784	7,696	41,970

Complete the following:

1. Open the **Blades1** workbook located in the Tutorial.03/Cases folder on your Data Disk, and then save the file as **Blades2** in the same folder.

2. Enter your name and the current date in the Documentation sheet. Switch to the Sales worksheet.

3. Change the font of the title in cell A1 to a 14–point, dark blue, boldface Arial font. Change the subtitle in cell A2 to a 12-point, dark blue, boldface Arial font.

Explore

4. Merge the cells in the range A4:A8, and align the contents of the cell with the upper-left corner of the cell. Repeat this for the following ranges: A9:A13, A14:A18, and A19:A23.

5. Change the background color of the cell range A4:I8 to light yellow. Change the background color of the range A9:I13 to light green. Change the background color of the range A14:I18 to light turquoise. Change the background color of the range A19:I23 to pale blue.

6. Reverse the color scheme for the subtotal values in the range B8:I8, so that instead of black on light yellow, the font color is light yellow on a black background. Reverse the subtotal values for the other products in the table.

7. Apply the gridlines as displayed in Figure 3-40 to the cells in the range A4:I23.

Explore

8. Rotate the column titles in the range C3:I3 by 45 degrees. Align the contents of each cell with the cell's bottom right border. Change the background color of these cells to white and add a border to each cell.

9. Set the print area as the range A1:K23.

10. Leave the page orientation as portrait, but center the worksheet horizontally on the page.

11. Remove any headers from the page. Create a custom footer with the the text "Filename: *name of the file*" left-aligned, and "Prepared by: *your name*" and "*the current date*" right-aligned, with your name and date on separate lines.

12. Print the worksheet.

13. Save and close the workbook, and then exit Excel.

Case 4. Oritz Marine Services Vince DiOrio is an information systems major at a local college. He works three days a week at a nearby marina, Oritz Marine Services, to help pay for his tuition. Vince works in the business office, and his responsibilities range from making coffee to keeping the company's books.

Recently, Jim Oritz, the owner of the marina, asked Vince if he could help computerize the payroll for the employees. He explained that the employees work a different number of hours each week at different rates of pay. Jim does the payroll manually now and finds it time-consuming. Moreover, whenever he makes an error, he is annoyed at having to take the additional time to correct it. Jim is hoping that Vince can help him.

Vince immediately agrees to help. He tells Jim that he knows how to use Excel and that he can build a worksheet that will save him time and reduce errors. Jim and Vince meet to review the present payroll process and discuss the desired outcome of the payroll spreadsheet. Figure 3-41 displays the type of information that Jim records in the spreadsheet.

Figure 3-41

Oritz Marine Service Payroll
Week Ending

Employee	Hours	Pay Rate	Gross Pay	Federal Withholding	State Withholding	Total Deductions	Net Pay
Bramble	16	9.50					
Juarez	25	12.00					
Smith	30	13.50					
DiOrio	25	12.50					
Smiken	10	9.00					
Cortez	30	10.50					
Fulton	20	9.50					
Total							

Complete the following:

1. Create a new workbook named **Payroll** and save it in the Tutorial.03/Cases folder on your Data Disk.

2. Name two worksheets Documentation and Payroll.

3. On the Documentation sheet, include the name of the company, your name, the date, and a brief description of the purpose of the workbook.

4. On the Payroll worksheet, enter the payroll table shown in Figure 3-41.

5. Use the following formulas in the table to calculate total hours, gross pay, federal withholding, state withholding, total deductions, and net pay:
   a. Gross pay is hours times pay rate
   b. Federal withholding is 15% of gross pay
   c. State withholding is 4% of gross pay
   d. Total deductions are the sum of federal and state withholdings
   e. Net pay is the difference between gross pay and total deductions

Explore 6. Format the appearance of the payroll table using the techniques you learned in this tutorial. The appearance of the payroll table is up to you; however, do not use an AutoFormat to format the table.

Explore 7. Format the printed page, setting the print area and inserting an appropriate header and footer. Only a few employees are entered into the table at present. However, after Jim Oritz approves your layout, many additional employees will be added, which will cause the report to cover multiple pages. Format your printout so that the page title and column titles will appear on every page.

8. Remove the hours for the seven employees, and enter the following new values: 18 for Bramble, 25 for Juarez, 35 for Smith, 20 for DiOrio, 15 for Smiken, 35 for Cortez, and 22 for Fulton.

9. Print the worksheet.

10. Save and close the workbook, and then exit Excel.

INTERNET ASSIGNMENTS

Student Union

The purpose of the Internet Assignments is to challenge you to find information on the Internet that you can use to create effective spreadsheets. The actual assignments are updated and maintained on the Course Technology Web site. Log on to the Internet and use your Web browser to go to the Student Union on the New Perspectives Series site at **www.course.com/NewPerspectives/studentunion**. Click the Online Companions link, and then click the link for this text.

QUICK CHECK ANSWERS

Session 3.1

1. Click the Currency Style button on the Formatting toolbar; or click Cells on the Format menu, click the Number tab, and then select Currency from the Category list box.
2. Excel will display the following:
   a. 5.8%
   b. $0.06
3. the Format Painter button and the Copy button
4. Increase the width of the column; decrease the font size of the text; or select the Shrink to fit check box or the Wrap text check box on the Alignment tab in the Format cells dialog box.
5. Select the range, click Cells on the Format menu, click the Alignment tab, and then choose Center Across Selection from the Horizontal list box.
6. Use the Borders button on the Formatting toolbar; use the Draw Borders tool in the Border gallery; or click Cells on the Format menu, click the Border tab, and then choose the border options in the dialog box.
7. Click Cells on the Format menu, click the Patterns tab, and then click the Pattern list arrow to choose the pattern type and color.

Session 3.2

1. Select the cells and either click the Merge and Center button on the Formatting toolbar; or click Cells on the Format menu, click the Alignment tab, and then click the Merge cells check box.
2. Select the cell, point to Clear on the Edit menu, and then click Formats.
3. Point to Sheet on the Format menu, and then click Background. Locate and select an image file to use for the background.
4. margins
5. Excel prints all parts of the active worksheet that contain text, formulas, or values.
6. To define a print area, select a range in the worksheet, point to Print Area on the File menu, and then click Set Print Area. To remove a print area, point to Print Area on the File menu, and then click Clear Print Area.
7. Select the first cell below the intended place for the page break, and then click Page Break on the Insert menu.

OBJECTIVES

In this tutorial you will:

- Create column and pie charts using the Chart Wizard
- Resize and move an embedded chart
- Create a chart sheet
- Modify the properties of your charts
- Format chart elements
- Create 3-D charts
- Insert drawing objects into your workbook
- Print a chart sheet

TUTORIAL 4

WORKING WITH CHARTS AND GRAPHICS

Charting Sales Data for Vega Telescopes

CASE

Vega Telescopes

Alicia Kendall is a sales manager at Vega Telescopes, one of the leading manufacturers of telescopes and optics. She has been asked to present information on last year's sales for four of Vega's top telescope models: the 6- and 8-inch BrightStars, and the 12- and 16-inch NightVisions. Her report should include the sales figures on each model organized by the United States, European, and Asian sales. Her presentation will be part of the sales conference that will be held next week in Charlotte, North Carolina.

Alicia has the basic sales information and knows that this kind of sales information is often best understood when presented visually, that is, in a graphical or pictorial form. Therefore, she wants you to help her create charts that will clearly and easily present the sales data. She would like to show the sales data in a column chart, but she would also like to use a pie chart that shows how each model contributes to Vega's overall sales of these top telescope models.

Alicia wants to format the charts so they are visually appealing. She wants to draw attention to the product that is the top-selling model. She also will need printouts of the charts.

In this tutorial you will create two charts: a column chart and a pie chart. You will format the charts and individual chart components. You will also add a drawing object that points out the top-selling telescope and then print the completed charts.

EXCEL   EX 4.02   TUTORIAL 4 WORKING WITH CHARTS AND GRAPHICS

SESSION 4.1

In this session, you will create a chart using Excel's Chart Wizard. You will learn about embedded charts and chart sheets. You will resize and move an embedded chart. You will work with pie charts by rotating them and exploding a pie slice.

Excel Charts

Alicia's sales data has already been entered into a workbook for you. Open the workbook and examine the data.

To open Alicia's workbook:

1. Start Excel, if necessary, and open the **Vega1** workbook located in the Tutorial.04/Tutorial folder on your Data Disk.

2. Enter your name and the current date in the Documentation sheet.

3. Save the workbook as **Vega2** in the same folder.

4. Switch to the Sales worksheet. See Figure 4-1.

Figure 4-1   THE SALES WORKSHEET FOR VEGA TELESCOPES

	A	B	C	D	E
1		*Vega Telescope Sales*			
2	Model	United States	Europe	Asia	Total
3	BrightStar 6	1,858,000	714,000	286,000	2,858,000
4	BrightStar 8	2,160,000	921,000	314,000	3,395,000
5	NightVision 12	1,194,000	460,000	184,000	1,838,000
6	NightVison 16	158,000	210,000	40,000	408,000
7	Total	5,370,000	2,305,000	824,000	$8,499,000

The Sales worksheet shows the annual sales, in dollars, for each of the four Vega telescope models. The sales data are broken down by world region. As Alicia has explained, she wants two charts. The first chart should show the sales for each telescope in each region represented by columns, in which the height of the column represents the sales volume for each model. The second should be a pie chart, in which the size of each slice is proportional to the total sales for each telescope model. The sketches of the charts Alicia wants to create are shown in Figure 4-2.

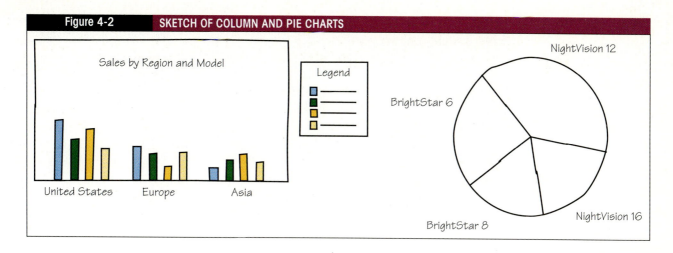

Charts, also referred to in Excel as graphs, provide visual representations of the workbook data. Excel makes it easy to create charts through the use of the **Chart Wizard**, a series of dialog boxes that prompt you for information about the chart you want to generate. You will use the Chart Wizard to create the first graph that Alicia sketched for you—the column chart of the sales figures broken down by region and telescope model.

Creating a Chart with the Chart Wizard

Before starting the Chart Wizard, you should (although it is not necessary) select the data that will be used in the chart. In this case, you will select the data in the range A2:D6. Note that you will not include any of the subtotals in the selection. The column chart that you need to create will only display the sales figures broken down by model type and region; it will not display any overall totals.

Once you start the Chart Wizard, you go through a series of four dialog boxes that prompt you for different information about the chart you are creating. Figure 4-3 describes each of the four dialog boxes.

Figure 4-3 — TASKS PERFORMED IN EACH STEP OF THE CHART WIZARD

DIALOG BOX	TASK OPTIONS
Chart Type	Select from list of available chart types and corresponding type sub-type, or choose to customize a chart type
Chart Source Data	Specify the worksheet cells that contain the data on which the chart will be based and the worksheet cells that contain the labels that will appear in the chart
Chart Options	Change the appearance of the chart by selecting the options that affect titles, axes, gridlines, legends, data labels, and data tables
Chart Location	Specify where the chart will be placed: embedded as an object in the worksheet containing the data or on a separate worksheet, also called a chart sheet

Note that you can quit the Chart Wizard at any time in the process, and Excel will complete the remaining dialog boxes for you, using the default configuration for the chart you have chosen.

REFERENCE WINDOW

Creating a Chart with the Chart Wizard
- Select the data you want to chart.
- Click the Chart Wizard button on the Standard toolbar.
- In the first step of the Chart Wizard, select the chart type and sub-type.
- In the second step, make any modifications or additions to the chart's data source.
- In the third step, make any modifications to the chart's appearance.
- In the fourth step, specify the location for the chart.
- Click the OK button.

Start the Chart Wizard.

To start the Chart Wizard:

1. Select the range **A2:D6**.

2. Click the **Chart Wizard** button on the Standard toolbar. The first step of the Chart Wizard is shown in Figure 4-4.

   TROUBLE? If the Chart Wizard button is not displayed on the toolbar, click the Toolbar Options button on the Standard toolbar, and then click.

Figure 4-4   STEP 1 OF THE CHART WIZARD

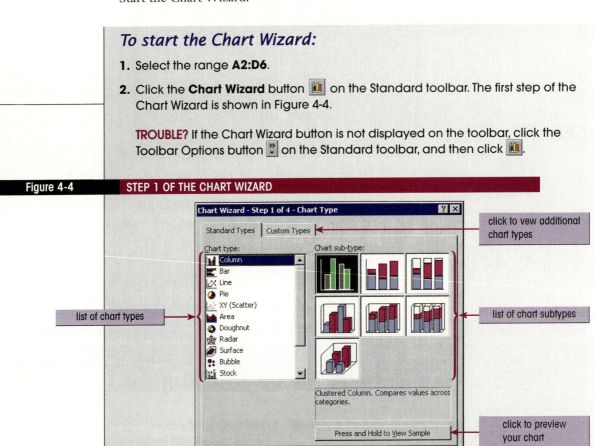

Choosing a Chart Type

The first step of the Chart Wizard provides the chart types from which you choose the one you think will best represent the data you want to present visually. Excel supports 14 types of charts ranging from the column chart, similar to the one shown in Alicia's first sketch, to stock market charts used to record the daily behavior of stocks. Figure 4-5 provides information about some of the chart types.

Figure 4-5 EXCEL CHART TYPES

ICON(S)	CHART TYPE(S)	DESCRIPTION
	Column	Compares values within different categories based on the height of the columns
	Bar	Compares values within different categories based on the width of the bars
	Line	Compares values using different lines for different categories
	Pie	Compares values within different categories based on the size of the pie slice
	XY (Scatter)	Shows the pattern or relationship between sets of (x, y) data points
	Area	Similar to the Line chart, except that the areas under the lines are filled in with color
	Stock	Displays stock market data, including the high, low, open, and close prices of a stock
	Cylinder, Cone, Pyramid	Similar to the Column chart, except that cylinders, cones, and pyramids are substituted for the columns

Each chart type has its own collection of sub-types that provide alternative formats for the chart. For example, the column chart type has seven different sub-types, including the clustered column and the stacked column. There are also 3-D, or three-dimensional, sub-types.

Excel also supports 20 additional "custom" chart types that either combine two of the 14 main chart types or that provide additional formatting of the chart's appearance. You can also create your own customized chart designs and add them to the custom chart list.

Alicia wants you to create a column chart for the sales data, in which values are arranged into separate columns. To see whether the chart you are creating is the right one, you can click a button to preview the chart before continuing in the Chart Wizard.

To select the chart type and preview it:

1. Verify that the Column chart type is selected in the Chart type list box and that the first sub-type, Clustered Column, is also selected.

2. Press the **Press and Hold to view Sample** button, but do not release the mouse button. Figure 4-6 shows the contents of the preview window.

Figure 4-6 PREVIEW OF THE CLUSTERED COLUMN CHART

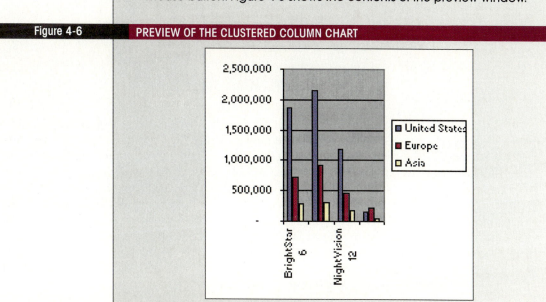

> A different colored column represents each region in this chart. The blue columns represent the United States sales, the maroon columns the European sales, and the yellow columns the Asian sales. Though the size of the Preview pane prevents you from viewing much of the chart detail, you can see that the columns are clustered into groups, where each group represents a different model. The first cluster represents sales for the BrightStar 6 telescope. The second cluster represents sales for the BrightStar 8 and so forth. Since this is the chart type that Alicia wants you to create, you can continue to the next step of the Chart Wizard.
>
> 3. Release the mouse button, and then click the **Next** button to go to step 2 of the Chart Wizard.

Choosing a Data Source

In the second step of the Chart Wizard, shown in Figure 4-7, you specify the data to be displayed in the chart, also known as the chart's **data source**. Excel organizes the data source into a collection of **data series**, where each data series is a range of data values that are plotted on the chart. A data series consists of data values, which are plotted on the chart's vertical axis, or y-axis. On the horizontal axis, or x-axis, are the data series' **category values**, or **x values**. A chart can have several data series, which are plotted against a common set of category values. For example, the column chart preview shown in Figure 4-7 illustrates the three data series that present the sales for the United States, Europe, and Asia. Those sales values are matched against the category values that indicate the telescope model.

| Figure 4-7 | SPECIFYING THE DATA SOURCE |

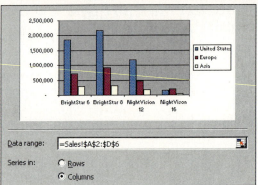

In Alicia's sketch, she has illustrated that she wants the category values to be the three regions, and not the four telescope models. Currently Excel has drawn the data from the range A2:D6, which is the range of data you selected before starting the Chart Wizard. By default, Excel organized these values by columns, so that the leftmost column contains the category values and the subsequent columns each contain a data series. The first row of the data used in the chart contains the labels that identify each data series. In general, if the data spans more rows than columns, then the Chart Wizard organizes the data series by columns, otherwise the Chart Wizard organizes the data series by rows. However, you can override this behavior and have Excel organize the data by rows. Therefore, the first row will contain the category values, and each subsequent row will contain a data series. The first column will then contain the label of each series.

To organize the data source by rows:

1. Click the **Rows** option button. Excel changes the orientation of the data source. The category values now represent the three regions rather than the four telescope models. See Figure 4-8.

Figure 4-8
CHANGING THE ORIENTATION OF THE DATA SOURCE

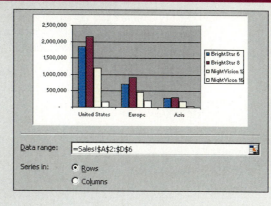

You can further define the data series used by the Chart Wizard using the Series tab. From this tab, you can add or remove data series from the chart or change the category values. Although it is recommended that you select the data series before starting the Chart Wizard, you do not have to since you can define all of the data series and chart values using the Series tab. However, selecting the data series first does save time.

To view the Series tab:

1. Click the **Series** tab. The Series tab lists all of the data series used in the chart and the cell references for the category labels. Note that the cell references include the name of the sheet from which the values are selected. See Figure 4-9.

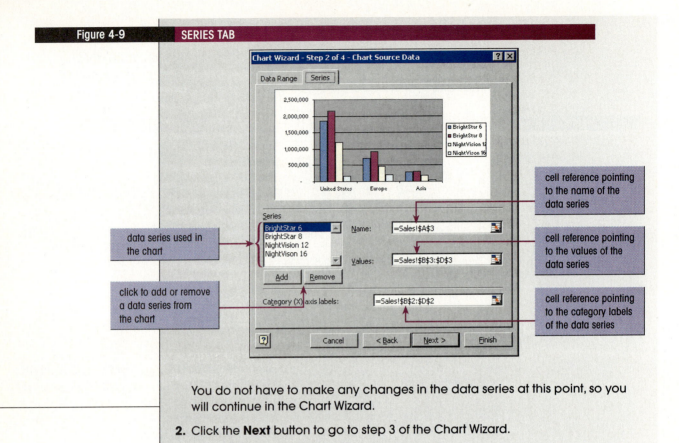

Figure 4-9 SERIES TAB

You do not have to make any changes in the data series at this point, so you will continue in the Chart Wizard.

2. Click the **Next** button to go to step 3 of the Chart Wizard.

Choosing Chart Options

The third step of the Chart Wizard provides the options that you can use to control the appearance of the chart. To better understand the options available to you, first explore the terminology that Excel uses with respect to charts. Figure 4-10 shows the elements of a typical Excel chart.

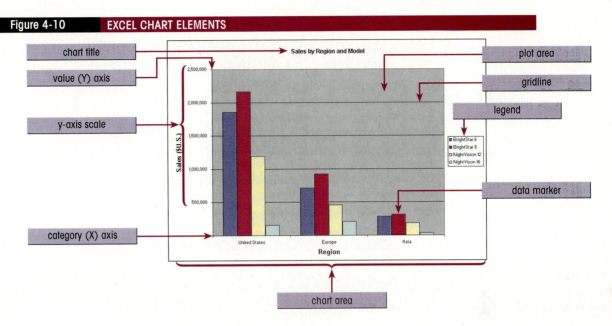

Figure 4-10 EXCEL CHART ELEMENTS

The basic element of the chart is the **plot area**, a rectangular area that contains a graphical representation of the values in the data series. These graphical representations are called **data markers**. The columns displayed in Column charts are examples of data markers. Other examples of data markers include the pie slices used in pie charts, or the points used in the XY (scatter) charts.

Most charts have two axes that border the plot area: a vertical, or y, axis and a horizontal, or x, axis. As mentioned earlier, values from the data series are plotted along the y-axis, whereas the category labels are plotted alongside the x-axis. Each axis can have a title that describes the values or labels displayed on the axis. In Figure 4-10, the x-axis title is "Region" and the y-axis title is "Sales ($U.S.)".

An axis covers a range of values, called a **scale**. The scale is displayed with values placed alongside the axes. Next to the values are **tick marks**, which act like the division lines on a ruler. Excel automatically displays a scale that represents the range of values in the data series. In the chart shown in Figure 4-10, the scale of the y-axis ranges from 0 up to 2,500,000. To make it easier to read the data markers on the axis scale, a chart might contain **gridlines**, which extend the tick marks into the plot area.

If several data series appear on the chart, a **legend** can be placed next to the plot area to identify each data series with a unique color or pattern. Above the plot area, Excel can display a **chart title** describing the contents of the plot and the data series. The entire chart and all of the elements discussed so far are contained in the **chart area**.

You can format these various elements of a chart in the Chart Wizard's third dialog box. You can also format these features later on, after the chart has been created. Figure 4-11 shows step 3 of the Chart Wizard. Excel divides the Step 3 dialog box into six tabs: Titles, Axes, Gridlines, Legend, Data Labels, and Data Table. Each tab provides tools for formatting different elements of your chart.

| Figure 4-11 | STEP 3 OF THE CHART WIZARD |

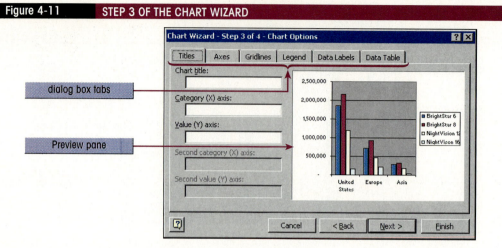

Alicia wants you to add descriptive titles to the chart and to each of the axes. She also wants you to remove the gridlines.

To insert titles into the chart:

1. Verify that the Titles tab is active.

2. Click the **Chart title** text box, type **Telescope Sales by Region**, and then press the **Tab** key. The Preview pane updates automatically to reflect the addition of the chart title to the chart area.

3. Type **Region** in the Category (X) axis box, and then press the **Tab** key.

4. Type **Sales ($U.S.)** in the Value (Y) axis box, and then press the **Tab** key. The Preview pane shows all of the new titles you entered into the chart.

5. Click the **Gridlines** tab.

6. Click the **Major gridlines** check box on the Value (Y) axes to remove the major gridlines from the chart.

7. Click the **Next** button.

Choosing the Chart Location

In the final step of the Chart Wizard, you choose a location for the chart. You have two choices: 1) you can save the chart as an embedded chart in a worksheet, or 2) you can create a sheet called a chart sheet that contains only the chart. Figure 4-12 shows both options.

Figure 4-12 EMBEDDED CHARTS AND CHART SHEETS

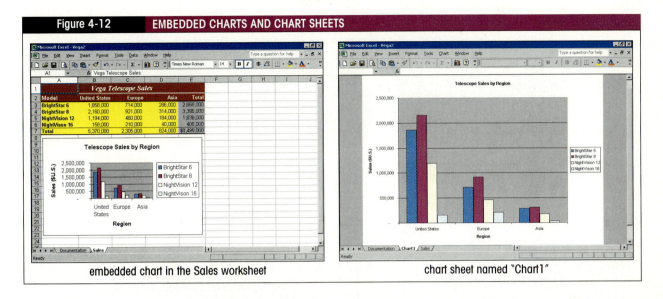

embedded chart in the Sales worksheet chart sheet named "Chart1"

An **embedded chart** is a chart that is displayed within a worksheet. The advantage of creating an embedded chart is that you can place the chart alongside the data source, giving context to the chart. On the other hand, a **chart sheet** is a new sheet that is automatically inserted in the workbook, occupying the entire document window and thus providing more space and details for the chart. For this chart, you will save it as an embedded chart in the Sales worksheet.

To save the chart:

1. Verify that the As object in option button is selected and that "Sales" is selected in the adjacent list box. See Figure 4-13.

Figure 4-13 STEP 4 OF THE CHART WIZARD

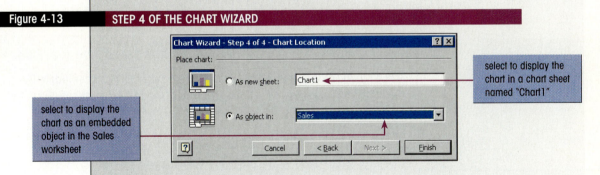

select to display the chart as an embedded object in the Sales worksheet

select to display the chart in a chart sheet named "Chart1"

2. Click the **Finish** button. Excel creates the column chart with the specifications you selected and embeds the chart in the Sales worksheet. Figure 4-14 shows the chart.

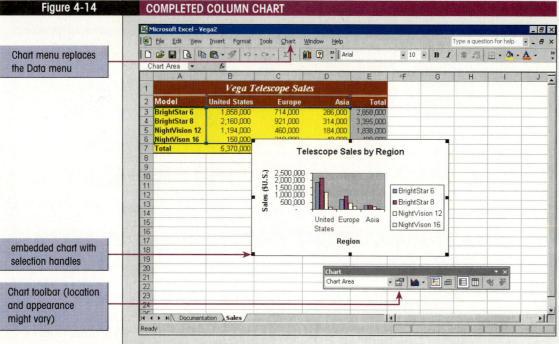

Figure 4-14 COMPLETED COLUMN CHART

- Chart menu replaces the Data menu
- embedded chart with selection handles
- Chart toolbar (location and appearance might vary)

When Excel creates the embedded chart, several things happen. First, note that the chart appears with selection handles around it. The selection handles indicate that the chart is an **active chart**, and it is ready for additional formatting. The Chart toolbar also appears automatically when the chart is selected (on some systems, where the Chart toolbar has been previously closed, this will not be true). Also note that the Chart menu has replaced the Data menu on Excel's menu bar. You will also find certain Excel commands are not available to you when a chart is the active object in the document window. When a chart is not active, the worksheet menus return and the Chart toolbar disappears.

To switch between the embedded chart and the worksheet:

1. Click anywhere in the worksheet outside of the chart to deselect it. The Chart toolbar disappears and the Data menu replaces the Chart menu on the menu bar. There are no selection handles around the chart.

2. Move the pointer over a blank area in the chart until the label, "Chart Area" appears, and then click the blank area. The Chart toolbar and the Chart menu reappear. Selection handles appear around the chart.

    TROUBLE? If you do not see the Chart toolbar, it may have been closed during a previous Excel session. Click View on the menu bar, point to Toolbars, and then click Chart to redisplay the toolbar.

    TROUBLE? If you clicked one of the chart's elements, you made that element active rather than the entire chart. Click a blank area in the chart area to select the entire embedded chart.

The new chart is obscuring some of the data from the sales table. The chart might also look better if it were bigger. You decide to make some additional changes to the chart's appearance.

Moving and Resizing an Embedded Chart

The Chart Wizard has a default size and location for embedded charts, which might not match what you want in your worksheet. The chart may be too small to accentuate relationships between the data markers, or labels might not be displayed correctly. An embedded chart is an object that you can move, resize, or copy. To work with an embedded chart, you first must make the chart active so that the selection handles appear.

Even though you are not sure where Alicia wants the chart to appear, you decide to move it so the chart appears directly under the worksheet.

To move the embedded chart:

1. Verify that the embedded chart is active and that the selection handles appear around the chart, and not around any element within the chart.
2. Move the pointer over a blank area of the chart so that the label "Chart Area" appears.
3. Drag the embedded chart so that the upper-left corner of the chart aligns with the upper-left corner of cell A8. Note that as you drag the chart with the pointer, an outline of the chart area appears. Use the outline as a guideline.
4. Release the mouse button. The chart moves to a new location in the worksheet.

To resize the chart, you drag the selection handles in the direction that you want the chart resized, that is, to increase or decrease the size of the chart. To keep the proportions of the chart the same, press and hold the Shift key as you drag one of the corner selection handles. Now that you have moved the chart, you can increase its size, which will improve its readability. Increasing the size of the chart will help to draw the audience's attention immediately to it.

To resize the embedded chart:

1. Move your mouse pointer over the lower-right corner selection handle until the pointer changes to ↘.
2. Press and hold down the mouse button.
3. Drag the lower-right corner of the embedded chart until that corner is aligned with the lower-right corner of cell F24.

    TROUBLE? If the Chart toolbar obscures cell F24, you can still move the pointer to the approximate location of cell F24, or you can release the mouse button, and then drag the Chart toolbar by its title bar to a new location on the worksheet, out of the way.

4. Release the mouse button. Figure 4-15 shows the final resized and moved chart.

Figure 4-15 — EMBEDDED CHART RESIZED AND MOVED TO A NEW LOCATION

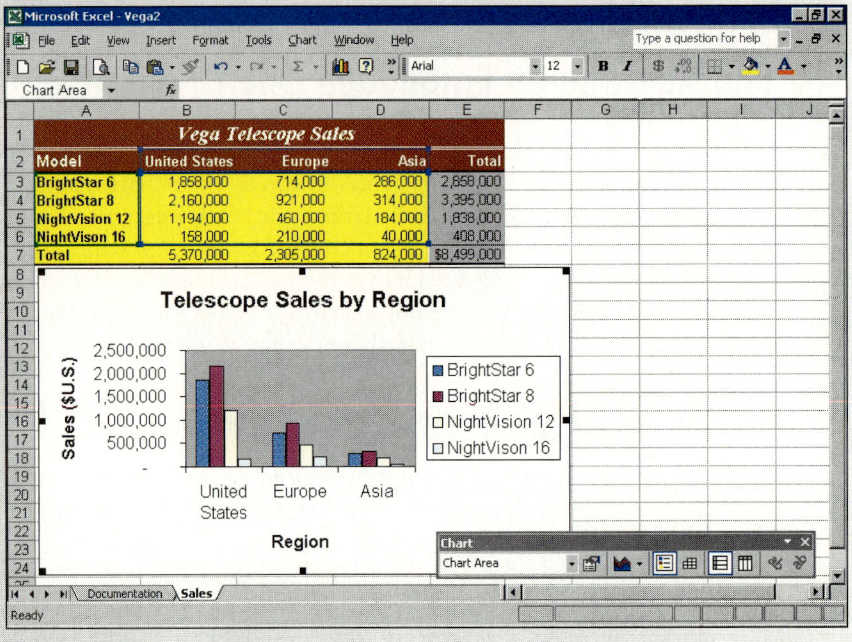

Updating a Chart

Every chart you create is linked to the data in a worksheet. As a result, if you change the data in the worksheet, Excel will automatically update the chart to reflect the change. This is true for category labels as well as for data values.

Alicia notices two mistakes in the Sales worksheet. First, the sales amount in cell C3 should be 914,000 and not 714,000. The second mistake is that the name of the telescope model in cell A6 is misspelled. The name of the telescope is "NightVision" and not "NightVison". You'll correct these mistakes and observe how the embedded chart is automatically updated.

To update the column chart:

1. Click cell **C3**, type **914000**, and then press the **Enter** key. The data marker corresponding to European sales for the BrightStar 6 changes to reflect the new sales value.

2. Click cell **A6**, type **NightVision 16**, and then press the **Enter** key. The entry in the chart's legend displays the correct spelling of the telescope.

Creating a Pie Chart

The second chart that Alicia sketched (shown in Figure 4-2) is a pie chart that shows the contribution of each telescope model to the total sales. In a pie chart, the size of each slice is determined by the value of a single data point to the sum of all values. Unlike the column chart you just created, a pie chart will have only one data series. In this case, the data series will contain the totals for each model across all regions. If you want to create a pie-like chart that contains several data series, you would choose the doughnut chart type in which the pie slices are nested inside one another.

The pie chart that you need to create will have four slices, each corresponding to one of the four telescope models. Alicia's sketch also shows percentages next to the slices, so that people viewing her report will be able to see instantly what percentage each model contributed to the total sales.

As with the column chart, you will create the pie chart using the Chart Wizard. You need to select two columns from the sales table. The first column, range A2:A6, contains the names of the different telescope models. The second column, range E2:E6, contains the totals sales for each model. Remember that a pie chart uses only one data series.

To create the pie chart:

1. Select the nonadjacent range **A2:A6;E2:E6**.

2. Click the **Chart Wizard** button on the Standard toolbar.

3. Click the **Pie** chart in the Chart type list box, and verify that the first chart subtype is selected.

4. Click the **Next** button.

   Since you already chose the data series for the chart, you do not have to make any changes, so you can bypass the second step of the Chart Wizard.

5. Click the **Next** button.

   According to Alicia's sketch, you need to add a title to the chart.

6. Verify that the Titles tab is active, double-click the **Chart title** text box, and then type **Total Telescope Sales** (which replaces the title "Total" that displayed automatically based on the data series in range E2:E6).

   Next you will add data labels to the chart that display the percentage of sales for each model.

7. Click the **Data Labels** tab, and then click the **Percentage** check box. See Figure 4-16.

Figure 4-16 DISPLAYING PERCENTAGE LABELS IN A PIE CHART

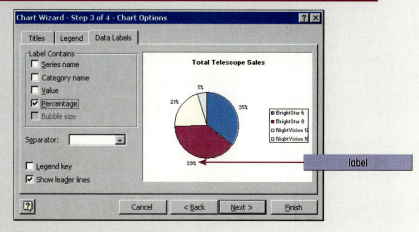

8. Click the **Next** button.

   Finally, you will place the pie chart in its own chart sheet and name the sheet "Pie Chart of Sales."

9. Click the **As new sheet** option button, and then type **Pie Chart of Sales** in the adjacent list box. The text you type in the text box appears as the name of the chart sheet on the tab.

10. Click the **Finish** button. Figure 4-17 shows the completed pie chart. Note that the chart sheet is inserted before the Sales sheet.

Figure 4-17   **PIE CHART OF TOTAL TELESCOPE SALES**

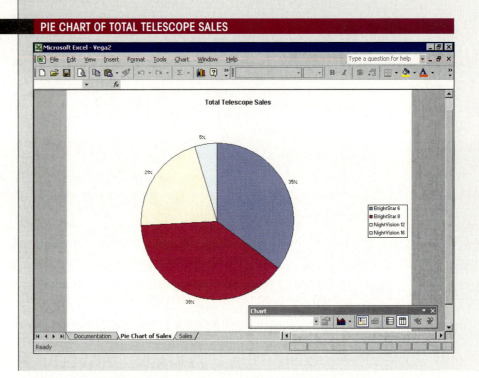

After reviewing the pie chart, Alicia has a few questions about the chart's appearance. She wonders why the slices are organized the way they are and whether the arrangement of the pie slices can be changed. The slices are arranged in a counter-clockwise direction following the order that they appeared in the table. The first entry is for the BrightStar 6 scope, the next is for the BrightStar 8, and so forth. Alicia asks whether it would be possible to move the BrightStar 6 slice away from the legend.

Rotating the Pie Chart

You cannot change the order in which the slices are arranged in the pie without changing their order in the data series, but you can rotate the chart. If you break the chart in 360 degree increments, starting from the top of the pie, the first slice starts at 0 degrees. You can specify a different starting point for the first slice.

Based on Alicia's suggestion, you decide to change the starting point to 180 degrees—the bottom of the chart.

To rotate the pie chart:

1. Double-click the pie in the pie chart. The Format Data Series dialog box opens.

2. Click the **Options** tab.

3. Double-click the value in the Angle of first slice box, and then enter **180** as the new value for the starting angle.

4. Press the **Tab** key. The Preview pane shows an updated view of the pie chart with the pie rotated 180 degrees. See Figure 4-18.

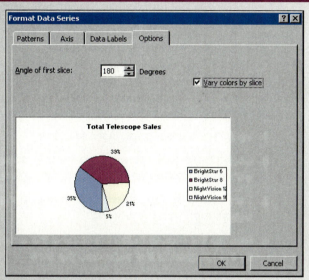

Figure 4-18   ROTATING THE PIE CHART 180 DEGREES

5. Click the **OK** button. The pie chart is updated to reflect the rotation.

Alicia tells you that the company is particularly interested in the sales performance of the BrightStar 6 telescope, since the company is considering replacing this scope with a 6-inch version of the NightVision. Alicia has seen pie charts in which a single slice is removed from the others to give it greater emphasis from the others. She wants the slice for the BrightStar 6 removed from the other slices to draw attention to this telescope.

Exploding a Slice of a Pie Chart

This method of emphasizing a particular pie slice over others is called separating or "exploding" the slice. An exploded slice is more distinctive because it is not connected to the other slices in the pie. Excel allows you to explode any or all of the slices in the pie. A pie chart with one or more pie slices separated from the whole is referred to as an **exploded pie chart**.

> **REFERENCE WINDOW**
>
> **Creating an Exploded Pie Chart**
>
> To explode one slice from a pie chart:
> - Click the pie chart.
> - Click the pie slice you want to explode.
> - Drag the selected pie slice away from the rest of the pie.
> - Release the mouse button.
>
> To explode all the pie slices in a pie chart:
> - Click the pie in the pie chart to select it.
> - Click and drag any pie slice to explode all the slices an equal distance apart.
> - Release the mouse button.

Next, you'll separate the BrightStar 6 telescope pie slice from the rest of the pie.

To explode the slice for the BrightStar 6 scope:

1. Verify that the pie chart is still selected.

2. Click the pie slice representing the total sales for the BrightStar 6. A ScreenTip with the corresponding worksheet cell information appears.

3. Click and drag the pie slice down and to the left. As you drag the pie slice, an outline marks your progress.

4. Release the mouse button, dropping the slice into its new position. See Figure 4-19 for the location of the exploded pie slice.

Figure 4-19   **EXPLODING A PIE SLICE**

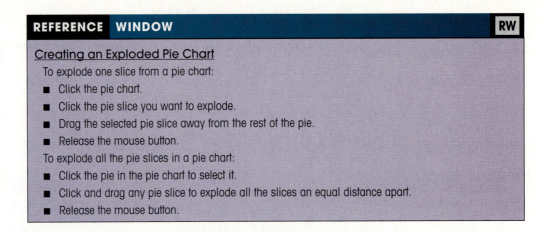

> You have created the two charts that Alicia wanted, so you can save your work, and then close the workbook and Excel.
>
> 5. Click the **Save** button on the Standard toolbar, and then click the **Close** button on the title bar to exit the program.

Rotating the pie and exploding a pie slice are both examples of formatting the appearance of an Excel chart after it has been created with the Chart Wizard. In the next session you will learn about the other formatting tools available to you.

Session 4.1 QUICK CHECK

1. What is the difference between a chart type and a chart sub-type?
2. Which chart would you most likely use to track the daily values of a stock?
3. What is a data series?
4. What is the difference between the plot area and the chart area?
5. What are gridlines?
6. Describe the two types of chart locations.
7. A chart that shows the contribution of each data value to the whole is called a(n) _____ chart.
8. A pie chart in which all slices are separated from one another is called a(n) _____ chart.

SESSION 4.2

In this session, you will modify the properties of the charts you created in the first session. You will change the chart's data source, location, options, and type. You will format individual chart elements and apply color fills. You will also work with 3-D charts and create drawing objects that you can place on your chart sheets or worksheets. Finally, you print a chart sheet.

Modifying a Chart

In the last session you used the Chart Wizard to create two charts. Although the Chart Wizard presents you with a variety of choices concerning your chart's appearance, the wizard does not provide every possibility. To make further modifications to your charts, you can use the formatting tools and commands available on the Chart toolbar and the Chart menu.

Editing the Data Source

After you create a chart, you can change the data that is used in the chart. You might need to change the data if the wrong information has been used or if you decide to display a different data series.

> **REFERENCE WINDOW**
>
> **Editing a Chart's Data Source**
> - Click Chart on the menu bar, and then click Source Data.
> - Click the Series tab.
> - To remove a data series, select the data series in the Series list box, and click the Remove button.
> - To add a data series, click the Add button, and then select the cell references for the new data series.
> - To revise a data series, select the data series in the Series list box, click the reference box for the data series, and then select a new cell reference.
> - Click the OK button.

Alicia can see from the charts that 16-inch telescopes comprise a small portion of Vega's sales due to their size and expense. For this reason, she wants you to remove the NightVision 16 from the two charts you created. You will begin by removing the NightVision 16 data series from the column chart.

To remove the NightVision 16 data series:

1. If you took a break after the previous session, make sure Excel is running and the Vega2 workbook is open. Click the **Sales** tab.

2. Click the embedded column chart to select it.

3. Click **Chart** on the menu bar, and then click **Source Data**. The Source Data dialog box opens.

4. Click the **Series** tab.

5. Click **NightVision 16** in the Series list box.

6. Click the **Remove** button.

7. Click the **OK** button. The NightVision 16 sales data is no longer represented in the column chart. See Figure 4-20.

Figure 4-20   REMOVING THE NIGHTVISION 16 FROM THE COLUMN CHART

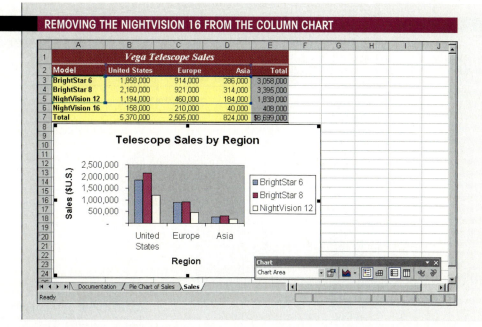

Removing the NightVision 16 pie slice from the pie chart presents a slightly different problem. Unlike the column chart (which has multiple data series), the pie chart has only one data series—there is not a separate data series for each model. To remove the NightVision 16 from the pie chart, you have to change the cell reference of the data series to exclude the NightVision 16 row.

To remove the NightVision 16 from the pie chart:

1. Click the **Pie Chart of Sales** tab.

2. Click **Chart** on the menu bar, and then click **Source Data**.

   There is only one data series, named "Total," in this chart. The cell reference for the values for this data series is found in the range E3:E6 on the Sales worksheet. The corresponding labels for the data series are found in the range A3:A6 on the same worksheet. To exclude the NightVision 16 from the chart, you have to change the references to range E3:E5 and range A3:A5, respectively.

3. Click the **Collapse Dialog Box** button for the Values box. Clicking the Collapse Dialog Box button collapses the dialog box so you can drag the pointer over a range of cells in the Sales worksheet that you need to select.

4. Select the range **E3:E5** and then click the **Expand Dialog Box** button.

5. Click for the Category Labels box.

6. Select the range **A3:A5** and then click.

7. Click the **OK** button. Figure 4-21 shows the revised pie chart.

Figure 4-21 — REMOVING THE NIGHTVISION 16 FROM THE PIE CHART

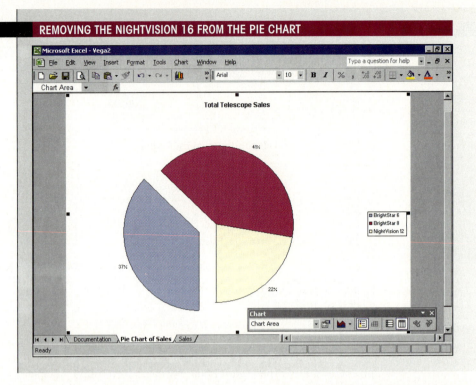

Note that, when you removed the NightVision 16 from the data series, the percentages in the pie chart changed as well to reflect a total sales figure based on only three models rather than on four.

Changing the Chart Location

Alicia has decided that she prefers the chart sheet to the embedded chart. She wants you to move the embedded column chart on the Sales worksheet to a chart sheet. Rather than re-creating the chart using the Chart Wizard, you will use the Location command on the Chart menu.

You will move the embedded chart to a chart sheet, which you will name "Column Chart of Sales."

To change the location of the column chart:

1. Click the **Sales** tab.
2. Verify that the embedded column chart is selected in the worksheet.
3. Click **Chart** on the menu bar, and then click **Location**.
4. Click the **As new sheet** option button, and then type **Column Chart of Sales** as the name of the chart sheet.
5. Click the **OK** button. The column chart moves into its own chart sheet.

Changing Chart Options

You may have noticed that the dialog boxes to change the chart's data source and location looked identical to the dialog boxes from steps 2 and 4 of the Chart Wizard. Dialog boxes from the remaining two Chart Wizard steps are also available through commands on the Chart menu. Recall that the third step of the Chart Wizard allowed you to format the chart's appearance by adding or removing chart titles, gridlines, legends, and labels.

Alicia wants to revisit some of the chart options selected earlier. After seeing that the percent labels in the pie chart provided useful information, she wants you to add labels to the column chart displaying the actual sales values on top of each column.

To revise the chart options for the column chart:

1. Click **Chart** on the menu bar, and then click **Chart Options**. The Chart Options dialog box opens. Note that the dialog box is identical to Step 3 of the Chart Wizard.

2. Click the **Data Labels** tab, if necessary.

3. Click the **Value** check box, and then click the **OK** button. The sales figures for each model now appear above the corresponding column. See Figure 4-22.

Figure 4-22   ADDING LABELS TO THE COLUMNS

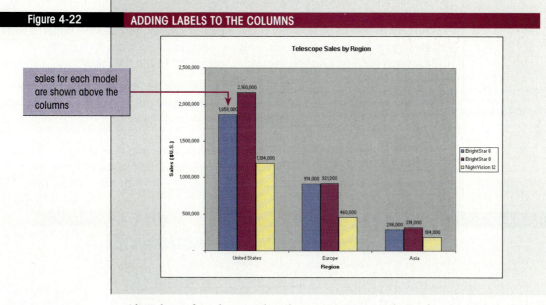

sales for each model are shown above the columns

Alicia has a few changes that she wants you to make to the chart labels. You cannot make these changes by modifying the chart options. Instead you have to format the individual elements within the chart.

Formatting Chart Elements

So far, all of the formatting that you have done has applied to the chart as a whole. You can also select and format individual chart elements, such as the chart title, legend, and axes. To format an individual chart element, you can click the element to select it and then format its appearance using the same tools on the Formatting toolbar you used to format worksheet cells; you can double-click the chart element to open a dialog box containing formatting shortcut menu to open the dialog box. Using the Formatting toolbar is usually quicker, but opening a format dialog box will provide you with more options and more control over the element's appearance.

Formatting Chart Text

Alicia wants you to change the alignment of the chart labels. She feels that the labels would look better if you changed their alignment from horizontal to vertical. Alicia also points out that the chart's background is gray. She is concerned that the black label text will be difficult to read for some people. She suggests that yellow text might show up better against the gray background.

To format the chart labels:

1. Double-click the chart label **1,858,000**, located above the first column in the chart. The Format Data Labels dialog box opens.

   The 1,858,000 chart label is part of the set of labels for the BrightStar 6 model. Any changes you make in this dialog box will apply to all of the labels for the BrightStar 6 telescope sales data (and not to the other labels on the chart). The Format Data Labels dialog box has four tabs. You use the Font and Number tabs to change font-related options to text and values and to apply number formats to values as you did in the previous tutorial. You use the Patterns tab to change the fill color, patterns, and borders around labels. You use the Alignment tab to change the alignment of the text in the label.

2. Click the **Font** tab (if necessary), click the **Color** list box, and then click the **Yellow** square located in the fourth row and third column of the color palette.

3. Click the **Alignment** tab.

4. Click the **red diamond** in the Orientation box, and then drag the diamond counterclockwise until the value in the Degrees box displays **90**. The text changes to a vertical orientation with an angle of 90 degrees. See Figure 4-23.

Figure 4-23   **CHANGING THE ORIENTATION OF THE COLUMN LABELS**

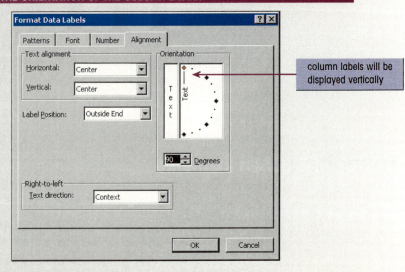

column labels will be displayed vertically

5. Click the **OK** button. The labels for the BrightStar 6 sales data have been rotated 90 degrees and now appear in a yellow font.

6. Double-click the **2,160,000** label above the second column in the chart, and then change the label to a yellow font, rotated 90 degrees.

7. Double-click the **1,194,000** label above the third column, and then format the label as you did the previous two labels. Figure 4-24 shows the revised labels.

Figure 4-24 **FORMATTED COLUMN LABELS**

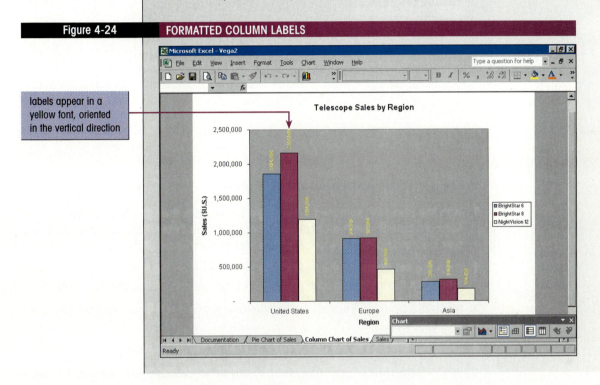

labels appear in a yellow font, oriented in the vertical direction

Inserting New Chart Text

Excel classifies chart text in three categories: label text, attached text, and unattached text. **Label text** includes the category names, the tick mark labels, and the legend text. Label text often is linked to cells in the worksheet. **Attached text** includes the chart title and the axes titles. Although the text appears in a predefined position, you can edit and move it. Unlike label text, attached text is not linked to any cells in the worksheet. Finally, **unattached text** is any additional text that you want to include in the chart. Unattached text can be positioned anywhere within the chart area and formatted with the same tools you use to format label and attached text.

To enter unattached text, you type the text in the Formula bar. Excel automatically creates a text box for the text entry and places the text box on the chart. You can then resize the text box and move it to another location in the chart area. You can format the text using the Format Text Box dialog box.

REFERENCE WINDOW

Inserting Unattached Text into a Chart
- Select the chart.
- In the Formula bar, type the text that you want to include in the chart.
- To resize the new unattached text box, click and drag one of the text box's selection handles.
- To move the unattached text box, click the border of the text box, and drag the text box to a new location in the chart area.
- To format the unattached text, select the text box and click the appropriate formatting buttons on the Formatting toolbar; or double-click the border of the text box to open the Format Text Box dialog box, and use the options provided on the dialog box tabs, and then click the OK button.

Alicia wants you to add the text "Vega Sales from the Last Fiscal Year" to the upper-right corner of the plot area. She wants the text in a yellow Arial font.

To create an unattached text entry:

1. With the chart still selected, type **Vega Sales from the Last Fiscal Year** in the Formula bar above the chart, and then press the **Enter** key. Excel places a text box containing the new unattached text in the middle of the plot area.

2. Click the **list arrow** for the **Font Color** button on the Formatting toolbar, and then click the **Yellow** square (fourth row, third column) in the color palette.

3. Move the pointer over the edge of the unattached text box until the pointer changes to.

4. Drag the text box to the upper-right corner of the chart area.

5. Release the mouse button and click outside of the text box to deselect it. See Figure 4-25.

Figure 4-25 FORMATTED COLUMN LABELS

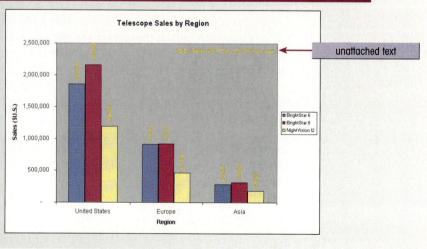

You can double-click an unattached text box at any time to open the Format Text Box dialog box in which you can change the font format, alignment, and color. You can also create a border around the text. Try this now by creating a yellow border.

To create a border for the text box:

1. Double-click the border of the selected text box.

   TROUBLE? If you double-clicked the text in the text box, the Format Text Box dialog box did not open. Double-click the border of the text box.

2. Click the **Colors and Lines** tab.

3. Click the **Color** list box in the Line section, and then click the **Yellow** square (fourth row, third column) in the color palette.

4. Click the **OK** button and then click outside the chart to deselect it. Figure 4-26 shows the revised text box with the yellow border.

Figure 4-26   **FORMATTED COLUMN LABELS**

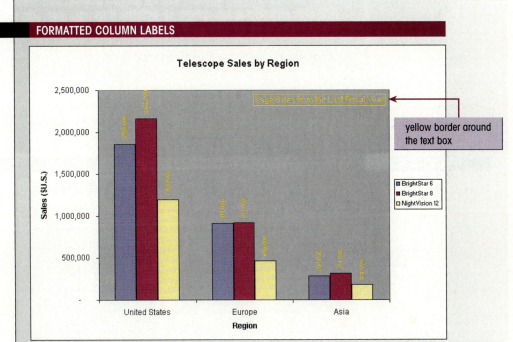

Now that you have formatted the chart labels and have added unattached text, you can turn to some of the other features of Excel charts that need modifying.

Working with Colors and Fills

You solved the problems with the chart labels, but Alicia feels that the column chart lacks visual appeal. Alicia has seen objects filled with a variety of colors that gradually blend from one color to another. She wonders if you can do the same thing for the columns in the column chart.

When you want to fill a column (or area) in a chart with a pattern or color, you are actually modifying the appearance of the data marker in the chart. You will concentrate only on the fill color used in the data marker. Other data markers have other patterns that you can modify. For example, in a scatter chart, the data markers are points that appear in the plot. You can specify the color of those data points, their size, whether a line will connect the data points, and if so the color, thickness, and style of that line.

To format the fill color of the chart columns:

1. Double-click the first column in the chart. The Format Data Series dialog box opens with the tabs that you can use to control one or more aspects of the selected data marker.

2. Click the **Patterns** tab. You can use the options provided on this tab to control the border style that appears around the column as well as the appearance of the column's interior. Currently, the column is formatted with a black border and filled with a pale blue color.

3. Click the **Fill Effects** button. The Fill Effects dialog box opens. The tabs in this dialog box provide a full range of options that you can use to create sophisticated and lush colors and patterns.

4. If necessary, click the **Gradient** tab.

You use the options on the Gradient tab to create fill effects that blend together different and varying amounts of color. Figure 4-27 displays the Gradient tab.

Figure 4-27 FILL EFFECTS

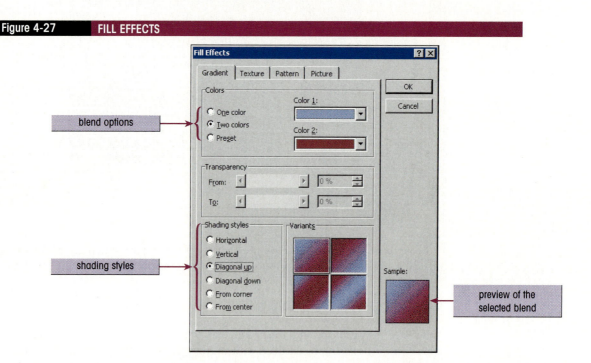

Note that you have three color options from which to choose:

- **One color**—Creates a blend that uses different shades of one color. You select the range of shades using a scroll bar.
- **Two colors**—Creates a blend from one color into another.
- **Preset**—Provides a list of predefined blend styles, including Early Sunset, Nightfall, Ocean, Rainbow, and Chrome.

You can also specify the direction of the blending effect, choosing from horizontal, vertical, diagonal up, diagonal down, from corner, and from center. For the selected column in the current chart, you will create a blend fill effect using a single color starting from a dark shade of the pale blue color. You will use a horizontal shading style to give the color dimension.

To create the fill effect:

1. Click the **One color** option button.
2. Drag the scroll box to the Dark end of the shading scale. Note that as you change the shading scale, the images in the Variants pane reflect the degree of shading.
3. Verify that the **Horizontal** option button in the Shading styles section is selected.
4. Click the **OK** button twice. Excel displays the first column series with a dark blue color at the bottom of the column, blending into the light blue color at the top.

   Create similar blends for the other columns.
5. Double-click the second column in the chart.
6. Click the **Fill Effects** button.
7. Click the **One color** option button, drag the shading scroll bar to the Dark end of the scale, and then click the **OK** button twice.
8. Double-click the third column, and then create the same blend fill effect you created for the first two data series, going from the dark end of the yellow scale to the light end.
9. Click outside the chart area. Figure 4-28 shows the revised column chart with blends for each of the three data series.

Figure 4-28 COLUMNS WITH BLENDED COLORS

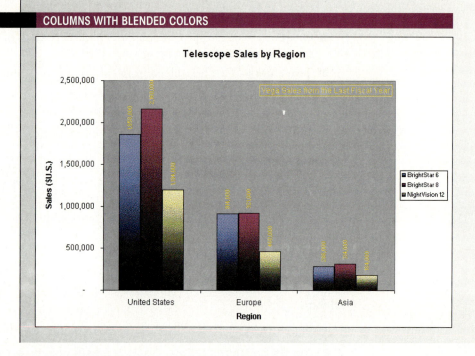

Using a Graphic Image as a Background

Alicia likes the change you made to the columns and now wants to change the background. Rather than just a solid gray background, she wants to use a graphic image in the background. She has a graphic file that shows an image from the Hubble telescope that she thinks would work well with the theme of telescope sales.

To insert this image into the chart, you need to change the fill options for the plot area of the chart.

To change the plot area fill:

1. Double-click any blank space inside the plot area (do not click one of the chart columns).
2. Click the **Fill Effects** button on the Patterns tab.
3. Click the **Picture** tab, and then click the **Select Picture** button.
4. Locate the Tutorial.04/Tutorial folder on your Data Disk, and then select the **Space** file.
5. Click the **Insert** button.
6. Click the **OK** button twice, and then click outside the chart area. Figure 4-29 shows the revised column chart with the new background image.

Figure 4-29 CHART WITH SPACE BACKGROUND IMAGE

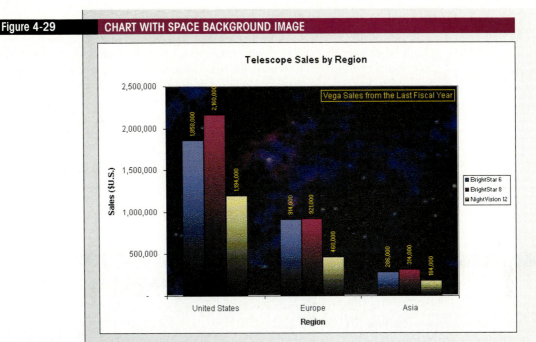

Graphic images can be applied to other elements in the chart. For example, you can replace the columns in the column chart with graphic images. To do so, you select the column and use the same Fill Effects dialog box that you used to create the background image for the chart. However, before you close the Fill Effects dialog box, you can also choose one of the stacking or stretching options available for the image in place of the column. Figure 4-30 shows the effect of the two Format options provided in the Fill Effects dialog box.

Figure 4-30 REPLACING COLUMNS WITH GRAPHICS

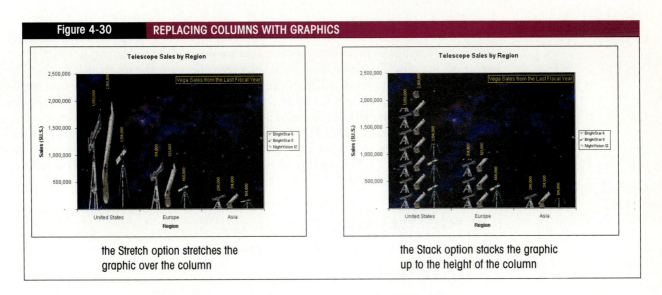

the Stretch option stretches the graphic over the column

the Stack option stacks the graphic up to the height of the column

Alicia is pleased with the appearance of the columns and does not require any additional changes to them.

Changing the Axis Scale

The final change that Alicia wants you to make to the column chart concerns the chart's scale. Excel chooses a default scale for the y-axis, usually designed to make the scale easy to read and to cover a range of reasonable values. Alicia wants you to examine the scale that Excel chose for this chart to see if a change is warranted.

To view the y-axis scale:

1. Double-click any of the values on the y-axis. The Format Axis dialog box opens. You can use this dialog box to format the scale's appearance and to change the range and increments used in the scale.

2. Click the **Scale** tab. See Figure 4-31.

Figure 4-31   SCALE TAB

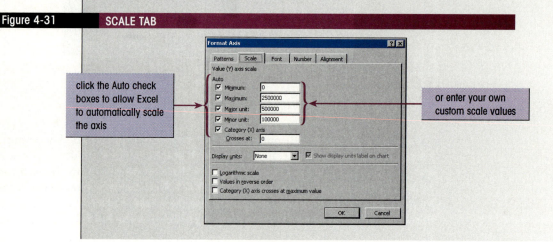

There are four values that comprise the scale: the minimum, maximum, major unit, and minor unit. The minimum and maximum values are the smallest and largest tick marks that appear on the axis. The major unit is the increment between the scale's tick marks. The chart also has a second set of tick marks called **minor tick marks** that may or may not be displayed. The difference between major and minor tick marks is that major tick marks are displayed alongside an axis value, whereas minor tick marks are not.

In the current chart, the scale that Excel displayed ranges from 0 to 2,500,000 in increments of 500,000. The minor tick mark increment is 100,000, but these tick marks are not displayed on the axes. Alicia would like to reduce the increment value to 250,000 in order to show more detail on the chart.

To revise the y-axis scale:

1. Double-click the current entry in the Major unit box.

2. Type **250000**.

3. Click the **OK** button. Figure 4-32 shows the revised y-axis scale.

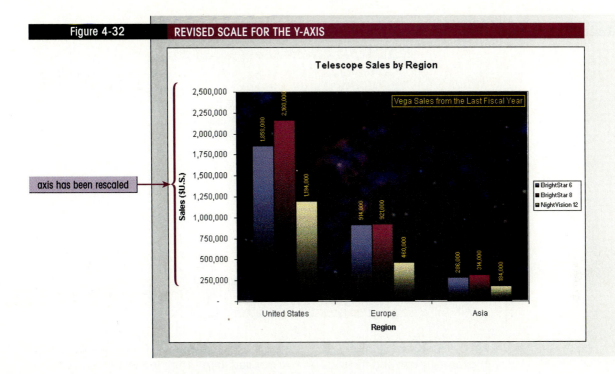

Figure 4-32 REVISED SCALE FOR THE Y-AXIS

axis has been rescaled

Alicia is happy with the latest version of the column chart. She now wants you to go back to the pie chart and make some modifications there.

Working with Three-Dimensional Charts

Many of the Excel charts can be displayed either as two-dimensional "flat" charts or as charts that appear three-dimensional. Alicia wants you to change the pie chart to a three-dimensional pie chart. To do this, you have to change the chart type.

To change the pie chart to 3-D:

1. Click the **Pie Chart of Sales** tab.

2. Click **Chart** on the menu bar, and then click **Chart Type**.

3. Click the second chart sub-type in the top row. See Figure 4-33.

| Figure 4-33 | CHANGING TO A 3-D PIE CHART |

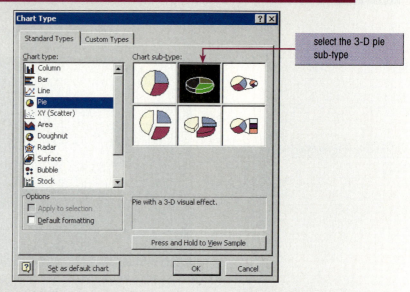

4. Click the **OK** button. Excel displays the pie chart in three dimensions. Note that Excel has retained the rotation you applied to the chart in the last session, and the BrightStar 6 slice is still exploded. See Figure 4-34.

| Figure 4-34 | 3-D PIE CHART |

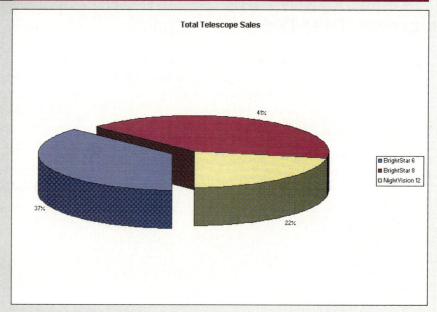

In a 3-D chart, you have several options to modify the 3-D effect. One of these is **elevation**, the illusion that you're looking at the 3-D chart from a particular height either above or below the chart. Another of these is **perspective**, which is the illusion that parts of the 3-D chart that are "farther" away from you decrease in size. Finally, you can rotate a 3-D chart to bring different parts of the chart to the forefront. In a pie chart, you can change the elevation and rotation, but not the perspective.

Alicia likes the 3-D view of the pie chart but feels that the angle of the pie is too low, causing the pie to appear flat despite its three dimensions. She wants the angle of the pie to be a little higher.

To increase the elevation above the pie chart:

1. Click **Chart** on the menu bar, and then click **3-D View**.

2. Click the **Elevation Up** button twice to increase the elevation to 25 degrees. See Figure 4-35.

Figure 4-35   **3-D VIEW DIALOG BOX**

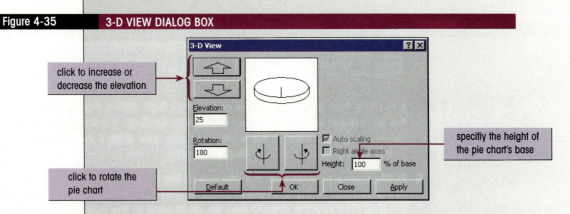

Note that there are also buttons that you can use to rotate the pie chart. Clicking one of the rotation buttons is similar to the rotation setting that you applied to the pie chart at the end of the first session.

3. Click the **OK** button. Excel redraws the pie chart, giving the illusion that the observer is at a higher elevation above the chart.

Alicia is happy with the appearance of the column chart and does not want you to apply any 3-D effects to that chart.

Using the Drawing Toolbar

One of the big stories from the past fiscal year was the successful introduction of the NightVision scopes, and Alicia wants to highlight the fact that the company had in excess of $1,800,000 in sales of the NightVision 12. She has seen charts that contain shapes, like star bursts and block arrows, that give added emphasis to details and facts that the chart author wants to include. Alicia wants to do something similar with the pie chart.

To create a graphical shape, Excel provides the Drawing toolbar. The Drawing toolbar is a common feature of all Office XP products. You can use the Drawing toolbar to add text boxes, lines, block arrows and other objects to charts and worksheets. A whole tutorial could be spent examining all of the features of the Drawing toolbar, but this tutorial just examines how to create and format a drawing object.

Displaying the Drawing Toolbar

Depending on your Excel configuration, the Drawing toolbar may or may not be displayed in the Excel window when you start Excel. (The default is to not show the toolbar.) As with all toolbars, you can choose to display or hide the Drawing toolbar.

To display the Drawing toolbar:

1. Click **View** on the menu bar, point to **Toolbars**, and then click **Drawing**. The Drawing toolbar appears, as shown in Figure 4-36.

Figure 4-36   DRAWING TOOLBAR

A toolbar that appears in a location other than along the very top or bottom of the worksheet window is called a **floating toolbar**. If a floating toolbar is obstructing your view of the worksheet, you can drag it to the bottom (or top) of the worksheet window to **anchor** it there.

2. Position your pointer over the title bar of the Drawing toolbar, drag the toolbar to the bottom of the worksheet window, and then release the mouse button. The Drawing toolbar should now be anchored to the bottom of the window.

Now you will use the Drawing toolbar to add a drawing object to the pie chart.

Working with AutoShapes

The Drawing toolbar contains a list of predefined shapes called **AutoShapes**. These AutoShapes can be simple squares or circles or more complicated objects such as flow chart objects and block arrows. Once you insert an AutoShape into a chart or worksheet, you can resize and move it, like any other object. You can modify the fill color of an AutoShape, change the border style, and even insert text.

TUTORIAL 4 WORKING WITH CHARTS AND GRAPHS   EX 4.37   EXCEL

> **REFERENCE WINDOW**   RW
>
> <u>Inserting an AutoShape</u>
> - Click the AutoShapes list arrow on the Drawing toolbar.
> - Point to the AutoShape category that you want to use, and then click the AutoShape that you want to create.
> - Position the crosshair pointer over the location for the AutoShape in the chart or worksheet, and then drag the pointer over the area where you want the shape to appear. To draw an AutoShape in the same proportion as the shape on the palette, press and hold the Shift key as you drag the pointer to draw the shape.
> - Release the mouse button.
> - To resize an AutoShape, click the shape to select it, and then drag one of the nine selection handles.
> - To rotate an AutoShape, click the green rotation handle that is connected to the shape, and drag the handle to rotate the shape.
> - To change the shape of the AutoShape, click the yellow diamond tool, and drag the tool to change the shape.

Alicia wants to add a multi-pointed star to the pie chart to highlight the success of the NightVision 12 telescope.

To add a multi-pointed star to the pie chart:

1. Click the **AutoShapes** list arrow on the Drawing toolbar.

2. Point to **Stars and Banners**, and then click the **16-Point Star** AutoShape located in the second row and second column of the AutoShapes palette.

   As you move the pointer over the worksheet, the pointer shape will change to ✢.

3. Move the pointer to the upper-right corner of the chart area, about one inch to the right of the chart title.

   To draw an AutoShape in the same proportion as the shape on the palette, you must press and hold the Shift key as you drag the pointer to draw the shape.

4. Press the **Shift** key as you drag the pointer down and to the right about one and one-half inches.

   Note that pressing the Shift key allows you to create a perfect 16-point star. If you do not press the Shift key as you drag the pointer, your star might be slightly lopsided.

5. Release the mouse button. A 16-point star appears in the upper-right corner of the chart area. See Figure 4-37.

   TROUBLE? If the AutoShape on your screen does not match the size and shape of the AutoShape shown in the figure, you can resize the object again by pressing and holding the Shift key as you drag a selection handle. Or click the Undo button on the Standard toolbar to delete the object, and then repeat Steps 1 through 5 to redraw the AutoShape. Make sure that you press and hold down the Shift key to draw the object proportionally.

Figure 4-37 ADDING AN AUTOSHAPE TO THE PIE CHART

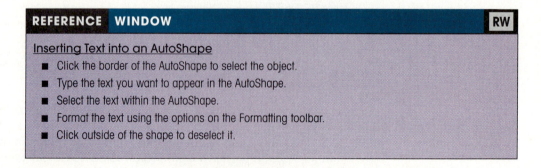

You probably noticed that the selection handles of the AutoShape appear as open circles and that there is also a diamond tool ◆. You can use the ◆ to change the shape of the AutoShape. For example, you can change the size of the jagged points of the star by dragging the diamond tool either in towards the center of the star (to increase the size of the points) or away from the star's center (to decrease the size of the points). You may have also noticed a green selection handle that is attached to the AutoShape through a vertical line. This is a rotation handle. By clicking and dragging this handle, you can rotate the AutoShape.

Formatting an AutoShape

In addition to modifying the shape, size, or rotation of an AutoShape, you can add text to it. To add text to an AutoShape, you first select it and then start typing the desired text. The text will be automatically placed within the boundaries of the shape.

REFERENCE WINDOW

Inserting Text into an AutoShape
- Click the border of the AutoShape to select the object.
- Type the text you want to appear in the AutoShape.
- Select the text within the AutoShape.
- Format the text using the options on the Formatting toolbar.
- Click outside of the shape to deselect it.

Alicia wants to add text to the AutoShape star that highlights the success of the NightVision 12.

To add text to the 16-point star:

1. Verify that the 16-point star AutoShape is still selected.
2. Type **NightVision 12 Sales Exceed $1,800,000!** (do *not* press the Enter key).
3. Click the **Center** button on the Formatting toolbar.
4. Click outside of the AutoShape to deselect it.

   TROUBLE? If the text does not wrap logically within the boundaries of the AutoShape, resize the star to better accommodate the text.

The star with the text adds value to the overall appearance of the chart. However, the star could use some background color to make it more visually interesting. You decide to format the AutoShape by adding a yellow background.

To change the background color of the AutoShape:

1. Click the border of the 16-point star AutoShape to select it.
2. Click the **list arrow** for the **Fill Color** button on the Drawing toolbar, and then click the **Yellow** square (fourth row, third column) in the color palette.

   TROUBLE? If the background color does not change to yellow, you may have selected the text in the star rather than the star itself. Click the Undo button, and then repeat Steps 1 and 2.

The AutoShape definitely looks better with the yellow background. You decide to try one more thing: you want to see if adding a shadow effect to the start will be too much or will add depth to the object. To add a shadow effect to an object, you can choose one of the available shadow effects provided on the Drawing toolbar.

To add a drop shadow:

1. Verify that the 16-point star is still selected.
2. Click the **Shadow Style** button on the Drawing toolbar to display the gallery of shadow options. See Figure 4-38.

Figure 4-38   SHADOW STYLE OPTIONS

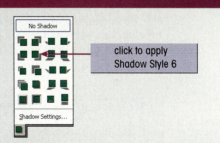

3. Click **Shadow Style 6** (second row, second column) in the shadow gallery.

4. Click outside the star to deselect it. Figure 4-39 shows the revised pie chart with the formatted AutoShape.

Figure 4-39 | **THE PIE CHART WITH THE STAR AUTOSHAPE**

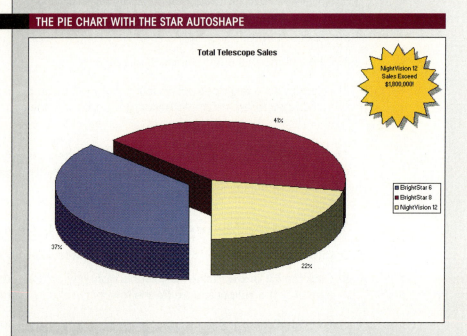

There are no other changes to be made, so you will hide the Drawing toolbar, which will increase the workspace on your screen. There are other shapes and objects on the Drawing toolbar that you can use to augment your charts and worksheets. For now though, Alicia is satisfied with the present appearance of the chart.

5. Click the **Drawing** button on the Formatting toolbar. The Drawing toolbar closes.

Printing Your Charts

Now that you have completed your work on the two charts for Alicia, you will make hard copies of them. Printing a chart sheet is similar to printing a worksheet. As when printing a worksheet, you should preview the printout before sending the worksheet to the printer. From the Print Preview window, you can add headers and footers and control the page layout, just as you do for printing the contents of your worksheets. You also have the added option of resizing the chart to fit within the confines of a single printed page.

To print more than one chart sheet at a time, you select both chart sheets, and then open the Print Preview window. Each chart will print on its own page.

To set up the two charts for printing:

1. Make sure the Pie Chart of Sales worksheet is the current sheet.

2. Press and hold the **Shift** key, and then click the **Column Chart of Sales** tab. Both chart sheets are selected.

3. Click the **Print Preview** button on the Standard toolbar. The Print Preview window opens, showing the pie chart on the first of two pages.

4. Click the **Setup** button on the Print Preview toolbar to open the Page Setup dialog box. The Page Setup options are similar to the options for printing a worksheet, except that a new dialog box tab, Chart, has been added.

5. Click the **Chart** tab. Figure 4-40 shows the Chart tab.

Figure 4-40 CHART TAB

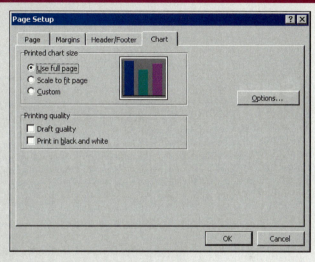

Excel provides three choices for defining the size of a chart printout. These are:

- **Use full page** in which the chart is resized to fit the full page, extending out to the borders of all four margins. The proportions of the chart may change since it is extended in all directions to fit the page. This is the default option.
- **Scale to fit page** in which the chart is resized until one of the edges reaches a margin border. The proportions of the chart remained unchanged, but it might not fit the entire page.
- **Custom** in which the dimensions of the printed chart are specified on the chart sheet outside of the Print Preview window.

You will use the Scale to fit page option because you do not want to have the charts resized disproportionately.

To set the size of the charts:

1. Click the **Scale to fit page** option button, and then click the **OK** button.
2. Click the **Next** button to preview the column chart printout.
3. Click the **Setup** button.
4. On the Chart tab, click the **Scale to fit page** option button, and then click the **OK** button.

5. Click the **Print** button to open the Print dialog box, and then send both chart sheets to the printer.

Now that you have finished your work, you can close the Vega2 workbook and exit Excel.

6. Click the **Save** button on the Standard toolbar, and then click the **Close** button on the title bar.

You show your final product to Alicia. She is pleased with the results. Alicia will get back to you with any other tasks she might need you to do before the sales meeting next week.

Session 4.2 QUICK CHECK

1. Describe how you would remove a data series from a column chart.
2. How would you change the location (either embedded or as a chart sheet) for a chart?
3. What is the difference between label text, attached text, and unattached text?
4. What is the difference between major tick marks and minor tick marks?
5. How would you change a column chart into a 3-D column chart?
6. What is an AutoShape?
7. Describe the three options for sizing a chart on the printed page.

REVIEW ASSIGNMENTS

Alicia has another workbook that shows the monthly United States sales for the three major telescope models. She wants you to create a chart for this worksheet, but this time a line chart. She wants the line chart to show the change in sales over the course of the last fiscal year. She prefers having a separate sheet for the chart with the legend placed at the bottom of the page.

To complete this task:

1. Start Excel and open the **VegaUSA1** workbook located in the Tutorial.04/Review folder on your Data Disk.
2. Save the workbook as **VegaUSA2** to the same folder.
3. Enter your name and the current date in the Documentation sheet, and then switch to the Monthly Sales worksheet.
4. Select the range A2:D14, and then start the Chart Wizard.
5. Use the Chart Wizard to create a line chart, using the first chart sub-type. Specify "United States Telescope Sales" as the chart title, "Month" as the x-axis title, and "Sales ($U.S.)" as the y-axis title. Position the legend at the bottom of the chart area. Place the chart on a chart sheet named "Monthly Sales Chart".
6. Format the x-axis labels, changing the alignment to 90 degrees.

Explore

7. Double-click the line for the BrightStar 6 model, and within the Patterns dialog box, change the color of the line to white.

8. Change the fill effect for the plot area to the preset fill style Nightfall.

Explore 9. Double-click the legend box, and change the fill color to dark blue and the color of the legend text to white.

Explore 10. Use the Drawing toolbar to create an 8-point star located in the upper-left corner of the chart area.

11. Insert the text "NightVision 12 sales remained high in Autumn!" into the 8-point star you just created.

12. Change the fill color of the 8-point star to tan, and apply Shadow Style 1 to the shape.

13. In the Print Preview window, scale the chart to fit the page.

14. Add a footer to the chart displaying your name and the date in the lower-right corner of the page. Save your changes, and then print the chart.

15. Close the workbook and exit Excel.

CASE PROBLEMS

Case 1. Cast Iron Concepts Andrea Puest, the regional sales manager of Cast Iron Concepts (CIC), a distributor of cast iron stoves, is required to present a report of the company's sales in her sales region, which includes the states of New Hampshire, Vermont, and Maine. She sells four major models: Star Windsor, Box Windsor, West Windsor, and Circle Windsor. The Circle Windsor is CIC's latest entry in the cast iron stove market.

Andrea will make a presentation of her sales figures next month and has asked for your help in creating a chart showing the sales results. She wants to create a 3-D column chart with each column representing the sales for a particular model and region.

To complete this task:

1. Open the **CIC1** workbook located in the Tutorial.04/Cases folder of your Data Disk, and then save the file as **CIC2** to the same folder.

2. Enter your name and the current date in the Documentation sheet. Switch to the Sales worksheet.

3. Select the range A2:D6, and then start the Chart Wizard.

4. Use the Chart Wizard to create an embedded 3-D Column chart that compares values across categories and across series. The data series in the chart should be organized by columns, not rows. Specify "Windsor Stove Sales" as the chart title. Do not specify titles for the axes. Do not include a legend.

5. Move the embedded chart so that the upper-left corner of the chart is located in cell A8, and then resize the chart so that it covers the range A8:E29.

6. Change the font of the chart title to a 14-point, bold, dark blue Arial.

7. Change the color of the chart area to tan.

Explore 8. Change the 3-D view of the chart so that its elevation equals 10 degrees, its rotation equals 120 degrees, and its perspective equals 15.

9. Change the font of the y-axis labels (the names of the state) to an 8-point regular Arial font.

10. Change the font of the x-axis labels (the model names) to an 8-point regular Arial font, displayed at a -90 degree angle.

Explore 11. Select the walls of the 3-D plot, and change the wall color to white.

12. Center the contents of the worksheet horizontally on the page, and then add a header that displays your name and the date in the upper-right corner of the worksheet.

13. Save your changes, and then print the worksheet.

14. Close the workbook, and then close Excel.

Case 2. Dantalia Baby Powder Kemp Wilson is a quality control engineer for Dantalia Baby Powder. Part of the company's manufacturing process involves a machine called a "filler," which pours a specified amount of powder into bottles. Sometimes the filling heads on the filler become partially clogged, causing the bottles to be under filled. If that happens, the bottles must be rejected. On each assembly line, there are a certain number of bottles rejected during each shift.

Kemp's job is to monitor the number of defective bottles and locate the fillers that may have clogged filler heads. One of the tools he uses to do this is a Pareto chart. A **Pareto chart** is a column chart in which each column represents the total number of defects assigned to different parts of the production process. In this case, the columns would represent the 24 different fillers in the assembly line. The columns are sorted so that the part that caused the most defects is displayed first; the second-most is displayed second, and so forth. Superimposed on the columns is a line that displays the cumulative percentage of defects for all of the parts. Thus by viewing the cumulative percentages, you can determine, for example, what percentages of the total defects are due to the three worst parts. In this way, Kemp can isolate the problem filler heads and report how much they contribute to the total defects.

Kemp has a worksheet listing the number of defects per filler head from a recent shift. The data is already sorted going from the filler head with the most defects to the one with the fewest. The cumulative percent values have also been already calculated. Kemp wants you to create a Pareto chart based on this data.

To complete this task:

1. Open the **Powder1** workbook located in the Tutorial.04/Cases folder of your Data Disk, and then save the file as **Powder2** to the same folder.

2. Enter your name and the current date in the Documentation sheet. Switch to the Quality Control worksheet.

3. Select the range A1:C25, and then start the Chart Wizard.

Explore 4. Use the Chart Wizard to create a custom chart, selecting the Line – Column on 2 Axes in the Custom Types list box. Specify "Filler Head Under Fills" as the chart title. Specify "Filler Head" as the x-axis title, "Count of Under Fills" as the y-axis title, and "Cumulative Percentage" as the second y-axis title. Do not include a legend. Place the chart on a chart sheet named "Pareto Chart".

5. Change the alignment of the x-axis labels to an angle of 90 degrees.

6. Change the alignment of the second y-axis title to –90 degrees.

Explore 7. Change the scale of the second y-axis so that the values range from 0 to 1.0.

Explore 8. Select the data series that displays the number of defects for each filler head, and add data labels that display the number of defects above each column. Do *not* display labels above the lines that represent the cumulative percentages. (*Hint*: Use the Data Labels tab in the Format Data Series dialog box.)

Explore 9. From the Format Data Series dialog box for the chart's columns, use the Options tab to reduce the gap separating the columns to 0 pixels.

10. Change the fill color of the chart columns and the plot area to white.

11. Examine the Pareto chart, and determine approximately what percentage of the total number of defects can be attributed to the three worst filler heads.

12. Add a header that displays your name and the date in the upper-right corner of the worksheet.

13. Save your changes to the file, and then print the Pareto chart.

14. Close the workbook, and then close Excel.

Case 3. Charting Stock Activity You work with Lee Whyte, a stock analyst who plans to publish a Web site on stocks. One component of the Web site will be a five-week record of the activity of various key stocks. Lee has asked for your help in setting up an Excel workbook to keep a running record of the trading volume, open, high, low, and close values of some of the stocks he's tracking.

Lee wants you to create a stock market chart of the activity of the Pixal Inc. stock as a sample. The last six weeks of the stock's performance have been saved in a workbook. He wants you to create a chart sheet for the data that has been entered.

To complete this task:

1. Open the **Pixal1** workbook located in the Tutorial.04/Cases folder of your Data Disk, and then save the file as **Pixal2** to the same folder.

2. Enter your name and the current date in the Documentation sheet. Switch to the Pixal Data worksheet.

3. Select the range A9:G39, and then start the Chart Wizard.

4. Use the Chart Wizard to create a stock chart using the Volume-Open-High-Low-Close sub-type. Specify "Pixal Inc." as the chart title. Specify "Date" as the x-axis title, "Volume (mil)" as the y-axis title, and "Price" as the second y-axis title. Remove the gridlines and do not include the legend. Place the chart in a chart sheet named "Pixal Chart".

5. Change the scale of the first y-axis so that the scale ranges from 0 to 5 with a major unit of 0.5.

6. Change the scale of the second y-axis so that the scale ranges from 15 to 21 with a major unit of 1.

7. Change the alignment of the second y-axis title to –90 degrees.

Explore 8. Change the scale of the x-axis so that the major unit occurs every seven days.

9. Double-click the column data series that displays the volume of shares traded, and using the Options tab, reduce the gap between adjacent columns to 0 pixels.

10. Change the fill color of the plot area to light yellow.

11. Change the font size of the chart title to 16 points.

Explore 12. In the upper-right corner of the plot area, insert the Rounded Rectangular Callout AutoShape from the Drawing toolbar. Enter "Pixal Inc. is experiencing a tough first quarter" in the area of the AutoShape, and then on a new line, enter "-Stock Reviews". Format the text in a bold red 14-point font. Resize the AutoShape if necessary.

13. Add the Shadow Style 6 drop shadow to the AutoShape.

14. Add your name and the date to the right section of the header. Scale the chart to fit the page in landscape orientation.

15. Save the changes, and then print the chart sheet.

Explore 16. Lee has a new week's worth of data for the Pixal worksheet. Enter the data shown in Figure 4-41 to the table of stock activity, and then modify that chart's data source to include the new data values for each data series.

Figure 4-41

DATE	VOLUME (MIL)	OPEN	HIGH	LOW	CLOSE
2/17/2003	0.35	16.30	16.95	16.75	16.85
2/18/2003	0.45	16.85	17.20	17.05	17.15
2/19/2003	0.52	17.15	17.45	17.25	17.25
2/20/2003	0.40	17.25	17.35	16.95	17.25
2/21/2003	0.38	17.25	17.55	16.75	16.95

17. Save your changes, and then reprint the chart sheet with the new data values.

18. Close the workbook and Excel.

Case 4. *Relating Cancer Rates to Temperature* A 1965 study analyzed the relationship between the mean annual temperature in 16 regions in Great Britain and the annual mortality rates in those regions for a certain type of breast cancer. Lynn Watson, a researcher at a British university, has asked you to chart the data from the sample. Figure 4-42 shows the sample values.

Figure 4-42

REGION	TEMPERATURE	MORTALITY
1	31.8	67.3
2	34.0	52.5
3	40.2	68.1
4	42.1	84.6
5	42.3	65.1
6	43.5	72.2
7	44.2	81.7
8	45.1	89.2
9	46.3	78.9
10	47.3	88.6
11	47.8	95.0
12	48.4	87.0
13	49.2	95.9
14	49.9	104.5
15	50.0	100.4
16	51.3	102.5

To complete this task:

1. Create a new workbook named **BCancer** that contains a Documentation sheet displaying your name, the date, and the purpose of the workbook, and a worksheet named "Breast Cancer Data" that contains the data from Figure 4-42 entered in the range A1:C17.

2. Select the temperature and mortality data, and then start the Chart Wizard.

3. Use the Chart Wizard to create an embedded XY (Scatter) chart with no data points connected. Specify "Mortality vs. Temperature" as the chart title. Specify "Temperature" as the title of the x-axis and "Mortality Index" as the title of the y-axis. Remove the gridlines. Do not include the legend. The scatter chart should be embedded on the Breast Cancer Data worksheet, with the chart covering the cell range D1:K23.

4. Change the scale of the x-axis to cover the temperature range 30 to 55 degrees.

5. Change the scale of the y-axis to cover the mortality index range 50 to 110.

Explore

6. Double-click one of the data points in the chart to open the Format Data Series dialog box, and make the following changes to the appearance of the data points:

   - Change the marker style to a circle that is 7 points in size.
   - Change the background color of the circle to white.
   - Change the foreground color of the circle to red.

Explore

7. Click Chart on the menu bar, and then click Add Trendline. On the Type tab, click the Linear trend line, and then click the OK button. The purpose of the linear trend line is to display whether a linear relationship exists between the 16 regions' mean annual temperature and their annual mortality index. Does it appear that such a relationship exists? What does a high mean annual temperature imply about the annual mortality index?

8. Change the fill color of the plot area to light yellow.

9. Set up the worksheet to print in landscape orientation. Center the worksheet horizontally and vertically on the page. Enter your name and the date in the right section of the page's header. Print the chart.

10. Save and close the workbook, and then close Excel.

INTERNET ASSIGNMENTS

Student Union

The purpose of the Internet Assignments is to challenge you to find information on the Internet that you can use to create effective spreadsheets. The actual assignments are updated and maintained on the Course Technology Web site. Log on to the Internet and use your Web browser to go to the Student Union on the New Perspectives Series site at **www.course.com/NewPerspectives/studentunion**. Click the Online Companions link, and then click the link for this text.

Quick Check Answers

Session 4.1

1. A chart type is one of the 14 styles of charts supported by Excel. Each chart type has various alternate formats, called chart sub-types.
2. stock chart
3. A data series is a range of data values that is plotted on the chart.
4. The plot area contains the actual data values that are plotted in the chart, as well as any background colors or images for that plot. The chart area contains the plot area and any other element (such as titles and legend boxes) that may be included in the chart.
5. Gridlines are lines that extend out from the tick marks on either axis into the plot area.
6. embedded charts, which are placed within a worksheet, and chart sheets, which contain only the chart itself
7. pie
8. exploded pie

Session 4.2

1. Click Chart on the menu bar, click Source Data, and then click the Series tab. Select the data series in the Series list box, and click the Remove button.
2. Click Chart on the menu bar, and then click Location. Select a new location from the dialog box.
3. Label text is text that consists of category names, tick mark labels, and legend text. Attached text is text that is attached to other elements of the chart, such as the chart title or axes titles. Unattached text is additional text that is unassociated with any particular element of the chart.
4. Major tick marks are tick marks that appear on the axis alongside the axis values. Minor tick marks do not appear alongside any axis value, but instead are used to provide a finer gradation between major tick marks.
5. Click Chart on the menu bar, and then click Chart Type. Select one of the 3-D chart sub-types for the column chart.
6. An AutoShape is a predefined shape available on the Drawing toolbar. You can add an AutoShape to any worksheet or chart. You can change the size or shape of an AutoShape, and you can change its fill color.
7. a) Use full page, which resizes the chart to fit the full size of the printed page; the proportions of the chart may change in the resizing, b) Scale to fit page, in which the chart is resized to fit the page, but it retains its proportions, c) Custom, in which the dimensions of the printed chart are specified in the chart sheet

OBJECTIVES

In this tutorial you will:

- Learn about the Internet and the World Wide Web
- Create a non-interactive Web page based on an Excel workbook
- Create an interactive Web page based on an Excel workbook

CREATING WEB PAGES WITH EXCEL

Publishing Workbooks to the Web

CASE

Premier Finance

David Kowlske is a financial officer at Premier Finance, a lending company that is increasing its presence on the World Wide Web. David wants to add a page to the company's Web site in which customers can view the current cost of a 20-year mortgage with a fixed interest rate. He also wants to create a second Web page in which customers can enter different values for the interest rate, the size of the mortgage, and the length of the loan to see how those values affect the cost of the mortgage. He has already created two Excel workbooks containing the values and formulas he wants to see transferred to the Web.

The most far-reaching and popular extended network today is the **Internet**. To share network information, the Internet uses hypertext documents. A **hypertext document** is an electronic file that contains elements called links that provide easy access to other hypertext documents. The collection of these hypertext documents is called the **World Wide Web**, or **Web** for short. Each hypertext document is referred to as a **Web page**; a collection of Web pages is called a **Web site**; Web sites are stored on computers called **Web servers**; and to view a Web page, a user must have a software program called a **Web browser** that retrieves the hypertext document from the Web server and then displays the document on the user's computer. The two major browsers are Netscape Navigator and Microsoft Internet Explorer.

David has asked for your help in creating the two Web pages.

Publishing a Non-Interactive Web Site

Microsoft provides tools to convert Excel workbooks into Web pages that can be placed on the Web to be viewed by others. You can create two types of Web pages: non-interactive and interactive. The **non-interactive Web page** allows users to scroll through the contents of an Excel workbook, but they cannot make any changes to the values displayed in the Web page. The **interactive Web page** provides tools to modify and format the values displayed in the Web page, though any changes a user makes in the Web page do not affect the original workbook, nor do those changes last from one browser session to another.

Your first task is to convert David's mortgage data into a non-interactive Web page that will display the current values for a $100,000 mortgage for twenty years at a fixed 7.50% annual interest rate. David has already placed this data into a workbook named "Mortgage1". Use this workbook as a basis for the non-interactive Web page.

To open the Mortgage1 workbook:

1. Start Excel, if necessary, and open the **Mortgage1** workbook located in the Web/Tutorial folder on your Data Disk.
2. On the Documentation sheet, enter the current date and your name.
3. Save the workbook as **Mortgage2** in the Web/Tutorial folder on your Data Disk.
4. Click the other sheet tabs to view the contents of the rest of the workbook, and then return to the Documentation sheet.

The Loan Values worksheet displays the current mortgage cost of a $100,000 loan along with two embedded charts that show the declining remaining balance on the principal over 240 payments and the breakdown between total interest payments and total principal payments. The Schedule worksheet displays a sample payment schedule for a 20-year mortgage.

Setting the Publishing Options

The process of creating a Web page based on a workbook involves opening the Save As dialog box. The first task you'll perform in that dialog box is to choose a non-interactive format for the Web page.

To start creating a non-interactive Web page:

1. Click **File** on the menu bar, and then click **Save as Web Page**. The Save As dialog box opens. See Figure 1.

| Figure 1 | SAVE AS DIALOG BOX |

(Save As dialog box screenshot with annotations:)
- click to publish either the selected sheet or the whole workbook
- click to create an interactive Web page
- click to specify publishing options for the Web page
- click to change the Web page's title

2. Verify that the Add interactivity check box is *not* selected.

Web pages will usually have a page title that appears in the title bar of the Web browser. You can set the page title for David's page in the Save As dialog box.

To specify the page title:

1. Click the **Change Title** button.

2. In the Set Page Title dialog box, type **Sample Mortgage Values**, and then click the **OK** button. The page title is displayed in the Save As dialog box above the File name list box.

   To avoid confusion with the Mortgage2 Excel workbook, you decide to change the filename of the Web page to Mortgage3.

3. Click the File name list box, and change the name of the Web page file to **Mortgage3.htm**.

The next step in setting up the page for publishing on the Web is to choose which components of the workbook to publish. From the current dialog box, you can choose from two option buttons to publish either the entire workbook or the current selection in the active worksheet. You can also click the Publish button, which opens the Publish as Web Page dialog box. From that dialog box you can further refine your publishing choices. You can publish the entire workbook; a selected worksheet in the workbook; an item on a selected worksheet, such as an embedded chart or pivot table; an adjacent range of cells in a worksheet; or a previously published selection from the workbook.

David wants only the Loan Values worksheet published to the company's Web site, and he wants to include both of the embedded charts on the sheet.

To select the Loan Values worksheet:

1. Click the **Publish** button. The Publish as Web Page dialog box opens. You use this dialog box to specify which components of the workbook to publish.

2. Click the **Choose** list arrow at the top of the dialog box. Excel displays a list of possible publishing options.

3. Click **Items on Loan Values** in the list. Excel displays three more options—each of which are based on the Loan Values worksheet. You can publish all of the contents of the Loan Values worksheet or either of the two embedded charts.

4. Click **Sheet All contents of Loan Values** in the list. See Figure 2.

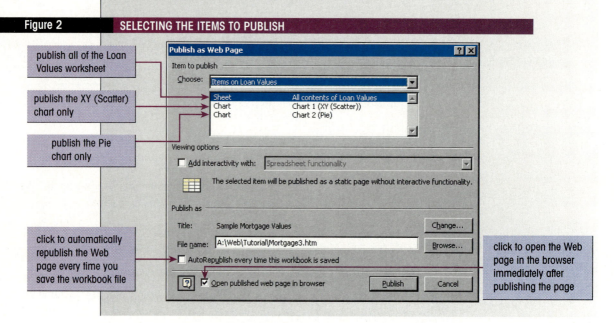

Figure 2   SELECTING THE ITEMS TO PUBLISH

Now that you've defined what you want to publish, you are ready to publish the Loan Values worksheet as a Web page.

Publishing the Web Page

David knows that he might need to update this particular workbook in the future. He wants the Web page to be updated automatically so that it always matches any changes made to the source workbook. You can ensure that the Web page will be automatically updated by turning on the **AutoRepublish** option. Enabling this option republishes the Web page with any changes that have been made to a workbook whenever the workbook is saved.

To turn on the AutoRepublish feature:

1. Click the **AutoRepublish every time this workbook is saved** check box.

   Rather than hunting around for the Web page after you publish it, you can have Excel launch your browser automatically.

2. Click the **Open published web page in browser** check box.

   You're now ready to publish the Web page.

3. Click the **Publish** button. Excel opens a Web page based on the contents of the Loan Values worksheet.

4. Click the **Maximize** button ☐ to maximize the browser window. Figure 3 shows the contents of the Web page.

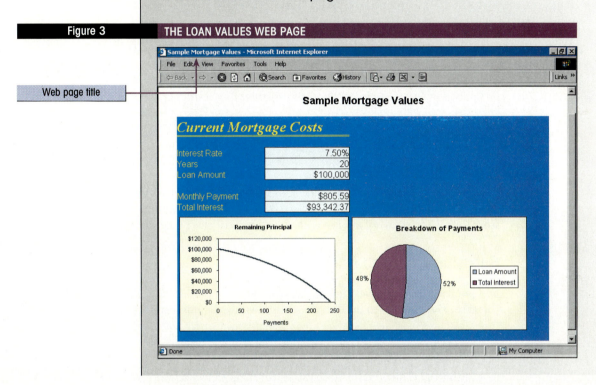

Figure 3 THE LOAN VALUES WEB PAGE

Web page title

Note that, unlike the previewed version you opened earlier, this Web page does not display boxes or symbols. These navigation tools are not needed because this Web page displays a single worksheet, not an entire workbook. Also note that the page title you specified, "Sample Mortgage Values," appears in the browser's title bar and above the worksheet.

You show the completed page to David, so you can close your Web browser and workbook.

To close your work:

1. Click the **Close** button ☒ to close the Web browser and return to the Mortgage2 workbook.

2. Click the **Save** button 🖫 on the Standard toolbar.

   Excel prompts you whether to disable or enable the AutoRepublish feature. Because you aren't about to make any additional changes to this workbook, you can safely disable the feature.

3. Verify that the Disable the AutoRepublish feature while this workbook is open option button is selected, and then click the **OK** button.

4. Click **File** on the menu bar, and then click **Close**.

Now that you've created a non-interactive Web page, you can create an interactive page.

Publishing an Interactive Web Site

David wants an interactive Web page in which customers can enter different mortgage values to see how the values affect the overall cost of the mortgage. He has created a workbook that you can use to create the interactive Web page.

To open the Calc1 workbook:

1. Open the file **Calc1**, located in the Web/Tutorial folder on your Data Disk.
2. On the Documentation worksheet, enter the current date and your name.
3. Save the workbook as **Calc2** in the Web/Tutorial folder on your Data Disk.
4. Review the contents of the workbook, and then return to the Documentation sheet.

There are a few differences between this workbook and the earlier Mortgage workbook. You can test different mortgage values using this workbook. Note that there are no charts in this workbook. Excel does not publish embedded charts or chart sheets in its interactive Web pages.

Publishing the Web Page

You publish an interactive page in the same way you published the non-interactive page. In this case, David wants to publish the entire workbook, not just one worksheet.

To begin publishing the Calc2 workbook:

1. Make sure the Documentation sheet is the active sheet.
2. Click **File** on the menu bar, and then click **Save as Web Page**.
3. Verify that the Entire Workbook option button is selected.
4. Click the **Add interactivity** check box.
5. Click the **Change Title** button, type **Mortgage Calculator** in the Set Title dialog box, and then click the **OK** button.
6. Click the File name list box, and change the name of the Web page file to **Calc3.htm**.

   As with the other workbook, David wants to republish the Web page each time the Calc2 workbook is saved.

7. Click the **Publish** button, and then click the **AutoRepublish every time this workbook is saved** check box.
8. Verify that the Open published Web page in the browser check box is selected.
9. Click the **Publish** button. The Web page opens in your Web browser.

   TROUBLE? If Netscape is your default browser, you will not be able to view the interactive Web page.

   TROUBLE? It may take a minute or so to create the interactive Web page based on this workbook.

Working with the Published Page

In an interactive Web page, the contents of the workbook are placed on the page as a Web component called the **spreadsheet component**. The initial size of the spreadsheet component is chosen to fit the initial dimensions of the Web browser window. If you change the size of the Web browser window, you might need to refresh the window to resize the workbook object to fit the new dimensions.

To view the interactive Web page:

1. Click the **Maximize** button on the Web browser. The Web browser enlarges to fit the entire monitor screen, but the spreadsheet component does not change size.

2. Click **View** on the menu bar, and then click **Refresh**. The spreadsheet component enlarges to match the new dimensions of the browser window. See Figure 4.

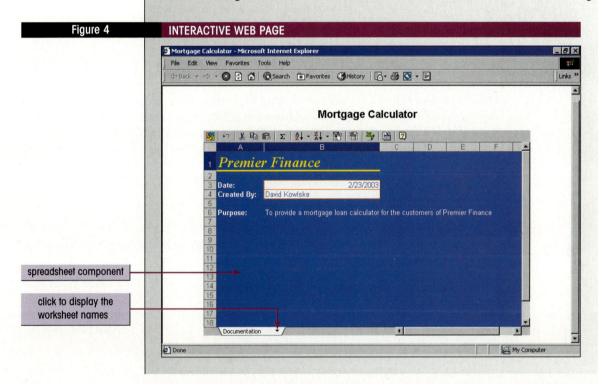

Figure 4 INTERACTIVE WEB PAGE

spreadsheet component

click to display the worksheet names

The spreadsheet component is a fully functioning object. You can enter new values or formulas, resize the rows or columns, and format the appearance of worksheet cells. The spreadsheet component does not have different tabs for the various worksheets. Instead you move between worksheets by selecting the worksheet from the single tab. You decide to test the interactive workbook by placing new values on the Calculator page.

To test the interactive workbook:

1. Click the **list arrow** for the Documentation tab, and then click **Calculator** in the list of worksheet names.

2. Select the current value in the Years box, type **15**, and then press the **Enter** key. The value of the monthly payment increases to $927.01, and the overall cost of the mortgage decreases to $66,862.22.

> 3. Click the **Close** button ⊠ to close your Web browser and return to the Calc2 workbook in Excel.
>
> You've completed your work for David. Save and close the Calc2 workbook before exiting Excel.
>
> 4. Click the **Save** button 🖫 on the Standard toolbar.
>
> 5. Close the workbook and then exit Excel.

The interactivity of this Web page also extends to the appearance of the workbook. You can sort the worksheet cells, filter the data, or export the data from the Web page back to an Excel workbook. You can also change the fill colors, fonts, or borders of individual cells in the workbook. However, none of the changes that you make to the workbook from the Web browser are permanent. The workbook will go back to its original appearance the next time you open the Web page.

REVIEW ASSIGNMENTS

David has placed the Web pages you helped him create on the company's Web server, and they've met with great success. David has a few additional workbooks that he wants you to convert to Web pages. These workbooks display sample values for a proposed college fund. David wants customers to have the ability to view the return from monthly investments in a college savings plan. As before, you'll create both a non-interactive and an interactive version of David's workbooks.

To complete this task:

1. Open the **Fund1** workbook located in the Web/Review folder on your Data Disk. Enter your name and the date in the workbook's Documentation sheet, and then save the workbook as **Fund2** in the same folder.

2. Create a non-interactive Web page based on the workbook using the following guidelines: a) enter "Sample College Fund" as the page title, b) enter **Fund3.htm** as the new filename, c) publish only the contents of the Fund Values worksheet, d) republish the Web page every time the Fund2 workbook is saved, and e) open the published Web page in the browser automatically.

3. Maximize the browser window so you can review the Web page, and then close your browser.

4. Close the workbook, saving your changes.

5. Open the **FCalc1** workbook located in the Web/Review folder on your Data Disk. Enter your name and the date in the Documentation sheet, and then save the workbook as **FCalc2** in the same folder.

6. Create an interactive Web page of the entire workbook with the page title "Fund Calculator" and the filename **FCalc3.htm**. Make sure the Web page is republished each time the FCalc2 workbook is saved, and make sure the Web page opens in the browser window automatically.

7. Maximize the browser window, refresh the screen, and then display the Calculator sheet.

8. Close your browser.

9. Save and close the **FCalc2** workbook, and then exit Excel.

BONUS

New Perspectives on

CREATING
A WORKSHEET IN
MICROSOFT®
EXCEL 2002

TUTORIAL 2 B-EX 2.03

Producing a Sales Comparison Report for MSI
Motorcycle Specialties Incorporated

Read This Before You Begin

To the Student

Data Disk
To complete the Excel Bonus Tutorial, you need **one** Data Disk. Your instructor will either provide you with a Data Disk or ask you to make your own.

If you are making your own Data Disk, you will need **one** blank, formatted high-density disk. You will need to copy a set of files and/or folders from a file server, standalone computer, or the Web onto your disk. Your instructor will tell you which computer, drive letter, and folders contain the files you need. You could also download the files by going to www.course.com and following the instructions on the screen.

The information below shows you which folders go on your disk, so that you will have enough disk space to complete the tutorial, Review Assignment, and Case Problems:

Write this on the disk label:
Data Disk: Excel Tutorial 2

Put this folder on the disk:
Bonus Tutorial.02

If necessary, ask your instructor or technical support person for assistance.

Using Your Own Computer
If you are going to work through this book using your own computer, you need:

- **Computer System** Microsoft Windows 98, NT, 2000 Professional, or higher must be installed on your computer. This book assumes a typical installation of Microsoft Excel.

- **Data Disk** You will not be able to complete the tutorials or exercises in this book using your own computer until you have your Data Disk.

Visit Our World Wide Web Site
Additional materials designed especially for you are available on the World Wide Web. Go to: www.course.com/NewPerspectives.

To the Instructor

The Data Disk Files and Course Labs are available on the Instructor's Resources CD-ROM for this title. Follow the instructions in the Help file on the CD-ROM to install the programs to your network or standalone computer. For information on creating Data Disk or the Course Labs, see the "To the Student" section above.

You are granted a license to copy the Data Files and Course Labs to any computer or computer network used by students who have purchased this book.

TUTORIAL 2

OBJECTIVES

In this tutorial you will:

- Plan, build, test, document, preview, and print a worksheet
- Enter labels, values, and formulas
- Calculate a total using the AutoSum button
- Copy formulas using the fill handle and Clipboard
- Learn about relative, absolute, and mixed references
- Use the AVERAGE, MAX, and MIN functions to calculate values in the worksheet
- Spell check the worksheet
- Insert a row or column
- Reverse an action using the Undo button
- Move a range of cells
- Format the worksheet using AutoFormat
- Center printouts on a page
- Customize a worksheet header and footer

CREATING A WORKSHEET

Producing a Sales Comparison Report for MSI

CASE

Motorcycle Specialties Incorporated

Motorcycle Specialties Incorporated (MSI), a motorcycle helmet and accessories company, provides a wide range of specialty items to motorcycle enthusiasts throughout the world. MSI has its headquarters in Atlanta, Georgia, but it markets products in North America, South America, Australia, and Europe.

The company's marketing and sales director, Sally Caneval, meets regularly with the regional sales managers who oversee global sales in each of the four regions in which MSI does business. This month, Sally intends to review overall sales in each region for the last two fiscal years and present her findings at her next meeting with the regional sales managers. She has asked you to help her put together a report that summarizes this sales information.

Specifically, Sally wants the report to show total sales for each region of the world for the two most recent fiscal years. Additionally, she wants to see the percentage change between the two years. She also wants the report to include the percentage each region contributed to the total sales of the company in 2003. Finally, she wants to include summary statistics on the average, maximum, and minimum sales for 2003.

SESSION 2.1

In this session you will learn how to plan and build a worksheet; enter labels, numbers, and formulas; and copy formulas to other cells.

Developing Worksheets

Effective worksheets are well planned and carefully designed. A well-designed worksheet should clearly identify its overall goal. It should present information in a clear, well-organized format and include all the data necessary to produce results that address the goal of the application. The process of developing a good worksheet includes the following planning and execution steps:

- determine the purpose of the workbook, what it will include, and how it will be organized
- enter the data and formulas into the worksheet
- test the worksheet
- edit the worksheet to correct any errors or make modifications
- document the worksheet
- improve the appearance of the worksheet
- save and print the completed worksheet

Planning the Worksheet

Sally begins to develop a worksheet that compares global sales by region over two years by creating a planning analysis sheet. Her planning analysis sheet helps her answer the following questions:

1. What is the goal of the worksheet? This helps to define the problem to solve.

2. What are the desired results? This information describes the output—the information required to help solve the problem.

3. What data is needed to calculate the desired results? This information is the input—data that must be entered.

4. What calculations are needed to produce the desired output? These calculations specify the formulas used in the worksheet.

Sally's completed planning analysis sheet is shown in Figure 2-1.

Figure 2-1   PLANNING ANALYSIS SHEET

Planning Analysis Sheet

My Goal
To development a worksheet to compare annual sales in each region for the last two fiscal years

What results do I want to see?
Sales by region for 2003 and for 2002
Total sales for 2003 and for 2002
Average sales for 2003
Maximum sales for 2003
Minimum sales for 2003
Percentage change for each region
Percentage of 2003 sales for each region

What information do I need?
Sales for each region in 2003
Sales for each region in 2002

What calculations do I perform?
Total sales for 2003 and for 2002
Average sales for 2003
Maximum sales for 2003
Minimum sales for 2003
Percentage change = Sales for 2003/Sales for 2002
Percentage of 2003 regional sales = (Sales for 2003 – Sales for 2002) / Sales for 2002

Next Sally makes a rough sketch of her design, including titles, column headings, row labels, and where data values and totals should be placed. Figure 2-2 shows Sally's sketch. With these two planning tools, Sally is now ready to enter the data into Excel and build the worksheet.

Figure 2-2   **SKETCH OF THE SALES COMPARISON WORKSHEET**

```
           Motorcycle Specialties Incorporated
              Sales Comparison 2003 with 2002

Region          Year 2003    Year 2002    % Change    % of 2003 Sales
North America    365000       314330        0.16          0.28
South America    354250       292120        0.21          0.27
Australia        251140       262000       -0.04          0.19
Europe           310440       279996        0.11          0.24
Total           1280830      1148446        0.12

Average     320207.5
Maximum      365000
Minimum      251140
```

Building the Worksheet

You use Sally's planning analysis sheet, Figure 2-1, and the rough sketch shown in Figure 2-2 to guide you in preparing the sales comparison worksheet. You begin by establishing the layout of the worksheet by entering titles and column headings. Next you work on inputting the data and formulas that will calculate the results Sally needs.

To start Excel and organize your desktop:

1. Start Excel.
2. Make sure your Data Disk is in the appropriate disk drive.
3. Make sure the Excel and Book1 windows are maximized.

Entering Labels

When you build a worksheet, it's a good practice to enter the labels before entering any other data. These labels help you identify the cells where you will enter data and formulas in your worksheet. As you type a label in a cell, Excel aligns the label at the left side of the cell. Labels that are too long to fit in a cell spill over into the cell or cells to the right, if those cells are empty. If the cells to the right are not empty, Excel displays only as much of the label as fits in the cell. Begin creating the sales comparison worksheet for Sally by entering the two-line title.

To enter the worksheet title:

1. If necessary, click cell **A1** to make it the active cell.
2. Type **Motorcycle Specialties Incorporated**, and then press the **Enter** key. Because cells B1, C1, and D1 are empty, the title in cell A1 spills over into the empty cells. Cell A2 is now the active cell.

TROUBLE? If you make a mistake while typing, remember that you can correct errors with the Backspace key. If you notice the error only after you have pressed the Enter key, double-click the cell to activate Edit mode, and use the keys on your keyboard to correct the error.

3. In cell A2 type **Sales Comparison 2003 with 2002**, and then press the **Enter** key.

Next you enter the column headings defined on the worksheet sketch in Figure 2-2.

To enter labels for the column headings:

1. If necessary, click cell **A3** to make it the active cell.
2. Type **Region** and then press the **Tab** key to complete the entry. Cell B3 is the active cell.
3. Type **Year 2003** in cell B3, and then press the **Tab** key.

   Sally's sketch shows that three more column heads are needed for the worksheet. Enter those next.

4. Enter the remaining column heads as follows:

   Cell C3: **Year 2002**

   Cell D3: **% Change**

   Cell E3: **% of 2003 Sales**

   See Figure 2-3.

   TROUBLE? If any cell does not contain the correct label, either edit the cell or retype the entry.

Figure 2-3 WORKSHEET WITH TITLES AND COLUMN HEADINGS ENTERED

	A	B	C	D	E
1	Motorcycle Specialties Incorporated				
2	Sales Comparison 2003 with 2002				
3	Region	Year 2003	Year 2002	% Change	% of 2003 Sales
4					
5					

Recall that MSI conducts business in four different regions of the world, and the spreadsheet needs to track the sales information for each region. So Sally wants labels reflecting the regions entered into the worksheet. Enter these labels next.

To enter the regions:

1. Click cell **A4**, type **North America**, and then press the **Enter** key.
2. In cell A5, type **South America**, and then press the **Enter** key.
3. Type **Australia** in cell A6, and then type **Europe** in cell A7.

The last set of labels entered identifies the summary information that will be included in the report.

To enter the summary labels:

1. In cell A8, type **Total** and then press the **Enter** key.
2. Type the following labels into the specified cells:

    Cell A9: **Average**

    Cell A10: **Maximum**

    Cell A11: **Minimum**

    See Figure 2-4.

Figure 2-4   **WORKSHEET WITH LABELS ENTERED**

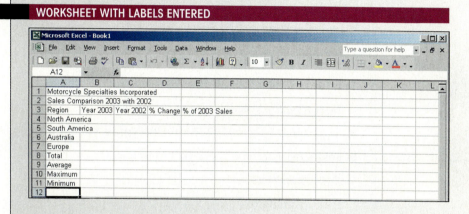

The labels that you just entered into the worksheet will help to identify where the data and formulas need to be placed.

Entering Data

Recall that values can be numbers, formulas, or functions. The next step in building the worksheet is to enter the data, which in this case are the numbers representing sales in each region during 2003 and 2002.

To enter the sales values for 2003 and 2002:

1. Click cell **B4** to make it the active cell. Type **365000** and then press the **Enter** key. See Figure 2-5. Notice that the region name, North America, is no longer completely visible in cell A4 because cell B4 is no longer empty. Later in the tutorial you will learn how to increase the width of a column in order to display the entire contents of cells.

Figure 2-5 LABEL TRUNCATED IN CELL

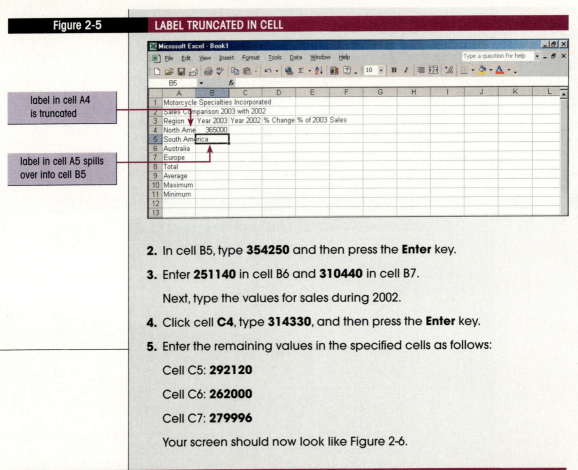

label in cell A4 is truncated

label in cell A5 spills over into cell B5

2. In cell B5, type **354250** and then press the **Enter** key.

3. Enter **251140** in cell B6 and **310440** in cell B7.

   Next, type the values for sales during 2002.

4. Click cell **C4**, type **314330**, and then press the **Enter** key.

5. Enter the remaining values in the specified cells as follows:

   Cell C5: **292120**

   Cell C6: **262000**

   Cell C7: **279996**

   Your screen should now look like Figure 2-6.

Figure 2-6 WORKSHEET WITH SALES DATA FOR 2003 AND 2002 ENTERED

Now that you have entered the labels and data, you need to enter the formulas that will calculate the data to produce the output, or the results. The first calculation Sally wants to see is the total sales for each year. To determine total sales for 2003, you would simply sum the sales from each region for that year. In the previous tutorial you used the SUM function to calculate the weighted total score for the Scottsdale golf site by typing that function into the cell. Similarly, you can use the SUM function to calculate total sales for each year for MSI's comparison report.

Using the AutoSum Button

Because the SUM function is used more often than any other function, Excel includes the AutoSum button on the Standard toolbar. This button automatically creates a formula that contains the SUM function. To do this, Excel looks at the cells adjacent to the active cell, makes an assumption as to which cells you want to sum, and displays a formula based on its best determination about the range you want to sum. You can press the Enter key to accept the formula, or you can select a different range of cells to change the range in the formula. You want to use the AutoSum button to calculate the total sales for each year.

To calculate total sales in 2003 using the AutoSum button:

1. Click cell **B8** because this is where you want to display the total sales for 2003.

2. Click the **AutoSum** button Σ on the Standard toolbar. Excel enters a SUM function in the selected cell and determines that the range of cells to sum is B4:B7, the range directly above the selected cell. See Figure 2-7. In this case, that's exactly what you want to do.

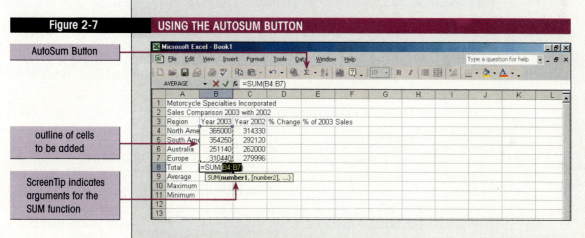

Figure 2-7 — USING THE AUTOSUM BUTTON
- AutoSum Button
- outline of cells to be added
- ScreenTip indicates arguments for the SUM function

3. Press the **Enter** key to complete the formula. The result, 1280830, appears in cell B8.

Now use the same approach to calculate the total sales for 2002.

To calculate total sales in 2002 using the AutoSum button:

1. Click cell **C8** to make it the active cell.

2. Click the **AutoSum** Σ button on the Standard toolbar.

3. Press the **Enter** key to complete the formula. The result, 1148446, appears in cell C8.

Next you need to enter the formula to calculate the percentage change in sales for North America between 2003 and 2002.

Entering Formulas

Recall that a formula is an equation that performs calculations in a cell. By entering an equal sign (=) as the first entry in the cell, you are telling Excel that the numbers or symbols that follow constitute a formula, not just data. Reviewing Sally's worksheet plan, you note that you need to calculate the percentage change in sales in North America. The formula for the percentage change in 2003 sales for North America *is equal to* the 2003 sales in North America *minus* the 2002 sales in North America *divided by* the 2002 sales in North America. In Excel, this formula is *=(B4-C4)/C4* because cell B4 contains the data for the 2003 sales in North America and cell C4 contains the data for the 2002 sales in North America.

If a formula contains more than one arithmetic operator, Excel performs the calculations in the standard order of precedence of operators, shown in Figure 2-8. The **order of precedence** is a set of predefined rules that Excel uses to unambiguously calculate a formula by determining which part of the formula to calculate first, which part second, and so on.

Figure 2-8	ORDER OF PRECEDENCE FOR ARITHMETIC OPERATIONS		
	ORDER	OPERATOR	DESCRIPTION
	First	^	Exponentiation
	Second	* or /	Multiplication or division
	Third	+ or -	Addition or subtraction

Exponentiation is the operation with the highest precedence, followed by multiplication and division, and finally addition and subtraction. For example, because multiplication has precedence over addition, the result of the formula =3+4*5 is 23.

When a formula contains more than one operator with the same order of precedence, Excel performs the operation from left to right. Thus, in the formula =4*10/8, Excel multiplies 4 by 10 before dividing the product by 8. The result of the calculation is 5. You can add parentheses to a formula to make it easier to understand or to change the order of operations. Enclosing an expression in parentheses overrides the normal order of precedence. Excel always performs any calculations contained in parentheses first. In the formula =3+4*5, the multiplication is performed before the addition. If instead you wanted the formula to add 3+4 and then multiply the sum by 5, you would enter the formula =(3+4)*5. The result of the calculation is 35. Figure 2-9 shows examples of formulas that will help you understand the order of precedence rules.

Figure 2-9	EXAMPLES ILLUSTRATING ORDER OF PRECEDENCE RULES	
FORMULA VALUE A1=10, B1=20, C1=3	ORDER OF PRECEDENCE RULE	RESULT
=A1+B1*C1	Multiplication before addition	70
=(A1+B1)*C1	Expression inside parentheses executed before expression outside	90
=A1/B1+C1	Division before addition	3.5
=A1/(B1+C1)	Expression inside parentheses executed before expression outside	.435
=A1/B1*C1	Two operators at same precedence level, leftmost operator evaluated first	1.5
=A1/(B1*C1)	Expression inside parentheses executed before expression outside	.166667

Now enter the percentage change formula as specified in Sally's planning analysis sheet.

To enter the formula for the percentage change in sales for North America:

1. Click cell **D4** to make it the active cell.

2. Type **=(B4-C4)/C4** and then press the **Enter** key. Excel performs the calculations and displays the value 0.1612 in cell D4. The formula is no longer visible in the cell. If you select the cell, the result of the formula appears in the cell, and the formula you entered appears in the Formula bar.

Next you need to enter the percentage change formulas for the other regions, as well as the percentage change for the total company sales. You could type the formula =(B5-C5)/C5 in cell D5, the formula =(B6-C6)/C6 in cell D6, the formula =(B7-C7)/C7 in cell D7, and the formula =(B8-C8)/C8 in cell D8. However, this approach is time consuming and error prone. Instead, you can copy the formula you entered in cell C4 (percentage change in North American sales) into cells D5, D6, D7, and D8. Copying duplicates the cell's underlying formula into other cells, automatically adjusting cell references to reflect the new cell address. Copying formulas from one cell to another saves time and reduces the chances of entering incorrect formulas when building worksheets.

Copying a Formula Using the Fill Handle

You can copy formulas using menu commands, toolbar buttons, or the fill handle. The **fill handle** is a small black square located in the lower-right corner of the selected cell, as shown in Figure 2-10. In this section you will use the fill handle to copy the formulas. In other situations you can also use the fill handle for copying values and labels from one cell or a group of cells.

Figure 2-10   **FILL HANDLE**

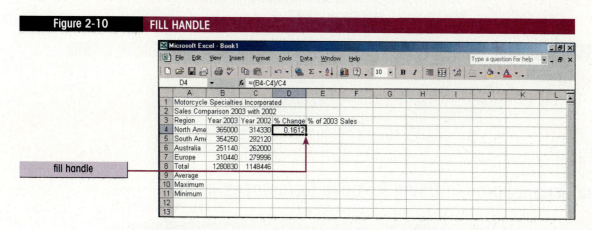

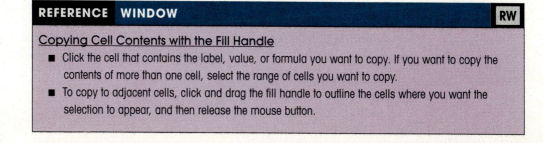

REFERENCE WINDOW

Copying Cell Contents with the Fill Handle
- Click the cell that contains the label, value, or formula you want to copy. If you want to copy the contents of more than one cell, select the range of cells you want to copy.
- To copy to adjacent cells, click and drag the fill handle to outline the cells where you want the selection to appear, and then release the mouse button.

You want to copy the formula from cell D4 to cells D5, D6, D7, and D8.

To copy the formula from cell D4 to cells D5, D6, D7, and D8:

1. Click cell **D4** to make it the active cell.
2. Position the pointer over the fill handle (in the lower-right corner of cell D4) until the pointer changes to +.
3. Click and drag the pointer down the worksheet to outline cells **D5** through **D8**.
4. Release the mouse button. Excel copies the formula from cell D4 to range D5:D8. Also note that a button appears in the lower-right corner of cell D8. This is the Auto Fill Options button. See Figure 2-11.

Figure 2-11   **COPYING A FORMULA USING THE FILL HANDLE**

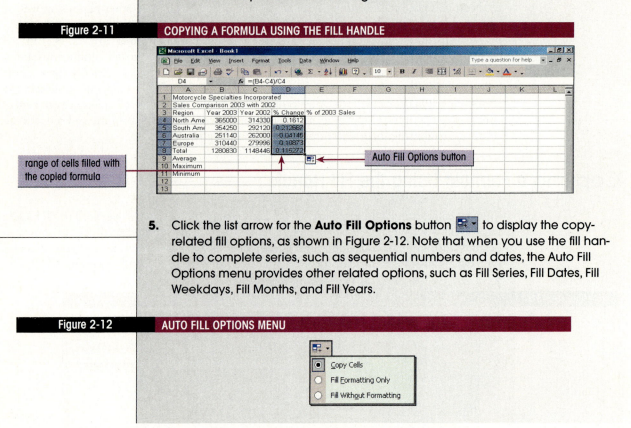

5. Click the list arrow for the **Auto Fill Options** button to display the copy-related fill options, as shown in Figure 2-12. Note that when you use the fill handle to complete series, such as sequential numbers and dates, the Auto Fill Options menu provides other related options, such as Fill Series, Fill Dates, Fill Weekdays, Fill Months, and Fill Years.

Figure 2-12   **AUTO FILL OPTIONS MENU**

Copying a Formula Using Relative References

When you copy a formula that contains cell references, Excel automatically adjusts the cell references for the new locations. For example, when Excel copied the formula from cell D4, =(B4-C4)/C4, it automatically changed the cell references in the formula to reflect the formula's new position in the worksheet. So in cell D5 the cell references adjust to =(B5-C5)/C5. Cell references that change when copied are called **relative cell references**.

Take a moment to look at the formulas in cells D5, D6, D7, and D8.

To examine the formulas in cells D5, D6, D7, and D8:

1. Click cell **D5**. The formula =(B5-C5)/C5 appears in the formula bar. When Excel copied the formula from cell D4 to cell D5, the cell references changed. The formula =(B4-C4)/C4 became =(B5-C5)/C5 when Excel copied the formula down one row to row 5.

2. Examine the formulas in cells D6, D7, and D8. Notice that the cell references were adjusted for the new locations.

Copying a Formula Using an Absolute Reference

According to Sally's plan, the worksheet should display the percentage that each region contributed to the total sales in 2003. For example, if the company's total sales were $100,000 and sales in North America were $25,000, then sales in North America would be 25% of total sales. To complete this calculation for each region, you need to divide each region's sales by the total company sales, as shown in the following formulas:

Contribution by North America	=B4/B8
Contribution by South America	=B5/B8
Contribution by Australia	=B6/B8
Contribution by Europe	=B7/B8

First enter the formula to calculate the percentage North America contributed to total sales.

To calculate North America's percentage of total 2003 sales:

1. Click cell **E4** to make it the active cell.

2. Type **=B4/B8** and then press the **Enter** key to display the value 0.284971 in cell E4.

Cell E4 displays the correct result. Sales in North America for 2003 were 365,000, which is approximately 28% of the 1,280,830 in total sales in 2003. Next, you decide to copy the formula in cell E4 to cells E5, E6, and E7.

To copy the percentage formula in cell E4 to cells E5 through E7:

1. Click cell **E4** and then move the pointer over the fill handle in cell E4 until the pointer changes to +.

2. Click and drag the pointer down to cell **E7**, and then release the mouse button. The error value "#DIV/0!" appears in cells E5 through E7. See Figure 2-13.

Figure 2-13 ERROR VALUES DISPLAYED AFTER COPYING A FORMULA

	A	B	C	D	E
1	Motorcycle Specialties Incorporated				
2	Sales Comparison 2003 with 2002				
3	Region	Year 2003	Year 2002	% Change	% of 2003 Sales
4	North Ame	365000	314330	0.1612	0.284971
5	South Ame	354250	292120	0.212687	#DIV/0!
6	Australia	251140	262000	-0.04145	#DIV/0!
7	Europe	310440	279996	0.10873	#DIV/0!
8	Total	1280830	1148446	0.115272	
9	Average				
10	Maximum				
11	Minimum				

Cell E4 formula: =B4/B8. This error value indicates that the formula is trying to divide by zero.

Something is wrong. Cells E5 through E7 display "#DIV/0!" a special constant, called an **error value.** Excel displays an error value when it cannot resolve the formula. **#DIV/0!**, which is one of seven error values, means that Excel was instructed to divide by zero. Take a moment to look at the formulas you copied into cells E5, E6, and E7.

To examine the formulas in cells E5 through E7:

1. Click cell **E5** and then look at the formula that appears in the Formula bar, =B5/B9. The first cell reference changed from B4 in the original formula to B5 in the copied formula. That's correct because the sales data for South America is entered in cell B5. The second cell reference changed from B8 in the original formula to B9, which is not correct. The correct formula should be =B5/B8 because the total sales are in cell B8, not cell B9.

2. Look at the formulas in cells E6 and E7 to see how the cell references changed in each formula.

As you observed, the cell reference to total company sales (B8) in the original formula was changed to B9, B10, and B11 in the copied formulas. The problem with the copied formulas is that Excel adjusted *all* the cell references relative to their new location.

Absolute Versus Relative Cell References

Sometimes when you copy a formula, you don't want Excel to change all cell references automatically to reflect their new positions in the worksheet. If you want a cell reference to point to the same location in the worksheet when you copy it, you must use an **absolute cell reference**. An absolute cell reference is a cell reference in a formula that does not change when copied to another cell.

To create an absolute cell reference, you insert a dollar sign ($) before the column and row of the cell reference. For example, the cell reference $B$8 is an absolute cell reference, whereas the cell reference B8 is a relative cell reference. If you copy a formula that contains the absolute cell reference $B$8 to another cell, the cell reference to $B$8 does not change. On the other hand, if you copy a formula containing the relative cell reference B8 to another cell, the reference to B8 changes. In some situations, a cell might have a **mixed cell reference**, such as $B8; in this case, when the formula is copied, the row number changes but the column letter does not.

To include an absolute cell reference in a formula, you can type a dollar sign when you type the cell reference, or you can use the F4 key to change the cell reference type while in Edit mode.

> **REFERENCE WINDOW**
>
> **Changing Absolute, Mixed, and Relative Cell References**
> - Double-click the cell that contains the formula you want to edit.
> - Use the arrow keys to move the insertion point to the part of the cell reference you want to change.
> - Press the F4 key until the cell reference is correct.
> - Press the Enter key to complete the edit.

To correct the problem in your worksheet, you need to use an absolute cell reference, instead of a relative cell reference, to indicate the location of total sales in 2001. That is, you need to change the formula from =B4/B8 to =B4/$B$8. The easiest way to make this change is in Edit mode.

To change a cell reference to an absolute cell reference:

1. Double-click cell **E4** to edit the formula in the cell. Notice that each cell reference in the formula in cell E4 appears in a different color and the corresponding cells referred to in the formula are outlined in the same color. This feature is called **Range Finder** and is designed to make it easier for you to check the accuracy of your formula.

2. Make sure the insertion point is to the right of the division (/) operator, anywhere in the cell reference B8.

3. Press the **F4** key to change the reference to $B$8.

    TROUBLE? If your reference shows the mixed cell reference B$8 or $B8, continue to press the F4 key until $B$8 appears.

4. Press the **Enter** key to update the formula in cell E4.

Cell E4 still displays .284971, which is the formula's correct result. But remember, the problem in your original formula did not surface until you copied it to cells E5 through E7. To correct the error, you need to copy the revised formula and then check the results. Although you can again use the fill handle to copy the formula, you can also copy the formula using the Clipboard and the Copy and Paste buttons on the Standard toolbar.

Copying Cell Contents Using the Copy-and-Paste Method

You can duplicate the contents of a cell or range by making a copy of the cell or range and then pasting the copy into one or more locations in the same worksheet, another worksheet, or another workbook.

When you copy a cell or range of cells, the copied material is placed on the Clipboard. You can copy labels, numbers, dates, or formulas.

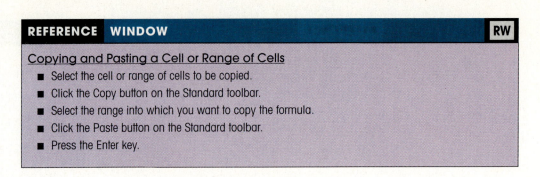

REFERENCE WINDOW

Copying and Pasting a Cell or Range of Cells
- Select the cell or range of cells to be copied.
- Click the Copy button on the Standard toolbar.
- Select the range into which you want to copy the formula.
- Click the Paste button on the Standard toolbar.
- Press the Enter key.

You need to copy the formula in cell E4 to the Clipboard and then paste that formula into cells E5 through E7.

To copy the revised formula from cell E4 to cells E5 through E7:

1. Click cell **E4** because it contains the revised formula that you want to copy.

2. Click the **Copy** button on the Standard toolbar. A moving dashed line surrounds cell E4, indicating that the formula has been copied and is available to be pasted into other cells.

3. Click and drag to select cells **E5** through **E7**.

4. Click the **Paste** button on the Standard toolbar. Excel adjusts the formula and pastes it into cells E5 through E7.

5. Click any cell to deselect the range and view the formulas' results. Press the **Esc** key to clear the Clipboard and remove the dashed line surrounding cell E4. See Figure 2-14.

Figure 2-14   **RESULTS OF COPYING A FORMULA WITH AN ABSOLUTE CELL REFERENCE**

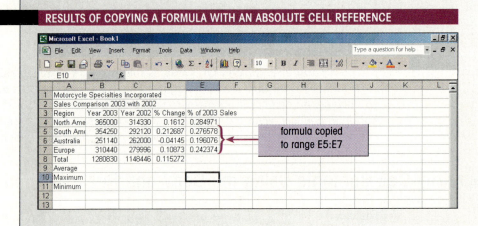

Copying this formula worked. When you pasted the formula from cell E4 into the range E5:E7, Excel automatically adjusted the relative reference (B4), while using the cell reference ($B$8) for all absolute references. You have now implemented most of the design as specified in the planning analysis sheet. Now rename the worksheet to accurately describe its contents, then save the workbook on your Data Disk before entering the formulas to compute the summary statistics.

Renaming the Worksheet

Before saving the workbook, look at the sheet tab in the lower-left corner of the worksheet window: the sheet is currently named Sheet1—the name Excel automatically uses when it opens a new workbook. Now that your worksheet is taking shape, you want to give it a more descriptive name that better indicates its contents. Change the worksheet name to Sales Comparison.

To change a worksheet name:

1. Double-click the **Sheet1** sheet tab to select it.
2. Type **Sales Comparison** and then press the **Enter** key. The sheet tab displays the name "Sales Comparison."

Saving the New Workbook

Now you want to save the workbook. Because this is the first time you have saved this workbook, you use the Save As command and name the file MSI Sales Report.

To save the workbook as MSI Sales Report:

1. Click **File** on the menu bar, and then click **Save As** to open the Save As dialog box.
2. In the File name text box, type **MSI Sales Report**, but don't press the Enter key yet.
3. Click the **Save in** list arrow, and then click the drive containing your Data Disk.
4. In the folder list, select the **Tutorial** folder for **Tutorial.02** into which you want to save the workbook. Your Save As dialog box should look like the dialog box in Figure 2-15.

Figure 2-15 SAVING THE WORKBOOK AS MSI SALES REPORT

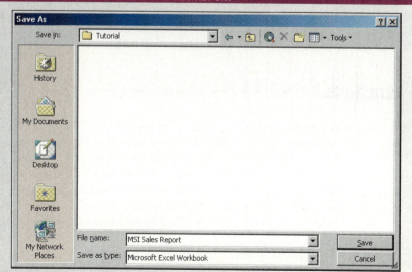

5. Click the **Save** button to save the workbook.

> **Trouble?** If you see the message "Replace Existing MSI Sales Report," Excel found a file with the same name on the current folder. Click the Yes button to replace the file on the folder with the current version.

You have planned and built the Sales Comparison worksheet by entering labels, values, and formulas. Next you will enter some functions and format the worksheet.

Session 2.1 QUICK CHECK

1. List the steps to follow to create a worksheet.
2. Describe how AutoSum works.
3. In cell D3 you have the formula =B3-C3. After you copy this formula to cell D4, the formula in cell D4 would appear in the Formula bar as _____.
4. The _____ is a small black square located in the lower-right corner of a selected cell.
5. In the formula =D10*C10, D10 and C10 are examples of _____ references.
6. In the formula =A8+(1+$C$1), $C$1 is an example of a(n) _____.
7. When you copy a formula using the Copy and Paste buttons on the Standard toolbar, Excel uses the _____ to temporarily store the formula.
8. Describe the steps you take to change the name of the sheet tab.
9. What is meant by order of precedence?

SESSION 2.2

In this session you will finish the worksheet. As you do this you will learn how to enter several statistical functions, increase the column width, insert a row between the titles and column headings, move the contents of a range to another location, and apply one of the Excel predefined formats to the report. You will also spell check the worksheet, preview, and print it.

Excel Functions

According to Sally's planning analysis sheet, you still need to enter the formulas for the summary statistics. To enter these statistics, you'll use three Excel functions, AVERAGE, MAX, and MIN. The many Excel functions help you enter formulas for calculations and other specialized tasks, even if you don't know the mathematical details of the calculations. As you recall, a function is a calculation tool that performs a predefined operation. You are already familiar with the SUM function, which adds the values in a range of cells. Excel provides hundreds of functions, including a function to calculate the average of a list of numbers, a function to find a number's square root, a function to calculate loan payments, and a function to calculate the number of days between two dates.

Each function has a **syntax**, which specifies the order in which you must type the parts of the function and where to put commas, parentheses, and other punctuation. The general syntax of an Excel function is FUNCTION NAME(*argument1,argument2,...*).

The syntax of most functions requires you to type the function name followed by one or more arguments in parentheses. The name of the function, such as SUM or AVERAGE, describes the operation the function performs. Function **arguments** specify the values the function must use in the calculation, or the cell references that Excel must include in the calculation. For example, in the function SUM(A1:A20) the function name is SUM and the argument is A1:A20, which is the range of cells you want to total.

You can use a function in a simple formula such as =SUM(A1:A20) or a more complex formula such as =SUM(A1:A20)*52. As with all formulas, you enter the formula that contains a function in the cell where you want to display the results. The easiest way to enter a function in a cell is to use the Insert Function button on the Formula bar, which leads you step-by-step through the process of entering a formula containing a function.

If you prefer, you can type the function directly into the cell. Although the function name is always shown in uppercase, you can type it in either uppercase or lowercase. Also, even though parentheses enclose the arguments, you need not type the closing parenthesis if the function ends the formula. Excel automatically adds the closing parenthesis when you press the Enter key to complete the formula.

Figure 2-16 shows a few of the functions available in Excel organized by category.

Figure 2-16 — SELECTED EXCEL FUNCTIONS

CATEGORY	FUNCTION NAME	SYNTAX	DEFINITION
Finance	PMT	PMT(rate,nper,pv,fv,type)	Calculates the payment for a loan based on constant payments and a constant interest rate
	FV	FV(rate,nper,pmt,pv,type)	Returns the future value of an investment based on periodic, constant payments and a constant interest rate
Math	ROUND	ROUND(number,num_digits)	Rounds a number to a specified number of digits
	RAND	RAND( )	Returns an evenly distributed random number greater than or equal to 0 and less than 1
Logical	IF	IF(logical_test,value_if_true, value_if_false)	Returns one value if a condition you specify evaluates to TRUE and another value if it evaluates to FALSE
	AND	AND(logical1,logical2, ...)	Returns TRUE if all its arguments are TRUE; returns FALSE if one or more arguments is FALSE
Lookup and Reference	VLOOKUP	VLOOKUP(lookup_value, table_array,col_index_num, range_lookup)	Searches for a value in the leftmost column of a table, and then returns a value in the same row from a column you specify in the table
	INDIRECT	INDIRECT(ref_text,a1)	Returns the reference specified by a text string–references are immediately evaluated to display their contents
Text	CONCATENATE	CONCATENATE (text1,text2,...)	Joins several text strings into one text string
	LEFT	LEFT(text,num_chars)	Returns the first (or leftmost) character or characters in a text string
Date and Time	TODAY	TODAY( )	Returns the serial number of the current date
	YEAR	YEAR(serial_number)	Returns the year corresponding to serial number–the year is given as an integer in the range 1900-9999
Statistical	COUNT	COUNT(value1,value2, ...)	Counts the number of cells that contain numbers and numbers within the list of arguments
	STDEV	STDEV(number1,number2,...)	Estimates standard deviation based on a sample

According to Sally's planning analysis sheet, the next step is to calculate the average regional sales for 2003.

AVERAGE Function

AVERAGE is a statistical function that calculates the average, or the arithmetic mean. The syntax for the AVERAGE function is AVERAGE(*number1,number2,...*).

Generally, when you use the AVERAGE function, *number* is a range of cells. To calculate the average of a range of cells, Excel sums the values in the range and then divides by the number of non-blank cells in the range.

> **REFERENCE WINDOW**
>
> **Using the Insert Function Button**
> - Click the cell in which you want to insert the function, and then click the Insert Function button on the Formula bar.
> - Type information about the function (or task you want to execute) in the search for a function box, and click the Go button, or click the Or select a category list arrow, and then select a category from the list.
> - Select the function you want to insert from the Select a function list box.
> - Click the OK button.
> - Enter the values for each required argument in the Function Arguments dialog box.
> - Click the OK button.

Sally wants you to calculate the average sales in 2003. You'll use the Insert Function button to enter the AVERAGE function.

To enter the AVERAGE function using the Insert Function button:

1. If you took a break after the last session, make sure Excel is running and the **MSI Sales Report** workbook is open. Click cell **B9** to select the cell in which you want to enter the AVERAGE function.

2. Click the **Insert Function** button on the Formula bar to open the Insert Function dialog box. Excel automatically inserts an equal sign (=), which signals the beginning of a formula, in cell B9.

   TROUBLE? If necessary, move the Insert Function dialog box so cell B9 is clearly visible.

3. Click the **Or select a category** list arrow, and then click **Statistical** in the list.

4. Click **AVERAGE** in the Select a function list box. See Figure 2-17. The syntax for the AVERAGE function appears below the list of functions.

| Figure 2-17 | INSERT FUNCTION DIALOG BOX |

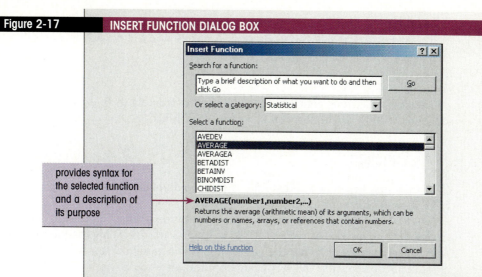

provides syntax for the selected function and a description of its purpose

5. Click the **OK** button to open the Function Arguments dialog box for the AVERAGE function. The dialog box displays the name of the function, a reference box for each argument, and the current values for the arguments, the current results of the function, and the current results of the entire formula. Notice that the range B4:B8 appears in the Number1 reference box, and =AVERAGE(B4:B8) appears in the Formula bar. See Figure 2-18.

| Figure 2-18 | FUNCTION ARGUMENTS DIALOG BOX |

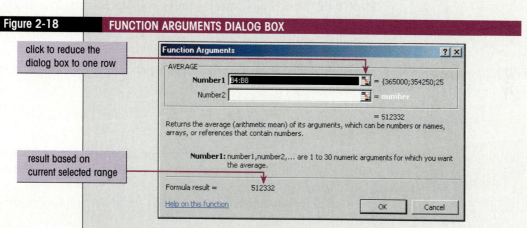

click to reduce the dialog box to one row

result based on current selected range

The range includes the total sales for 2003 (cell B8), which should not be included if you are calculating the average of the sales.

6. Click the **Collapse Dialog Box** button to collapse the dialog box to the size of one row. This makes it easier for you to select the correct range for the argument.

7. Position the pointer over cell **B4**, and then click and drag to select the range **B4:B7**. As you drag the mouse over the range, notice that the message "4Rx1C" appears in a ScreenTip, indicating that you have selected four rows and one column.

8. Click the **Expand Dialog Box** button to restore the collapsed dialog box. The correct range, B4:B7, appears in the Number1 reference box, the formula =AVERAGE(B4:B7) appears in the Formula bar, and the result of the formula appears at the bottom on the dialog box.

> 9. Click the **OK** button to close the dialog box and return to the worksheet. The average, 320207.5, now appears in cell B9 and the completed function appears in the Formula bar.

According to your plan, you need to enter a formula to find the largest regional sales amount in 2003. To do this, you'll use the MAX function.

MAX Function

MAX is a statistical function that finds the largest number. The syntax of the MAX function is MAX(*number1,number2,...*).

In the MAX function, *number* can be a constant number such as 345, a cell reference such as B6, or a range of cells such as B5:B16. You can use the MAX function to simply display the largest number or to use the largest number in a calculation. Although you can use the Paste Function to enter the MAX function, this time you'll type the MAX function directly into cell B10.

> ### To enter the MAX function by typing directly into a cell:
>
> 1. If necessary, click cell **B10** to select it as the cell into which you want to type the formula that uses the MAX function.
>
> 2. Type **=MAX(B4:B7)** and then press the **Enter** key. Cell B10 displays 365000, the largest regional sales amount in 2003.

Next you need to find the smallest regional sales amount in 2003. For that, you'll use the MIN function.

MIN Function

MIN is a statistical function that finds the smallest number. You can use the MIN function to display the smallest number or to use the smallest number in a calculation. The syntax of the MIN function is MIN(*number1,number2,...*).

You'll enter the MIN function directly into cell B11 using the pointing method.

Building Formulas by Pointing

Excel provides several ways to enter cell references into a formula. One is to type the cell references directly, as you have done so far in all the formulas you've entered. Another way to enter a cell reference in a formula is to point to the cell you want to include while building the formula. To use the **pointing method** to enter the formula, you click the cell or select the range of cells whose cell references you want to include in the formula. You may prefer to use this method to enter formulas because it minimizes typing errors.

Now use the pointing method to enter the formula to calculate the minimum sales.

> ### To enter the MIN function using the pointing method:
>
> 1. If necessary, click cell **B11** to move to the cell where you want to enter the formula that uses the MIN function.

2. Type **=MIN(** to begin the formula.

3. Position the pointer in cell **B4**, and then click and drag to select cells **B4** through **B7**. See Figure 2-19.

Figure 2-19 — ENTERING A FORMULA USING THE POINTING METHOD

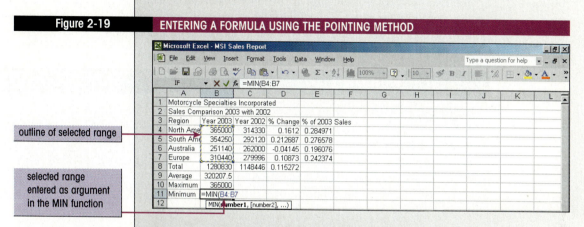

outline of selected range

selected range entered as argument in the MIN function

4. Release the mouse button, and then press the **Enter** key. Cell B11 displays 251140, the smallest regional sales amount for 2003.

Now that the worksheet labels, values, formulas, and functions have been entered, Sally reviews the worksheet.

Testing the Worksheet

Before trusting a worksheet and its results, you should test it to make sure you entered the correct formulas. You want the worksheet to produce accurate results.

Beginners often expect their Excel worksheets to work correctly the first time. Sometimes they do work correctly the first time, but even well-planned and well-designed worksheets can contain errors. It's best to assume that a worksheet has errors and test it to make sure it is correct. While there are no rules for testing a worksheet, here are some approaches:

- Entering **test values**, numbers that generate a known result, to determine whether your worksheet formulas are accurate. For example, try entering a 1 into each cell. After you enter the test values, you compare the results in your worksheet with the known results. If the results on your worksheet don't match the known results, you probably made an error.

- Entering **extreme values**, such as very large or very small numbers, and observing their effect on cells with formulas.

- Working out the numbers ahead of time with pencil, paper, and calculator, and comparing these results with the output from the computer.

Sally used the third approach to test her worksheet. She had calculated her results using a calculator (Figure 2-2) and then compared them with the results on the screen (Figure 2-19). The numbers agree, so she feels confident that the worksheet she created contains accurate results.

Spell Checking the Worksheet

You can use the Excel spell check feature to help identify and correct spelling and typing errors. Excel compares the words in your worksheet to the words in its dictionary. If Excel finds a word in your worksheet not in its dictionary, it shows you the word and some suggested corrections, and you decide whether to correct it or leave it as is.

> **REFERENCE WINDOW** RW
>
> **Checking the Spelling in a Worksheet**
> - Click cell A1 to begin the spell check from the top of the worksheet.
> - Click the Spelling button on the Standard toolbar.
> - Change the spelling or ignore the spell check's suggestion for each highlighted word.
> - Click the OK button when the spell check is complete.

You have tested your numbers and formulas for accuracy. Now you can check the spelling of all text entries in the worksheet.

To check the spelling in a worksheet:

1. Click cell **A1** to begin spell checking in the first cell of the worksheet.

2. Click the **Spelling** button 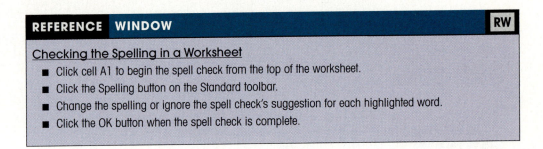 on the Standard toolbar to check the spelling of the text in the worksheet. A message box indicates that Excel has finished spell checking the entire worksheet. No errors were found.

   TROUBLE? If a spelling error is found, use the Spelling dialog box options to correct it.

3. Click the **OK** button.

Improving the Worksheet Layout

Although the numbers are correct, Sally wants to present a more polished-looking worksheet. She feels that there are a number of simple changes you can make to the worksheet that will improve its layout and make the data more readable. Specifically, she asks you to increase the width of column A so that the entire region names are visible, insert a blank row between the titles and column headings, move the summary statistics down three rows from their current location, and apply one of the predefined Excel formats to the worksheet.

Changing Column Width

Changing the column width is one way to improve the appearance of the worksheet, making it easier to read and interpret data. In Sally's worksheet, you need to increase the width of column A so that all of the labels for North America and South America appear in their cells.

Excel provides several methods for changing column width. For example, you can click a column heading or click and drag the pointer to select a series of column headings and then use the Format menu. You can also use the dividing line between column headings in the column header row. When you move the pointer over the dividing line between two column headings, the pointer changes to ↔. You can then use the pointer to drag the dividing line to a new location. You can also double-click the dividing line to make the column as wide as the longest text label or number in the column.

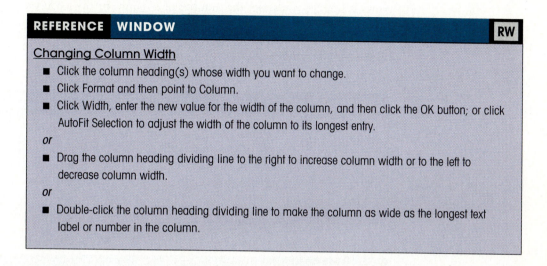

| REFERENCE WINDOW | RW |

Changing Column Width
- Click the column heading(s) whose width you want to change.
- Click Format and then point to Column.
- Click Width, enter the new value for the width of the column, and then click the OK button; or click AutoFit Selection to adjust the width of the column to its longest entry.

or

- Drag the column heading dividing line to the right to increase column width or to the left to decrease column width.

or

- Double-click the column heading dividing line to make the column as wide as the longest text label or number in the column.

Sally has asked you to change the width of column A so that the complete region name is visible.

To change the width of column A:

1. Position the pointer over the right edge of the column A heading until the pointer changes to ↔.

2. Click and drag the pointer to the right, increasing the column width 12 characters or 89 pixels, as indicated in the ScreenTip that appears on the screen. See Figure 2-20.

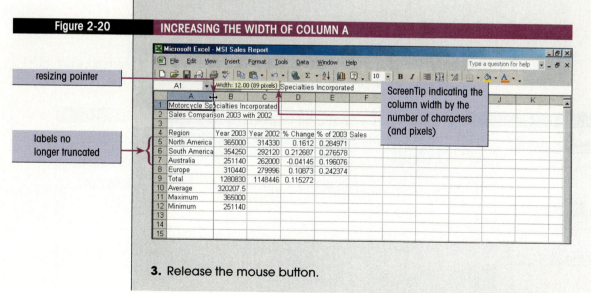

Figure 2-20 — INCREASING THE WIDTH OF COLUMN A

- resizing pointer
- labels no longer truncated
- ScreenTip indicating the column width by the number of characters (and pixels)

3. Release the mouse button.

Next you need to insert a row between the title and the column heading.

Inserting a Row or Column into a Worksheet

At times you may need to add one or more rows or columns to a worksheet to make room for new data or to make the worksheet easier to read. The process of inserting columns and rows is similar; you select the number of columns or rows you want to insert and then use the Insert command to insert them. When you insert rows or columns, Excel repositions other rows and columns in the worksheet and automatically adjusts cell references in formulas to reflect the new location of values used in calculations.

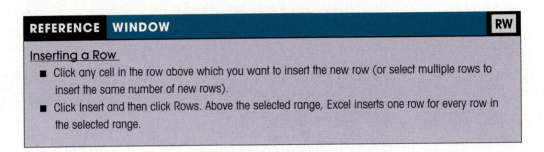

REFERENCE WINDOW

Inserting a Row
- Click any cell in the row above which you want to insert the new row (or select multiple rows to insert the same number of new rows).
- Click Insert and then click Rows. Above the selected range, Excel inserts one row for every row in the selected range.

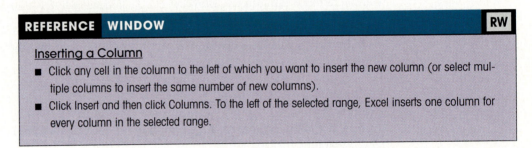

REFERENCE WINDOW

Inserting a Column
- Click any cell in the column to the left of which you want to insert the new column (or select multiple columns to insert the same number of new columns).
- Click Insert and then click Columns. To the left of the selected range, Excel inserts one column for every column in the selected range.

Sally wants one blank row between the titles and column headings in her worksheet.

To insert a row into a worksheet:

1. Click cell **A2**.

2. Click **Insert** on the menu bar, and then click **Rows**. Excel inserts a blank row above the original row 2. All other rows shift down one row. See Figure 2-21.

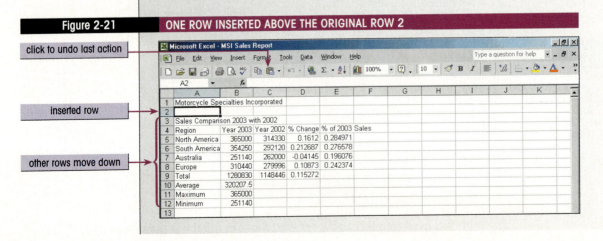

Figure 2-21 ONE ROW INSERTED ABOVE THE ORIGINAL ROW 2

click to undo last action

inserted row

other rows move down

The blank row isn't really where you wanted it. You inserted a row between the two lines of the title instead of between the title and the column heading. To correct this error you can either delete the row or use the Undo button. If you need to delete a row or column, select the row(s) or column(s) you want to delete, then click Delete on the Edit menu, or press the Delete key on your keyboard. You use the Undo button because it is a feature you find valuable in many situations.

Using the Undo Button

The Undo button lets you cancel recent actions one at a time. Click the Undo button to reverse the last command or delete the last entry you typed. To reverse more than one action, click the list arrow next to the Undo button and click the action you want to undo from the list.

Now use the Undo button to reverse the row insertion.

To reverse the row insertion:

1. Click the **Undo** button on the Standard toolbar to restore the worksheet to its status before the row was inserted.

Now you can insert the blank row in the correct place—between the second line of the worksheet title and the column heads.

To insert a row into a worksheet:

1. Click cell **A3** because you want to insert one row above row 3. If you wanted to insert several rows, you would select as many rows as you wanted to insert immediately below where you want the new rows inserted before using the Insert command.

2. Click **Insert** on the menu bar, and then click **Rows**. Excel inserts a blank row above the original row 3. All other rows shift down one row.

Adding a row changed the location of the data in the worksheet. For example, the percentage change in North American sales, originally in cell D4, is now in cell D5. Did Excel adjust the formulas to compensate for the new row? Check cell D5 and any other cells you want to view to verify that the cell references were adjusted.

To examine the formula in cell D5 and other cells:

1. Click cell **D5**. The formula =(B5-C5)/C5 appears in the Formula bar. You originally entered the formula =(B4-C4)/C4 in cell D4 to calculate percentage change in North America. Excel automatically adjusted the cell reference to reflect the new location of the data.

2. Inspect other cells below row 3 to verify that their cell references were automatically adjusted when the new row was inserted.

Sally has also suggested moving the summary statistics down three rows from their present location to make the report easier to read. So you will need to move the range of cells containing the average, minimum, and maximum sales to a different location in the worksheet.

Moving a Range Using the Mouse

To place the summary statistics three rows below the other data in the report, you could use the Insert command to insert three blank rows between the total and average sales. Alternatively, you could use the mouse to move the summary statistics to a new location. Because you already know how to insert a row, try using the mouse to move the summary statistics to a new location. This technique is called drag and drop.

REFERENCE WINDOW

Moving a Range Using the Mouse
- Select the cell or range of cells you want to move.
- Place the mouse pointer over any edge of the selected range until the pointer changes to a double-headed arrow.
- Click and drag the outline of the range to the new worksheet location.
- Release the mouse button.

Sally has asked you to move the range A10 through B12 to the new destination area A13 through B15.

To move a range of cells using the drag-and-drop technique:

1. Select the range of cells **A10:B12**, which contains the sales summary statistics you want to move.

2. Position the mouse pointer over any edge of the selected range until the pointer changes to ✥. See Figure 2-22.

Figure 2-22   SELECTED RANGE TO BE MOVED

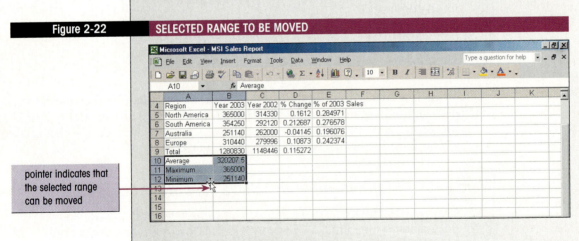

pointer indicates that the selected range can be moved

3. Press and hold the mouse button as you drag the outline of the three rows down to range **A13:B15**. Notice how Excel displays a gray outline and a box with a range reference that shows the destination of the selection.

4. Release the mouse button. Excel moves the selected cells to the range A13:B15. See Figure 2-23.

Figure 2-23   **SELECTED RANGE MOVED TO NEW LOCATION**

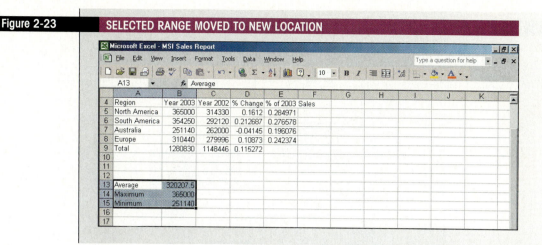

Next Sally wants you to use the Excel AutoFormat feature to improve the worksheet's appearance by emphasizing the titles and aligning numbers in cells.

Using AutoFormat

The **AutoFormat** feature lets you change the appearance of your worksheet by selecting from a collection of predefined worksheet formats. Each worksheet format in the AutoFormat collection gives your worksheet a more professional appearance by applying attractive fonts, borders, colors, and shading to a range of data. AutoFormat also adjusts column widths, row heights, and the alignment of text in cells to improve the appearance of the worksheet.

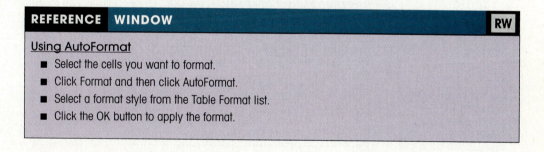

REFERENCE WINDOW

Using AutoFormat
- Select the cells you want to format.
- Click Format and then click AutoFormat.
- Select a format style from the Table Format list.
- Click the OK button to apply the format.

Now you'll use AutoFormat's Simple format to improve the worksheet's appearance.

To apply AutoFormat's Simple format:

1. Select range **A1:E9**. You must select the cells before you can apply an AutoFormat.

2. Click **Format** on the menu bar, and then click **AutoFormat**. The AutoFormat dialog box opens. See Figure 2-24.

Figure 2-24 AUTOFORMAT DIALOG BOX

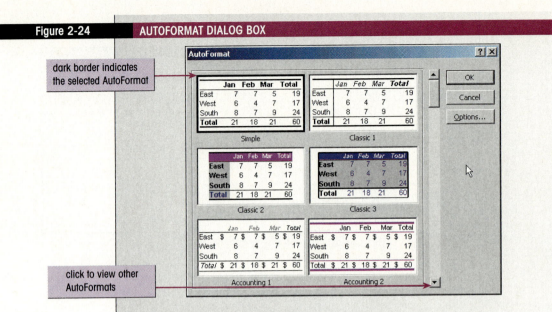

dark border indicates the selected AutoFormat

click to view other AutoFormats

The dialog box displays a preview of how each format will appear when applied to a worksheet. Notice the dark border around the Simple format indicating it is the selected format.

3. Click the **OK** button to apply the Simple format.

4. Click any cell to deselect the range. See Figure 2-25.

Figure 2-25 SIMPLE AUTOFORMAT APPLIED TO SELECTED RANGE

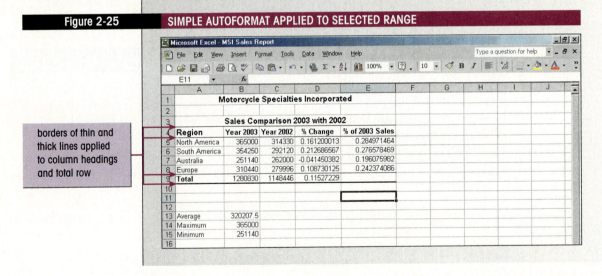

borders of thin and thick lines applied to column headings and total row

You show the worksheet to Sally. She's impressed with the improved appearance and decides to hand it out to the regional sales managers at their next meeting. She asks you to print it so she can make copies.

Previewing the Worksheet Using Print Preview

Before you print a worksheet, you can use the Excel Print Preview window to see how it will look when printed. The Print Preview window shows you margins, page breaks, headers, and footers that are not always visible on the screen. If the preview isn't what you want, you can close the Print Preview window and change the worksheet before printing it.

To preview the worksheet before you print it:

1. Click the **Print Preview** button to display the worksheet in the Print Preview window. See Figure 2-26.

   TROUBLE? If you do not see the Print Preview button on the Standard toolbar, click the Toolbar Options button at the end of the Standard toolbar, click Add or Remove Buttons, point to Standard, and then click Print Preview in the list. Click anywhere in the worksheet to close the menus, and then repeat Step 1.

Figure 2-26 **PRINT PREVIEW OF SALES COMPARISON WORKSHEET**

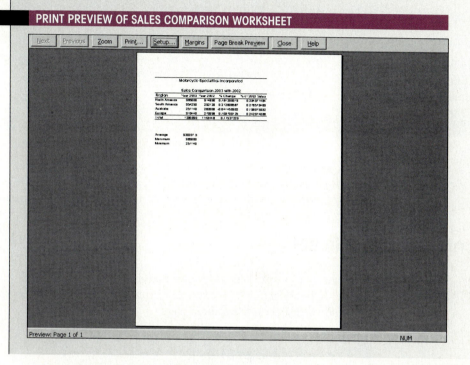

When Excel displays a full page in Print Preview, you might have difficulty seeing the text of the worksheet because it is so small. Don't worry if the preview isn't completely readable. One purpose of Print Preview is to see the overall layout of the worksheet and how it will fit on the printed page. If you want a better view of the text, you can use the Zoom button.

To display an enlarged section of the Print Preview window:

1. Click the **Zoom** button on the Print Preview toolbar to display an enlarged section of the Print Preview.

2. Click the **Zoom** button again to return to the full-page view.

Notice that the Print Preview toolbar contains several other buttons. Figure 2-27 describes each of these buttons.

Figure 2-27 — PRINT PREVIEW TOOLBAR BUTTONS

CLICKING THIS BUTTON	RESULTS IN
Next	Moving forward one page
Previous	Moving backward one page
Zoom	Magnifying the Print Preview window to zoom in on any portion of the page; click again to return to full-page preview
Print	Printing the document
Setup	Opening the Page Setup dialog box
Margins	Changing the width of margins, columns in the worksheet and the position of headers and footers
Page Break Preview	Showing where page breaks occur in the worksheet and which area of the worksheet will be printed; you can adjust where data will print by inserting or moving page breaks
Close	Closing Print Preview
Help	Starting Help

Looking at the worksheet in Print Preview, you observe that it is not centered on the page. By default, Excel prints a worksheet at the upper-left of the page's print area. You can specify that the worksheet be centered vertically, horizontally, or both.

Centering the Printout

Worksheet printouts generally look more professional centered on the printed page. You decide that Sally would want you to center the sales comparison worksheet both horizontally and vertically on the printed page.

To center the printout:

1. Click the **Setup** button on the Print Preview toolbar to open the Page Setup dialog box.
2. Click the **Margins** tab. See Figure 2-28. Notice that the preview box displays a worksheet positioned at the upper-left edge of the page.

Figure 2-28 — MARGINS TAB IN THE PAGE SETUP DIALOG BOX

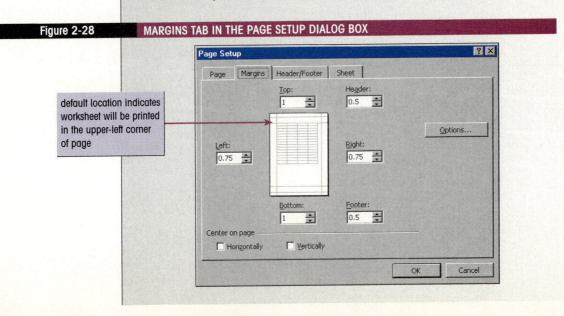

default location indicates worksheet will be printed in the upper-left corner of page

3. Click the **Horizontally** check box in the Center on page section to place a check in it.

4. Click the **Vertically** check box to place a check in it.

   Notice that the sample window shows that the worksheet is now centered vertically and horizontally on the page.

5. Click the **OK** button. Notice that the output appears in the Print Preview window centered vertically and horizontally.

   TROUBLE? If the worksheet is enlarged, click the Zoom button to view the entire page.

Adding Headers and Footers

Headers and footers can provide useful documentation on your printed worksheet, such as the name of the person who created the worksheet, the date it was printed, and its filename. The **header** is text printed in the top margin of every worksheet page. A **footer** is text printed in the bottom margin of every page. Headers and footers are not displayed in the worksheet window. To see them, you must preview or print the worksheet.

Excel uses formatting codes in headers and footers to represent the items you want to print. Formatting codes produce dates, times, and filenames that you might want a header or footer to include. Using formatting codes instead of typing the date, time, filename and so on provides flexibility. For example, if you use a formatting code for date, the current date appears on the printout whenever the worksheet is printed. You can type these codes, or you can click a formatting code button to insert the code. Figure 2-29 shows the formatting codes and the buttons for inserting them.

Figure 2-29 HEADER AND FOOTER FORMATTING BUTTONS

BUTTON	BUTTON NAME	FORMATTING CODE	ACTION
A	Font	none	Sets font, text style, and font size
#	Page number	&[Page]	Inserts page number
	Total pages	&[Pages]	Inserts total number of pages
	Date	&[Date]	Inserts current date
	Time	&[Time]	Inserts current time
	Filename	&[File]	Inserts filename
	Sheet name	&[Tab]	Inserts name of active worksheet

Sally asks you to add a custom header that includes the filename and today's date. She also wants you to add a custom footer that displays the preparer's name.

To add a header and a footer to your worksheet:

1. Click the **Setup** button on the Print Preview toolbar to open the Page Setup dialog box, and then click the **Header/Footer** tab.

2. Click the **Custom Header** button to open the Header dialog box.

3. With the insertion point in the Left section box, click the **Filename** button. The code &(File) appears in the Left section box.

   TROUBLE? If you clicked the wrong code, double-click the code, press the Delete key, and then repeat Steps 2 and 3.

4. Click in the **Right section** box to move the insertion point.

5. Click the **Date** button. The code &(Date) appears in the Right section box. See Figure 2-30.

Figure 2-30   INSERTING FORMATTING CODES INTO THE HEADER DIALOG BOX

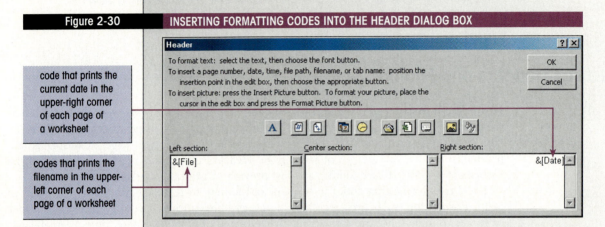

- code that prints the current date in the upper-right corner of each page of a worksheet
- codes that prints the filename in the upper-left corner of each page of a worksheet

TROUBLE? If you clicked the wrong code, double-click the code, press the Delete key, and then repeat Step 5.

6. Click the **OK** button to complete the header and return to the Page Setup dialog box. Notice that the header shows the filename on the left and the date on the right.

7. Click the **Custom Footer** button to open the Footer dialog box.

8. Click in the **Center section** box to move the insertion point to the Center section box.

9. Type **Prepared by** *your name*.

10. Click the **OK** button to complete the footer and return to the Page Setup dialog box. Notice that the footer shows your name in the bottom, center of the page.

11. Click the **OK** button. The new header and footer appear in the worksheet.

12. Click the **Close** button to exit Print Preview and return to the worksheet.

You'll use the Print button on the Standard toolbar to print one copy of the worksheet with the current settings. First, save the worksheet before printing it.

To save your page setup settings with the worksheet and print the worksheet:

1. Click the **Save** button on the Standard toolbar.

2. Click the **Print** button on the Standard toolbar. See Figure 2-31.

> **TROUBLE?** If you see a message that indicates that you have a printer problem, click the Cancel button to cancel printing. Check your printer to make sure it is turned on and is online; also make sure it has paper. Then go back and try Step 2 again. If you have no printer available, click the Cancel button.

Figure 2-31 **PRINTOUT OF THE SALES COMPARISON WORKSHEET**

MSI Sales Report   1/30/2004

Motorcycle Specialties Incorporated
Sales Comparison 2003 with 2002

Region	Year 2003	Year 2002	% Change	% of 2003 Sales
North America	365000	314330	0.161200013	0.284971464
South America	354250	292120	0.212686567	0.276578469
Australia	251140	262000	-0.041450382	0.196075982
Europe	310440	279996	0.108730125	0.242374086
Total	1280830	1148446	0.11527229	

Average   320207.5
Maximum   365000
Minimum   251140

Sally Caneval

Sally reviews the printed worksheet and is satisfied with its appearance. Now she asks for a second printout without the average, minimum, and maximum statistics.

Setting the Print Area

By default, Excel prints the entire worksheet. There are situations in which you are interested in printing a portion of the worksheet. To do this, you first select the area you want to print, and then use the Set Print Area command to define the print area.

To print a portion of the worksheet:

1. Select range **A1:E9**.

2. Click **File** on the menu bar, point to **Print Area**, and then click **Set Print Area**.

3. Click the **Print Preview** button on the Standard toolbar. Notice the average, minimum and maximum values are not included in the Print Preview window.

4. Click the **Close** button on the Print Preview toolbar to return to the worksheet.

5. Click any cell outside the highlighted range. Notice the range A1: E9 is surrounded with a dashed line indicating the current print area for the worksheet.

6. Click the **Print** button on the Standard toolbar.

If you want to print the entire worksheet once a print area has been set, you need to remove the current print area. Point to Print Area on the File menu, and click the Clear Print Area to remove the print area. Now the entire worksheet will print.

Documenting the Workbook

Documenting the workbook provides valuable information to those using the workbook. Documentation includes external documentation as well as notes and instructions within the workbook. This information could be as basic as who created the worksheet and the date it was created, or it could be more detailed, including formulas, summaries, and layout information.

Depending on the use of the workbook, the required amount of documentation varies. Sally's planning analysis sheet and sketch for the sales comparison worksheet are one form of external documentation. This information can be useful to someone who would need to modify the worksheet in any way because it states the goals, required input, output, and the calculations used.

One source of internal documentation might be a worksheet placed as the first worksheet in the workbook, such as the documentation sheet described in Tutorial 1; to determine the best location for the new Inwood golf course. In more complex workbooks, this sheet may also include an index of all worksheets in the workbook, instructions on how to use the worksheets, where to enter data, how to save the workbook, and how to print reports. This documentation method is useful because the information is contained directly in the workbook and can easily be viewed upon opening the workbook, or printed if necessary. Another source of internal documentation is the **Properties** dialog box. This dialog box enables you to electronically capture information such as the name of the workbook's creator, the creation date, the number of revisions, and other information related to the workbook.

If you prefer, you can include documentation on each sheet of the workbook. One way is to attach notes to cells by using the Comments command to explain complex formulas, list assumptions, and enter reminders.

The worksheet itself can be used as documentation. Once a worksheet is completed, it is a good practice to print and file a hardcopy of your work as documentation. This hardcopy file should include a printout of each worksheet displaying the values and another printout of the worksheet displaying the cell formulas.

Sally asks you to include a note in the worksheet that will remind her that the sales in Europe do not include an acquisition that was approved in December. You suggest inserting a cell comment.

Adding Cell Comments

Cell comments can help users remember assumptions, explain complex formulas, or place reminders related to the contents of a specific cell.

REFERENCE WINDOW

Inserting a Comment
- Select the cell in which you want to add the comment.
- Click Insert from the menu bar, and then click Comment to display a text box.
- Type your comment in the text box.
- Click any cell outside the box to store the comment.

Insert the comment for Sally.

To add a comment to a cell:

1. Click cell **B8**.

2. Click **Insert** on the menu bar and then click **Comment**. A text box appears.

   TROUBLE? If the Comment command does not appear on the Insert menu, click ⌄ to view additional items on the Insert menu.

   Now enter your comment in the text box.

3. Type **Does not include sales from company acquired in December**. See Figure 2-32.

Figure 2-32 **INSERTING A COMMENT IN A CELL**

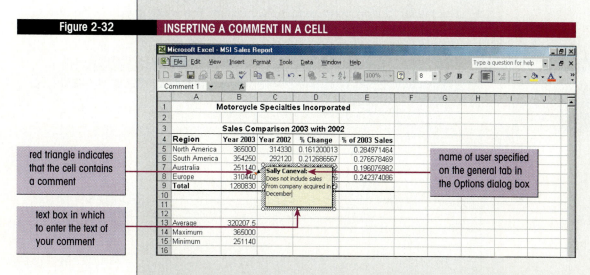

red triangle indicates that the cell contains a comment

text box in which to enter the text of your comment

name of user specified on the general tab in the Options dialog box

4. Click any cell outside the text box. The comment may or may not remain on the screen. Notice, however, that a tiny red triangle appears in the upper-right corner of the cell indicating the cell contains a comment. If the comment does remain on the screen, you can hide it.

5. If necessary, right-click cell **B8** and then click **Hide Comment** on the shortcut menu. Once the comment is hidden, all you have to do is position the pointer over the cell to redisplay the comment.

6. Move the pointer over cell **B8**. The comment appears.

7. Move the pointer over to another cell. The comment disappears.

8. Save the workbook.

Once a comment is inserted, you can edit or delete the comment by right-clicking the cell and selecting Edit Comment or Delete Comment from the shortcut menu.

Now Sally asks for a printout of the worksheet formulas for her file.

Displaying and Printing Worksheet Formulas

You can document the formulas you entered in a worksheet by displaying and printing them. When you display formulas, Excel shows the formulas you entered in each cell instead of showing the results of the calculations. You want a printout of the formulas in your worksheet for documentation.

To display worksheet formulas:

1. Click **Tools** on the menu bar, and then click **Options** to open the Options dialog box.

2. If necessary, click the **View** tab, and then click the **Formulas** check box in the Window options section to select it.

3. Click the **OK** button to return to the worksheet. The width of each column nearly doubles to accommodate the underlying formulas. See Figure 2-33.

Figure 2-33 DISPLAYING FORMULAS IN A WORKSHEET

columns automatically adjust to accommodate the width of the formulas

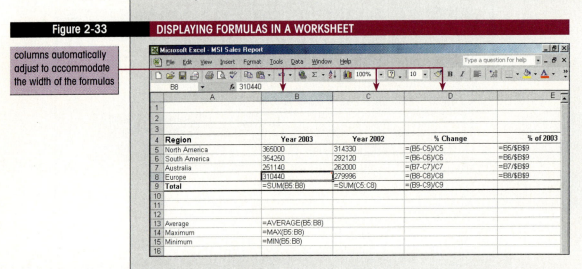

You may find the keyboard shortcut, Ctrl + grave accent (`) (the grave accent key is found next to the 1 in the upper-left area of the keyboard) easier to use when displaying formulas. Press the shortcut key once to display formulas and again to display results.

Now print the worksheet displaying the formulas. Before printing the formulas, you need to change the appropriate settings in the Page Setup dialog box to show the gridlines and the row/column headings, center the worksheet on the page, and fit the printout on a single page.

To adjust the print setups to display formulas:

1. Click **File** on the menu bar, and then click **Page Setup** to open the Page Setup dialog box.

2. Click the **Sheet** tab to view the sheet options, and then click the **Row and column headings** check box in the Print section to print the row numbers and column letters along with the worksheet results.

3. Click the **Gridlines** check box to select that option.

4. Click the **Page** tab and then click the **Landscape** option button. This option prints the worksheet with the paper positioned so it is wider than it is tall.

5. Click the **Fit to** option button in the Scaling section of the Page tab. This option reduces the worksheet when you print it, so it fits on the specific number of pages in the Fit to check box. The default is 1.

6. Click the **Print Preview** button. Notice that the worksheet does not include the formulas for average, minimum and maximum because the print area is still set for the range A1:E9.

7. Click the **Print** button and then click the **OK** button. See Figure 2-34.

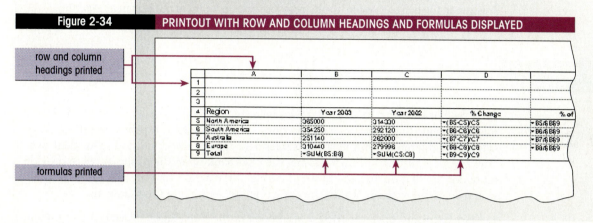

Figure 2-34 — PRINTOUT WITH ROW AND COLUMN HEADINGS AND FORMULAS DISPLAYED

After printing the formulas, return the worksheet so it displays the worksheet values.

To display the worksheet values:

1. Press **Ctrl + grave accent** key (`) to display the worksheet values.
2. Save and close the workbook, and then exit Excel.

Session 2.2 Quick Check

1. What is meant by syntax?
2. In the function MAX(A1:A8), identify the function name. Identify the argument(s).
3. Describe how you use the pointing method to create a formula that includes the SUM function.
4. Describe how to insert a row or a column.
5. To reverse your most recent action, which button should you click?
   a. 🖫
   b. 📂
   c. ↩
6. To move a range of cells, you must _____ the range first.
7. _____ is a command that lets you change your worksheet's appearance by selecting a collection of predefined worksheet formats.
8. A _____ is text that is printed in the top margin of every worksheet page.

9. A _____ is a tiny red triangle in the upper-right corner of a cell that indicates the cell contains a _____.

10. To display formulas instead of values in your worksheet, what command should you choose?

11. If your worksheet has too many columns to fit on one printed page, you should try _____ orientation.

You have planned, built, formatted, and documented Sally's sales comparison worksheet. It is ready for her to present to the regional sales managers at their next meeting.

REVIEW ASSIGNMENTS

After Sally meets with the regional sales managers for MSI, she decides it would be a good idea to provide the managers with their own copy of the sales report workbook, so they can update the report with next year's sales data and also modify it to use for their own sales tracking purposes. Before passing the workbook on to them, she wants to provide more documentation and add some additional information that the managers thought would be useful to them. To update the workbook, complete the following:

1. Start Excel and open the **MSI-2** workbook in the Tutorial.02\Review folder on your Data Disk. Be sure to maximize both windows if necessary.

2. Save the workbook as **MSI Sales Report 2** in the same folder.

3. Switch to Sheet 2 and enter the information about the workbook as shown in Figure 2-35.

Figure 2-35

increase the width of column A to 12 characters

enter the current date

enter your name

	A	B	C	D	E	F	G	H	I	J	K
1	Motorcycle Specialties Incorporated										
2											
3	Created by:	Sally Caneval									
4	Date Created:	1/30/2004									
5											
6	Purpose:	To compare by region sales for 2003 with sales for 2002									
7											
8											

4. Rename the sheet "Documentation", move the worksheet to the beginning of the workbook, and then print the worksheet.

5. Switch to the Sales Comparison sheet.

6. Insert a row between Australia and Europe, and then enter the following information: "Africa" in cell A8, "125000" in cell B8, and "100000" in cell C8.

7. Copy the formula for the % Change and the % of 2003 Sales values to the row containing the new data for Africa.

Explore

8. Insert a column between columns C and D, and then enter "Change" in cell D4 as the column heading.

9. In cell D5, enter a formula that calculates the difference (or change) in sales for North America for 2003 and 2002.

10. Copy the formula to range D6:D9 using the fill handle. Copy the formula in cell C10 to cell D10 to calculate the total for the Change column.

11. Calculate the summary statistics for 2002, displaying the average in cell C14, the maximum in cell C15, and the minimum in cell C16.

Explore 12. Insert the comment "Divide 2003 sales in each region by the total sales in 2003" in cell F4, and then use Help to find out how to print the comments on a worksheet. Print the worksheet with the comments displayed, and then hide the comments before continuing to the next step. (*Hint*: You might need to clear the print area before printing the worksheet with the comments displayed.)

Explore 13. Apply the Classic 3 AutoFormat to range A1:F10, and then apply the List 3 AutoFormat to range A14:C16. Resize any column as needed after applying the List 3 AutoFormat. (*Hint*: The width of column C changed when you applied the List 3 AutoFormat.)

14. Preview the layout of the Sales Comparison worksheet, and then set up the worksheet to print in landscape orientation on one page, with the row and column headings displayed, and with the filename and the current date in the header and your name centered at the bottom of the printout. Print the worksheet.

15. Save and close the workbook, and then exit Excel.

CASE PROBLEMS

Case 1. Annual Stockholders' Meeting at MJ Incorporated Jeanne Phelp, chief financial officer (CFO) of MJ Incorporated is responsible for preparing the annual financial reports and mailing them to stockholders before the annual stockholder's meeting. She has completed some of the work for the annual meeting and is now in the process of finishing a report comparing the changes in net income between the current year and last year. Complete the following.

1. Start Excel, open the **MJ Inc** workbook located in the Tutorial.02\Cases folder on your Data Disk, and then save the workbook as **MJ Income** in the same folder. The title of the worksheet, labels, and column headings have already been entered.

2. Resize column A to 24 characters, and then enter the values in the 2003 and 2002 columns as shown in Figure 2-36.

Figure 2-36

	A	B	C	D
1	MJ Incorporated Income Statement			
2				
3		2003	2002	Percentage Change
4	Net Sales	1818500	1750500	
5	Cost of Goods Sold	1005500	996000	
6	Gross Profit			
7	Selling and Admin Expenses	506000	479000	
8	Income From Operations			
9	Interest Expense	18000	19000	
10	Income Before Taxes			
11	Income Tax Expense	86700	77000	
12	Net Income			
13	Outstanding Shares	20000	20000	
14	Earnings per Share			
15				
16				

3. Enter the following formulas for 2003:
    - Gross Profit = Net Sales − Cost of Goods Sold
    - Income From Operations = Gross Profit − Selling and Admin Expenses
    - Income Before Taxes = Income From Operations − Interest Expense
    - Net Income = Income Before Taxes − Income Tax Expense

4. Enter a formula that calculates the Earnings per Share for 2003. (*Hint*: The earnings per share is equal to the net income divided by the outstanding shares.)

5. Copy the formulas in column B to the appropriate cells in column C for 2002.

6. Enter a formula that calculates the percentage change between the two years for each item in the income statement.

Explore

7. Enter the comment "These results have not been audited." in cell B4. Change the color of the comment text box to a light yellow. (*Hint*: To display comment-related options, right-click the comment text box.) Hide the comment if necessary.

8. Apply the List 3 AutoFormat to the cells that contain values.

9. Rename the sheet "Income" and then make cell A1 active.

10. Prepare a Documentation sheet, including the name of the company, your name as the person who prepared the workbook, the current date, and a purpose statement. Be sure this worksheet is the first sheet in the workbook.

11. Switch to the Income sheet and enter your name and the date in a custom footer. Center the worksheet horizontally and vertically on the page. Change the page orientation to landscape and fit the worksheet on one page. Print the worksheet.

12. Display the formulas on the worksheet, and then print the worksheet. Hide the formulas after you've printed the worksheet.

13. Switch to the Documentation sheet, make cell A1 active, save and close the workbook, and then exit Excel.

Case 2. Compiling Data on the U.S. Airline Industry The editor of *Aviation Week and Space Technology* has asked you to research the current status of the U.S. airline industry. The editor wants you to calculate the total and average revenue-miles and passenger-miles for six airlines that she feels best represent the U.S. airline industry. She also wants to know the share of the total revenue-miles and passenger-miles held by each airline. To provide the requested information, complete the following:

1. Start Excel, open the **Airline** workbook located in the Tutorial.02\Cases folder on your Data Disk, and then save the workbook as **Airline Data** in the same folder. The title of the worksheet, labels, and column headings have already been entered, and columns B and C have been resized for you.

2. Enter the values in columns B and C as shown in Figure 2-37.

Figure 2-37

	A	B	C
1	Airline	Revenue-Miles	Passenger-Miles
2		In 1000s	In 1000s
3	American	26000	2210000
4	Continental	9300	620500
5	Delta	21500	1860000
6	Northwest	20800	1900500
7	US Airways	9850	1540000
8	United	35175	3675000
9			
10			

3. In cell A9, enter the label "Total" and enter the label "Average" in cell A10. In cells B9 and B10, enter the formulas that will calculate the following results:

- Total revenue-miles
- Average revenue-miles

4. Select range B9:B10 and then, using the fill handle, copy the formulas to range C9:C10.

5. In cell D1, enter "Share of Total" and then enter "Revenue-Miles" in cell D2. Enter "Share of Total" in cell E1 and "Passenger-Miles" in cell E2. Resize columns D and E to 16 characters.

6. Enter a formula in column D that calculates for each airline its share of the total revenue-miles.

7. Enter a formula in column E that calculates each airline's share of the total passenger-miles.

8. Apply the Classic 3 AutoFormat to the cells that contains values. Resize columns as needed.

9. Rename the sheet "Mileage Data" and then make cell A1 active.

10. Display the formulas on the worksheet, enter your name and the current date in a custom header, center the worksheet horizontally on the page, change the page orientation to landscape, and then print the worksheet on one page.

11. Hide the formulas and make cell A1 the active cell.

12. Save and close the workbook, and then exit Excel.

Case 3. Fresh Air Sales Incentive Program   Carl Stambaugh is assistant sales manager at Fresh Air Inc., a manufacturer of outdoor and expedition clothing. Fresh Air sales representatives contact retail chains and individual retail outlets to sell the Fresh Air line.

This year, to stimulate sales, Carl has decided to run a sales incentive program for sales representatives. Each sales representative has been assigned a sales goal 12% higher than his or her total sales last year. All sales representatives who reach this new goal will be awarded an all-expenses-paid trip for two to Cozumel, Mexico.

Carl has asked you to track the results of the sales incentive program using an Excel workbook. Complete the following:

1. Start Excel, open the **Fresh Air** workbook located in the Tutorial.02\Cases folder on your Data Disk, and then save the workbook as **Fresh Air Sales Incentive** in the same folder.

2. In the appropriate cells in columns H, I, and J, enter the following formulas:
    - Actual Total 2003 = Total of the actual sales for each quarter
    - 2003 Sales Goal = 2002 Sales * (1 + Sales Goal % Increase)
    - % Goal Reached = Actual Total 2003 / 2003 Sales Goal

4. Copy the three formulas to calculate the values for each sales rep. (*Hint*: Be sure you have used absolute cell references as needed.)

5. In row 45, enter the formulas that calculate the average sales each quarter, the maximum sales each quarter, and the minimum sales each quarter. Enter appropriate labels in column A.

6. In cell C4, insert the comment "Enter a sales goal value between 10 and 15%." Hide the comment.

7. Apply the List 2 AutoFormat to the range of cells A1:J47.

8. Preview the worksheet and then set it up to print on one page in landscape, centered horizontally on the page, with your name and today's date in the header, and with the filename centered in the footer. Print the worksheet.

Explore 9. Change the Sales Goal % Increase to 14% (0.14). Scroll down the worksheet to see how the values have changed. Note that as you scroll the worksheet, the column headings (which appear above row 8) are no longer visible. Use Help to find out how to keep the column headings visible as you scroll through a worksheet.

10. Display the formulas in the worksheet, set the print area to include only the cells in columns H, I and J that contain formulas, and then print the selection of cells.

11. Hide the formulas and make cell A1 the active cell.

12. Save and close the workbook, and then exit Excel.

Case 4. Stock Portfolio for Juan Cortez Your close friend, Juan Cortez, works as an accountant at a local manufacturing company. While in college, with a double major in accounting and finance, Juan dabbled in the stock market and expressed an interest in becoming a financial planner and running his own firm. To that end, he has continued his professional studies in the evenings with the aim of becoming a certified financial planner. He has already begun to provide financial planning services to a few clients. Because of his hectic schedule as a full-time accountant, part-time student, and part-time financial planner, Juan finds it difficult to keep up with the data-processing needs for his clients. Juan asks you to set up a worksheet to keep track of a stock portfolio for one of his clients.

1. Start Excel and enter the column headings, row labels, and values as shown in Figure 2-38. (*Hint*: You can resize the columns as needed at this time. You will be resizing the columns again later in this case.)

Figure 2-38

	A	B	C	D	E	F	G
1	Stock	No of Shares	Purchase Price	Cost	Current Price	Current Value	Gains/Losses
2	Excite	100	67.5		55.5		
3	Yahoo	250	121		90.625		
4	Netscape	50	24.5		26.375		
5	Microsoft	100	89.875		105.375		
6	Intel	50	69		83		

2. In the appropriate cells, enter the following formulas:
   - Cost = No of Shares * Purchase Price
   - Current Value = No of Shares * Current Price
   - Gains/Losses = Current Value – Cost

3. Copy the formulas to calculate values for each stock.

4. Enter the necessary formulas to calculate totals for the number of shares, cost, current value, and gains/losses. Include an appropriate label for the totals.

5. In cell E1, insert the comment "As of 9/1/2004." Hide the comment.

6. Apply an appropriate AutoFormat to improve the overall appearance of the worksheet. (*Hint*: You might have to try several different AutoFormats before deciding which format best suits your data.)

Explore 7. Using the Column Width command on the Format menu, resize columns B, C, E, F, and G to 15 characters and column D to 9 characters. (*Hint*: To select multiple columns, click a column heading and then press and hold the Ctrl key as you click the other column headings.)

8. Rename the sheet "Stock Data".

9. Provide documentation for anyone who might use this workbook in the future. Make the documentation sheet the first sheet in the workbook.

10. Save the workbook as **Portfolio** in the Tutorial.02\Cases folder on your Data Disk.

11. Switch to the Stock Data sheet, print the worksheet in landscape, centered horizontally on one page, with your name and today's date in the header, and with the filename centered in the footer.

12. Clear the values in the Current Price column, and then enter the following new values:

Excite	57.250
Yahoo	86.625
Netscape	30.75
Microsoft	102.375
Intel	84.375

13. Print the worksheet with the new values.

14. Print the worksheet with the formulas and the row and column headings displayed.

15. Hide the formulas and then save the workbook.

Explore

16. Using the financial section of your newspaper, look up the current price of each stock and enter the current prices in the worksheet. (*Hint*: You will find these stocks listed on the NASDAQ Stock Exchange.) Add three more stocks and their current prices. Print the worksheet with the formulas displayed. How did the formula for the total Current Value change? Close the workbook without saving it.

INTERNET ASSIGNMENTS

Student Union

The purpose of the Internet Assignments is to challenge you to find information on the Internet that you can use to create effective spreadsheets. The actual assignments are updated and maintained on the Course Technology Web site. Log on to the Internet and use your Web browser to go to the Student Union on the New Perspectives Series site at **www.course.com/NewPerspectives/studentunion**. Click the Online Companions link, and then click the link for this text.

QUICK CHECK ANSWERS

Session 2.1

1. Determine the purpose of the worksheet, enter the data and formulas, test the worksheet; correct errors, improve the appearance, document the worksheet, save and print.

2. Select the cell where you want the sum to appear. Click the AutoSum button. Excel suggests a formula that includes the SUM function. To accept the formula press the Enter key.

3. =B4-C4

4. fill handle

5. Cell references; if you were to copy the formula to other cells, these cells are relative references.

6. absolute reference
7. Windows clipboard
8. Double-click the sheet tab, then type the new name, and then press the Enter key or click any cell in the worksheet to accept the entry.
9. Order of precedence is a set of predefined rules that Excel uses to unambiguously calculate a formula by determining which part of the formula to calculate first, which part second, and so on.

Session 2.2

1. Syntax specifies the set of rules that determine the order and punctuation of formulas and functions in Excel.
2. MAX is the function name; A1:A8 is the argument.
3. Assuming you are entering a formula with a function, select the cell where you want to place a formula, type an equal sign followed by the function name and a left parenthesis, select the range of cells to be used in the formula, and then press the Enter key.
4. Click any cell in the row above which you want to insert a row. Click Insert and then click Rows.
5. c
6. select
7. AutoFormat
8. header
9. comment indicator, comment
10. Click Tools, click Options, click the View tab, and then click the Formula check box.
11. landscape

BONUS

OBJECTIVES

In this tutorial you will:

- Learn about Financial functions
- Learn about Date and Time functions
- Learn about Statistical functions
- Learn about Lookup and Reference functions
- Learn about Database functions
- Learn about Text functions
- Learn about Logical functions
- Learn about Mathematical and Trigonometric functions
- Learn about Information functions

EXCEL FUNCTIONS REFERENCE

A Hands-on Guide

An Introduction to Some of Excel's Specialized Functions

Excel provides over 300 built-in functions. These functions are prewritten formulas that perform complex calculations quickly and easily. The textbook tutorials focus on more commonly used functions, such as SUM, AVERAGE, PMT, and NOW, that are used to analyze problems in many fields—business, health, government, etc. There may be times when you need to use other functions to help with certain specialized tasks or problems. This reference will introduce you to several functions that are used by people in professions that need these specialized functions.

An accountant, for instance, might calculate depreciation by using the SYD (sum of year's digit) function, or a computer engineer might use the DEC2HEX function to convert decimal numbers to hexadecimals. Other functions appeal to many fields but only in special situations, for example, advanced statistical functions such as TTEST, FTEST and ZTEST.

Since functions are used in formulas, each function, like any formula, begins with an equal sign (=), followed by a name describing its operation, such as SUM or AVERAGE. Most functions require additional information called arguments in order for Excel to perform the calculations and return a result.

If you are familiar with the syntax of a particular function, you can type that function and its arguments directly into a cell. If you need assistance in deciding which function to select or if you are not familiar with the syntax of a function, click Insert Function *fx*, and use the Insert Function dialog box to assist you in locating the function you need to complete the formula. The dialog box provides you with the correct spelling of the function name as well as the required and optional arguments that are used in each function.

Student Data Files

▽ **Reference folder**
Functns.xls

Function Categories

To find the function you are looking for more easily, Excel groups all functions into ten categories: Financial, Date and Time, Statistical, Lookup and Reference, Database, Text, Logical, Math and Trigonometric, Information, and Engineering (not covered in this tutorial).

In this section several functions from each category are presented in a tabular format. In addition, your Data Disk contains an Excel file, **Functns.xls,** which includes an example of each function listed in figures R-1 to R-9.

Financial Functions

Includes functions that perform various financial calculations.
   These functions allow you to:

- Calculate depreciation of an asset
- Determine the amount of interest paid on an investment
- Compute the present value of an investment

Figure R-1 lists some commonly used Financial functions. To see examples of these functions refer to the Financial tab in the Functns.xls file on your Data Disk.

Figure R-1	FINANCIAL FUNCTIONS	
FUNCTION NAME	DESCRIPTION	SYNTAX
FV	Returns the future value of an investment based on periodic, constant, payments, and constant interest rate	FV(Rate,Nper,Pmt,PV,Type)
PV	Returns the present value of an investment. The present value is the total amount that a series of future payments is worth now	PV(Rate,Nper,Pmt,FV,Type)
DDB	Returns the depreciation of an asset for a specified period using the double-declining balance method	DDB(Cost,Salvage,Life,Period)
SYD	Returns the sum-of-years' digits depreciation of an asset for a specified period	SYD(Cost,Salvage,Life,Period)
IPMT	Returns the interest paid a specified period	IPMT(Rate,Per,Nper,PV,FT,Type)
NPV	Returns the net present value of an investment with a discount rate and a series of future payments and incomes	NPV(Rate,Value1,Value2,...)

Date and Time Functions

Includes functions that enable you to analyze and work with date and time values in formulas.
   These functions allow you to:

- Determine the day of the week on which a specific date falls
- Manipulate date and time values to return specific portions of a date
- Build a date using values from other cells

Figure R-2 lists some commonly used Date and Time functions. To see examples of these functions refer to the Date and Time tab in the Functns.xls file on your Data Disk.

Figure R-2	DATE AND TIME FUNCTIONS	
FUNCTION NAME	DESCRIPTION	SYNTAX
DATE	Returns a serial number that represents a date from 3 values—year, month, day—which is then formatted as date	DATE(year,month,day)
YEAR	Returns a year (1900 to 9999) from a date	YEAR(date)
MONTH	Returns a month (1 to 12) from a date	MONTH(date)
DAY	Returns the day number (1 to 31) from a date	DAY(date)
WEEKDAY	Returns the day of the week as an integer that corresponds to a date	WEEKDAY(date)
HOUR	Returns the hour of a time value. The hour is given as an integer ranging from 0 (12:00 AM) to 23 (11:00 PM)	HOUR(serial_number)
MINUTE	Returns the minutes of a time value. The minute in given as an integer ranging from 0 to 59	MINUTE(serial_number)
TIME	Returns a decimal number from 3 numbers—hour, minute, and second. The decimal number is a value ranging from 0:00:00 to 23:59:59	TIME(hour,minute,second)

Statistical Functions

Includes functions that perform statistical analysis on a range of data. These functions allow you to:

- Summarize a single data set
- Summarize relationships between data sets
- Calculate probabilities for different statistical distributions
- Make statistical inferences

Figure R-3 lists some commonly used Statistical functions. To see examples of these functions refer to the Statistical tab in the Functns.xls file on your Data Disk.

Figure R-3	STATISTICAL FUNCTIONS	
FUNCTION NAME	DESCRIPTION	SYNTAX
CORREL	Returns the correlation coefficient of the array1 and array2 cell ranges	CORREL(array1,array2)
COVAR	Returns covariance, the average of the products of deviations for each data point pair for all elements of the array	COVAR(array1,array2)
MEDIAN	Returns the median of the given numbers. The median is the number in the middle of a set of numbers	MEDIAN(number1,number2,...)
MODE	Returns the most frequently occurring, or repetitive, value in an array or range of data	MODE(number1,number2,...)
PERCENTILE	Returns the k-th percentile of values in a range	PERCENTILE(array,k)
STDEV	Returns the standard deviation of a sample by measuring how far the numeric values are from the mean	STDEV(number1,number2,...)

Lookup and Reference Functions

Includes functions for looking up and referencing specific values within a range.

These functions allow you to:

- Select specific values
- Create a reference to a specific cell
- Transpose a range of cells

Figure R-4 lists some commonly used Lookup and Reference functions. To see examples of these functions refer to the Lookup and Reference tab in the Functns.xls file on your Data Disk.

Figure R-4	LOOKUP AND REFERENCE FUNCTIONS	
FUNCTION NAME	**DESCRIPTION**	**SYNTAX**
CHOOSE	Returns a value from the list of value arguments based on the index_num	CHOOSE(Index_num,value1,value2,...)
MATCH	Returns the relative position of an item in an array that matches a specified value. Use MATCH instead of one of the LOOKUP functions when you need the position of an item in a range instead of the item itself	MATCH(lookup_value,lookup_array,match_type)
INDEX	Returns a value or the reference to a value from within a table or range	INDEX(array,row_num,column_num)
ROW	Returns the row number of a reference	ROW(cell)
COLUMNS	Returns the number of columns in a reference	COLUMNS(cell)
OFFSET	Returns the reference to a cell that is that is the specified number of rows and columns for the specified cells	OFFSET(reference,row,cols,height,width)

Database Functions

Includes functions designed to return summary statistics based on filtering criteria when working with lists.

These functions allow you to:

- Determine the number of values in a specific list
- Find a minimum or maximum value in a list
- Find the sum or average of a list

Figure R-5 lists some commonly used Database functions. To see examples of these functions refer to the Database tab in the Functns.xls file on your Data Disk.

Figure R-5 — DATABASE FUNCTIONS

FUNCTION NAME	DESCRIPTION	SYNTAX
DAVERAGE	Returns the average of the values in a column of a list or database that match conditions you specify	DAVERAGE(database, field, criteria range)
DCOUNT	Returns a count of the cells that contain numbers in a column of a list or database that match conditions you specify	DCOUNT(database, field, criteria range)
DMAX	Returns the largest number in a column of a list or database that matches conditions you specify	DMAX(database, field, criteria range)
DSUM	Returns the sum of the numbers in a column of a list or database that match conditions you specify	DSUM(database, field, criteria range)

Text Functions

Includes functions that enable you to manipulate and convert strings of characters. These functions allow you to:

- Join multiple text strings together
- Determine location of text within a string
- Remove unprintable characters from text
- Find the length of a string
- Replace text within a string

Figure R-6 lists some commonly used Text functions. To see examples of these functions refer to the Text tab in the Functns.xls file on your Data Disk.

Figure R-6 — TEXT FUNCTIONS

FUNCTION NAME	DESCRIPTION	SYNTAX
LEFT	Returns the specified number of characters from the beginning of the text string	LEFT(text, num_chars)
RIGHT	Returns the specified number of characters from the end of the text string	RIGHT(text, num_chars)
MID	Returns a specified number of characters from a text string, starting at the position you specify, based on the number of characters you specify	MID(text, start_position, num_chars)
REPLACE	Replaces part of a text string, based on the number of characters you specify, with a different text string	REPLACE(old_text, start_pos, num_chars, new_text)
LEN	Returns the number of characters in a text string	LEN(text)
PROPER	Capitalizes the first letter in a text string and any other letters in text that follow any character other than a letter. Converts all other letters to lowercase letters	PROPER(text)
UPPER	Converts text to uppercase	UPPER(text)

Logical Functions

Includes functions that return logical values.
These functions allow you to:

- Compare two logical expressions
- Return TRUE if all arguments evaluate to TRUE
- Return TRUE if at least one arguments evaluates to TRUE

Figure R-7 lists some commonly used Logical functions. To see examples of these functions refer to the Logical tab in the Functns.xls file on your Data Disk.

Figure R-7: LOGICAL FUNCTIONS

FUNCTION NAME	DESCRIPTION	SYNTAX
IF	Returns one value if a condition you specify evaluates to TRUE and another value if it evaluates to FALSE	IF(logical_test,value_if_true,value_if_false)
AND	Returns TRUE if all its arguments are TRUE; returns FALSE if one or more argument is FALSE	AND(logical1,logical2,…)
OR	Returns TRUE if any argument is TRUE; returns FALSE if all arguments are FALSE	OR(logical1,logical2,…)

Math and Trigonometry Functions

Includes functions that perform mathematical and trigonometric calculations.
These functions allow you to:

- Make sure a numeric value is positive
- Round numbers up or down
- Make sure a numeric value is an even number
- Determine the square root of a number

Figure R-8 lists some commonly used Math and Trigonometric functions. To see examples of these functions refer to the Math tab in the Functns.xls file on your Data Disk.

Figure R-8: MATHEMATICAL AND TRIGONOMETRIC FUNCTIONS

FUNCTION NAME	DESCRIPTION	SYNTAX
ABS	Returns the absolute value of a number	ABS(number)
INT	Rounds a number down to the nearest integer	INT(number)
LN	Returns the natural logarithm of a number	LN(number)
MOD	Returns the remainder after a number is divided by the divisor	MOD(number,divisor)
RAND	Returns an evenly distributed random number greater than or equal to 0 and less than 1	RAND()
ROUND	Returns a number rounded to a number of digits	ROUND(number,num_digits)
SIN	Returns the sine of the given angle	SIN(number)
SQRT	Returns a positive square root	SQRT(number)

Information Functions

Includes functions that return information about your worksheet and computer system. These functions allow you to:

- Determine the type of error contained in a cell
- Determine the formatting of a cell
- Convert the value in a cell to a number
- Determine the type of error contained in a cell

Figure R-9 lists some commonly used Information functions. To see examples of these functions refer to the Information tab in the Functns.xls file on your Data Disk.

Figure R-9: INFORMATION FUNCTIONS

FUNCTION NAME	DESCRIPTION	SYNTAX
CELL	Returns information about the formatting, location, or contents of the upper-left cell in a reference	CELL(Information_type,Reference)
ISERROR	Returns TRUE if value refers to any error value (#N/A, #VALUE!, #REF!, #DIV/0!, #NUM!, #NAME?, or #NULL!), otherwise returns FALSE	ISERROR(value)
ISNUMBER	Returns TRUE if a value in a cell is a number, otherwise returns FALSE	ISNUMBER(value)
ISEVEN	Returns TRUE if number is even, otherwise returns FALSE	ISEVEN(value)
N	Converts a non-number value to a number, a date to a serial number, TRUE to 1	N(value)
TYPE	Returns an integer representing the data type of the cell content value: number = 1, text = 2, logical value = 4, error value 16, and array = 64	TYPE(value)

Summary

In this reference you are introduced to several useful Excel functions that assist you in solving specialized tasks. If you need additional information about Excel functions, there are many resources available to help. For instance, within Excel, use the Insert Function dialog box and the Microsoft Office Excel Help feature to get more information. Another useful source of information is the Internet where you can access Microsoft's Web site, Excel newsgroups, and list servs.

INDEX

Special Characters
$ (dollar sign), B-EX 2.14
* (asterisk), B-EX 2.10
+ (plus sign), B-EX 2.10
− (minus sign), B-EX 2.10
/ (slash), B-EX 2.10
= (equal sign), B-EX 2.10
^ (caret), B-EX 2.10

A

absolute references, copying formulas, B-EX 2.12–2.14
Access, in general, OFF 6
addition operator (+), B-EX 2.10
AND function, B-EX 2.19
arguments
  Excel functions, EX 2.03, B-EX 2.19
  optional, EX 2.04
arithmetic mean, calculating, B-EX 2.20–2.22
arithmetic operations, order of precedence, B-EX 2.10–2.11
arithmetic operator, in formulas, EX 1.22
Ask a Question box, OFF 21
Auto Fill, EX 2.16. *See also* filling
  options, EX 2.18
AutoFormat feature, EX 3.31–3.32, B-EX 2.29–2.30. *See also* format; formatting
AutoRepublish, WEB 4
AutoShapes
  formatting, EX 4.38–4.40
  working with, EX 4.36–4.38
AutoSum button, EX 2.25–2.27, B-EX 2.09–2.10
average, calculating, B-EX 2.20–2.22
AVERAGE function, B-EX 2.20–2.22
axis scale. *See also* Excel charts
  charts, EX 4.32–4.33

B

background, graphic image for, EX 4.30–4.31
background color and pattern. *See also* color
  formatting, EX 3.23–3.24
  setting, EX 3.18–3.20

border. *See also* cell border
  text box, EX 4.27
button, Office, OFF 13

C

category values, EX 4.06. *See also* values
cell. *See also* cell border; cell reference; range
  active cell, EX 1.08
  aligning cell contents
    in general, EX 3.11–3.12
    indenting and wrapping text, EX 3.12–3.14
  Excel, EX 1.07
  inserting into row or column, EX 1.26–1.27
  merging cells into one cell EX 3.21–3.22
    hiding rows and columns, EX 3.22–3.23
  moving a selection of cells, EX 1.18–1.19
cell border, adding, EX 3.14–3.17
cell comments, B-EX 2.36–2.37
cell content
  copying using copy-and-paste method, B-EX 2.15–2.16
cell range, EX 1.15. *See also* range
  moving, B-EX 2.28–2.29
cell reference, EX 1.08
  absolute, EX 2.14–2.15, B-EX 2.13–2.15
  mixed, EX 2.14–2.15, B-EX 2.14–2.15
  relative, EX 2.14–2.15, B-EX 2.12, B-EX 2.14
centering
  worksheet printouts, B-EX 2.32–2.33
Chart Wizard. *See* Excel charts
charts. *See* Excel charts
clearing, row and column, EX 1.27–1.29, B-EX 2.26
clipboard, Excel functions, EX 2.12
Close button, Print Preview window, B-EX 2.32
closing, Office, OFF 16–18
color
  background color and pattern, EX 3.18–3.20
  in charts, EX 4.27–4.30
  in general, EX 3.09–3.11
column
  changing width, B-EX 2.24–2.25
  clearing or deleting, EX 1.27–1.29, B-EX 2.27
  entering, EX 1.26–1.27

entering labels for headings, B-EX 2.05
hiding, EX 3.22–3.23
increasing width, EX 1.29–1.30
reducing width, EX 3.13

comments, adding to cells, B-EX 2.36–2.37
comparison operator, EX 2.22
CONCATENATE function, B-EX 2.19
copy-and-paste method, B-EX 2.15–2.16
copying
cell contents, using copy-and-paste method, B-EX 2.15–2.16
formats, EX 3.06–3.07
formulas. *See* copying formulas

copying formulas, EX 2.10–2.14, EX 2.16–2.18
absolute references, B-EX 2.13–2.14
copy-and-paste method, B-EX 2.15–2.16
fill handle, B-EX 2.11–2.12
relative references, B-EX 2.12, B-EX 2.14

correcting errors. *See* error correction
COUNT function, B-EX 2.19
Currency format, applying, EX 3.04–3.05, 3.09

D

data. *See* worksheet data
data markers, chart, EX 4.09
data source
for charts EX 4.06–4.08
category values, EX 4.06
data series, EX 4.06
editing, EX 4.19–4.22
X values, EX 4.06

database, OFF 6
database program, OFF 6
Date button, B-EX 2.33
date functions, using, EX 2.27–2.29
dates
entering into worksheet, EX 1.21
filling, EX 2.19–2.21
TODAY function, EX 2.28

decimal places, increasing, EX 3.05–3.06
deleting, row and column, EX 1.27–1.29, B-EX 2.26
dimensional chart. *See also* Excel charts
working with, EX 4.33–4.35

displaying
formulas, B-EX 2.38–2.39

division operator (/), B-EX 2.10
document
entering text into, OFF 16–17
hypertext document, WEB 1
Word, OFF 4

documentation sheet, worksheet, EX 1.33
documenting workbooks, B-EX 2.36
dollar signs ($)
absolute references, B-EX 2.13

drag-and-drop technique, moving cell ranges, B-EX 2.28–2.29
Drawing toolbar
Autoshapes, EX 4.36–4.38
formatting, EX 4.38–4.40
displaying, EX 4.36
in general, EX 4.35

E

edit mode. *See also* editing
working in, EX 1.31–1.32
worksheet, EX 1.31

editing
worksheet
edit mode, EX 1.31–1.32
in general, EX 1.31
undoing action, EX 1.32–1.33

elevation, chart, EX 4.34
embedded chart, EX 4.11. *See also* Excel charts
moving and resizing, EX 4.13–4.14

entering. *See also* inserting
data in worksheets, B-EX 2.07–2.08
formulas. *See* entering formulas
functions, B-EX 2.18–2.19
worksheet labels, B-EX 2.05–2.06
worksheet titles, B-EX 2.05–2.06

entering formulas, B-EX 2.10–2.11
equal sign (=), formulas, B-EX 2.10
error correction, EX 1.32–1.33
spelling errors, B-EX 2.24
Undo button, EX 1.32, B–EX 2.27

error values, B-EX 2.13

Excel
  exiting, EX 1.19
  in general, OFF 4
  introduction, EX 1.04
    workbook, EX 1.05
    worksheet, EX 1.05
  saving, EX 2.29
  spreadsheets, in general, EX 1.04–1.05
  starting, OFF 10–11, EX 1.06

Excel charts
  active chart, EX 4.12
  chart options
    changing options, EX 4.23
    chart area, EX 4.09
    chart location, EX 4.10–4.13, EX 4.22
    chart title, EX 4.09
    data markers, EX 4.09
    gridlines, EX 4.09
    legend, EX 4.09
    plot area, EX 4.09
    scale, EX 4.09
    tick marks, EX 4.09, EX 4.32
  chart sheet, EX 4.11
  creating with Chart Wizard
    choosing chart options, EX 4.08–4.10
    choosing chart type, EX 4.04–4.06
    choosing data source, EX 4.06–4.08
    in general, EX 4.03–4.04
  dimensional chart, EX 4.33–4.35
    elevation, EX 4.34
    perspective, EX 4.34
  embedded chart, EX 4.11
    moving and resizing, EX 4.13–4.14
  formatting
    changing axis scale, EX 4.32–4.33
    chart text, EX 4.24–4.25
    colors and fills, EX 4.27–4.30
    in general, EX 4.23–4.24
    graphic image as background, EX 4.30–4.31
    inserting new chart text, EX 4.25–4.27
  in general, EX 4.02–4.03
  modifying
    data source editing, EX 4.19–4.22
    in general, EX 4.19
  pie chart
    exploding a slice of, EX 4.17–4.19
    in general, EX 4.14–4.16
    rotating, EX 4.16–4.17
  printing, EX 4.40–4.42
  saving, EX 4.11
  updating, EX 4.14

Excel functions
  date functions, EX 2.27–2.29
  financial functions, EX 2.05
  function syntax, EX 2.03–2.04
  in general, EX 2.02–2.03
  inserting, EX 2.06–EX 2.10
  logical functions, EX 2.21–2.25
    comparison operator, EX 2.22

Excel window
  cell, EX 1.07
  discussed, EX 1.05–1.08
  workbook window, EX 1.07
  worksheet window, EX 1.07

exponential operator (^), B-EX 2.10
extreme values, B-EX 2.23

F

file
  closing, OFF 18
  modifying, OFF 18
  opening, OFF 18–20
  printing, OFF 20–21
  saving, OFF 18
  switching between, OFF 12–13

file extension, OFF 16
Filename button, B-EX 2.33
filename, OFF 16
filenames
  renaming worksheets, B-EX 2.17

fill handle, EX 2.16. *See also* **filling**
  copying formulas, B-EX 2.11–2.12
  using, EX 3.07

filling
  charts, EX 4.27–4.30
  dates, EX 2.19–2.21
  formulas, EX 2.16
  series, EX 2.18–2.19

financial functions, Excel, EX 2.05
font. *See also* **text**
  bold typeface, EX 3.10
  in general, EX 3.09–3.11
  italic typeface, EX 3.10

Font button, B-EX 2.33
font name, EX 3.09
footer. *See also* **text**
   adding, B-EX 2.33–2.34
   in general, EX 3.35–3.37
Format Cells dialog box
   Merge and Center option, EX 3.11–3.12
   using, EX 3.07–3.09
Format Painter button, using, EX 3.06–3.07
formatting. *See also* **AutoFormat; format**
   clearing and replacing, EX 3.25–3.28
   copying, EX 3.06–3.07
   Currency format, EX 3.04–3.05, EX 3.09
   definition, EX 3.03
   General format, EX 3.03
   other options, EX 3.14
   Percent format, EX 3.05–3.06
   tabs, EX 3.24–3.25
   worksheet
      background, EX 3.23–3.24
      headers and footers, B-EX 2.33–2.35
      hiding rows and columns, EX 3.22–3.23
      merging cells into one cell, EX 3.21–3.22
      opening Print Preview window, EX 3.32–3.33
      tabs, EX 3.24–3.25
      worksheet data, in general, EX 3.02–3.03
Formatting toolbar, using, EX 3.03–3.06
formulas
   copying, EX 2.16–2.18
   copying. *See* copying formulas
   copying and pasting, EX 2.10–2.14
   displaying, B-EX 2.38–2.39
   editing, EX 1.31–1.32
   entering. *See* entering formulas
   entering into worksheet, EX 1.22–1.25
      order of precedence, EX 1.23
   filling in, in general, EX 2.16
   pointing method for building, B-EX 2.22–2.23
functions, B-EX 2.18–2.22
   arguments, B-EX 2.19
   entering, B-EX 2.20–2.21
   syntax, B-EX 2.18–2.19
FV function, B-EX 2.19

gridlines, chart, EX 4.09

H

header. *See also* **text**
   adding, B-EX 2.33–2.35
   in general, EX 3.35–3.37
Help button, Print Preview window, B-EX 2.32
Help, Office, OFF 21–23
hypertext document, WEB 1

I

IF function, B-EX 2.19
INDIRECT function, B-EX 2.19
inserting. *See also* **entering; entering formulas**
   cell comments, B-EX 2.36–2.37
   headers and footers in worksheets, B-EX 2.33–2.35
   rows in worksheets, B-EX 2.26–2.27
integration, Office, OFF 7–9
Internet, WEB 1

K

keyboard shortcut, Office, OFF 13

L

label, entering into worksheet, EX 1.20–1.21, B-EX 2.05–2.07
label text, EX 4.25
layout
   worksheets, B-EX 2.24–2.30
LEFT function, B-EX 2.19
legend, charts, EX 4.09
logical functions
   in general, EX 2.21–2.25
      comparison operator, EX 2.22

M

Margins button, Print Preview window, B-EX 2.31
MAX function, B-EX 2.22
mean, arithmetic, calculating, B-EX 2.18–2.20

menu
   Office, OFF 13–16
   personalized, OFF 13–14
menu command, OFF 13
Microsoft Access 2002. *See* **Access**
Microsoft Excel 2002. *See* **Excel**
Microsoft Office XP. *See* **Office**
Microsoft Outlook 2002. *See* **Outlook**
Microsoft PowerPoint 2002. *See* **PowerPoint**
Microsoft Word 2002. *See* **Word**
MIN function, B-EX 2.22
mistakes. *See* **error correction**
mixed references, B-EX 2.14
mouse
   moving cell ranges, B-EX 2.28–2.29
moving
   cell ranges, B-EX 2.28–2.29
multiplication operator (*), B-EX 2.10

N

name(s), files. *See* **filenames**
Next button, Print Preview window, B-EX 2.32
non-interactive Web site. *See also* **Web site**
   publishing
      AutoRepublish, WEB 4
      in general, WEB 2, WEB 4–5
      options, WEB 2–4
number(s)
   entering in worksheets, B-EX 2.07–2.08
   largest, finding, B-EX 2.22
   smallest, finding, B-EX 2.22

O

Office
   closing, OFF 16–18
   exiting programs, OFF 23
   in general, OFF 4–7
   Help, OFF 21–23
   menus and toolbars, OFF 13–16
   opening file, OFF 18–20
   program integration, OFF 7–9
   saving, OFF 16–18
   speech recognition, OFF 15
   starting, OFF 9–12
   switching between programs and files, OFF 12–13
Office Assistant, OFF 21
order of precedence for arithmetic operations, B-EX 2.10–2.11
order of precedence, formula, EX 1.23
Outlook, in general, OFF 6

P

Page Break Preview button, Print Preview window, B-EX 2.31
page break, inserting, EX 3.37–3.40
Page number button, B-EX 2.33
page orientation
   worksheet, EX 3.33–3.35
      landscape orientation, EX 3.34
      portrait orientation, EX 3.34
Page Setup dialog box, B-EX 2.32–2.33
Page Setup settings, saving, B-EX 2.34
parenthesis, for formula, EX 1.23
Paste Function button, entering functions, B-EX 2.20–2.21
pattern, for title, EX 3.18–3.20
Percent format, applying, EX 3.05–3.06
perspective, chart, EX 4.34
pie chart. *See also* **Excel charts**
   exploding a slice of, EX 4.17–4.19
   in general, EX 4.14–4.16
   rotating, EX 4.16–4.17
planning
   worksheets, B-EX 2.04–2.05
plot area, chart, EX 4.09
PMT function, B-EX 2.19
pointing method for building formulas, B-EX 2.22–2.23
PowerPoint, in general, OFF 5
presentation, in general, OFF 5
presentation graphics program, OFF 5
previewing worksheets, B-EX 2.30–2.31
Previous button, Print Preview window, B-EX 2.32
print area, EX 3.37
Print button, Print Preview window, B-EX 2.32

Print Preview window
  buttons, B-EX 2.32
  previewing worksheets, B-EX 2.30–2.31
Print Preview window, opening, EX 3.32–3.33
printing
  charts, EX 4.40–4.42
  file, OFF 20–21
printing worksheets, EX 1.36, B-EX 2.34–2.35
  centering printouts, B-EX 2.32–2.33
  creating page breaks, EX 3.37–3.40
  defining page setup, EX 3.33–3.35
  displaying formulas, B-EX 2.38
  headers and footers, B-EX 2.33–2.34
  setting print area, EX 3.37–3.40, B-EX 2.35
programs. *See also specific programs*
  exiting, OFF 23
  switching between, OFF 12–13
Properties dialog box, B-EX 2.36

R

RAND function, B-EX 2.19
range, EX 1.15. *See also* **cell**
  adjacent range, EX 1.15
  nonadjacent range, EX 1.15
  selecting, EX 1.15–1.17
    other selection techniques, EX 1.17–1.18
range reference, EX 1.15
relative references, copying formulas, B-EX 2.12, B-EX 2.14
removing. *See* **deleting**
renaming. *See* **filenames**
ROUND function, B-EX 2.19
row
  clearing or deleting, EX 1.27–1.29, B-EX 2.26
  hiding, EX 3.22–3.23
  increasing height of, EX 1.29–1.30
  inserting, EX 1.26–1.27, B-EX 2.26–2.27

S

Save As command, B-EX 2.17
saving workbooks, B-EX 2.17
saving
  Excel, EX 2.29
  Excel chart, EX 4.11
  Office, OFF 16–18
  Page Setup settings, B-EX 2.34
  workbook, EX 1.12–1.15
scale, chart, EX 4.09
ScreenTip, Office, OFF 21
series, filling, EX 2.18–2.19
Setup button, Print Preview window, B-EX 2.32
sheet(s). *See* **worksheet**
Sheet name button, B-EX 2.33
Simple format, B-EX 2.29–2.30
speech recognition, Office, OFF 15
spell checking worksheets, B-EX 2.24
spreadsheet
  defined, EX 1.04
  in general, EX 1.04–1.05
spreadsheet component, Web page, WEB 7
spreadsheet program, OFF 4
starting
  Excel, OFF 10–11
  Office, OFF 9–12
  Word, OFF 11–12
STDEV function, B-EX 2.19
styles
  applying, EX 3.29–3.31
  creating, EX 3.28–3.29
  in general, EX 3.28
subtraction operator (-), B-EX 2.10
SUM function, B-EX 2.08–2.09, B-EX 2.19
syntax
  Excel functions EX 2.03–2.04, B-EX 2.18
    arguments, EX 2.03

T

tabs, formatting, EX 3.24–3.25
testing worksheets, B-EX 2.23
test values, B-EX 2.23
text. *See also* **font**
  entering into document, OFF 16–17
  entering into worksheet, EX 1.20–1.21
  formatting in chart, EX 4.24–4.25
  indenting and wrapping, EX 3.12–3.14
  inserting new chart text, EX 4.25–4.27
    attached text, EX 4.25
    label text, EX 4.25
    unattached text, EX 4.25

text box, border, EX 4.27
tick marks, chart, EX 4.09, EX 4.32
Time button, B-EX 2.33
title
   centering, EX 3.11
   for chart, EX 4.09
   color and pattern for, EX 3.18–3.20
   worksheets, entering, B-EX 2.05–2.06
   wrapping within cell, EX 3.13
TODAY function, EX 2.28, B–EX 2.19
toolbar
   Office, OFF 13–16
      personalized, OFF 14–15
Total pages button, B-EX 2.33
totals, calculation using AutoSum button, B-EX 2.09
typeface, EX 3.09

U

Undo button, EX 1.32, B-EX 2.27
updating, Excel charts, EX 4.14

V

values. *See also* number(s)
   category values, EX 4.06
   definition, EX 1.21
   entering into worksheet, EX 1.21–1.22
   error, B-EX 2.14
   extreme, B-EX 2.23
   filling in, in general, EX 2.16
   test, B-EX 2.23
   X values, EX 4.06
VLOOKUP function, B-EX 2.19

W

Web browser, WEB 1
Web page, WEB 1
   spreadsheet component, WEB 7
Web. *See* World Wide Web
Web server, WEB 1
Web site, WEB 1. *See also* non-interactive Web site
   interactive, publishing, WEB 6–8

What's This? command, OFF 21
Word
   in general, OFF 4
      documents, OFF 4
   starting, OFF 11–12
word processing program, OFF 4
workbook, EX 1.05
   documenting, B-EX 2.36
   Excel, OFF 4
   inserting worksheet into, EX 1.34
   navigating in, in general, EX 1.08
   navigating in worksheet, EX 1.08–1.11
   opening and saving, EX 1.12–1.15
   saving, with different name, EX 1.13–1.14
   saving workbooks, B-EX 2.17
workbook window, EX 1.07
worksheet. *See also* worksheet data
   adding or removing, EX 1.33–1.34
      documentation sheet, EX 1.33
   developing, B-EX 2.04
   editing
      in general, EX 1.31
      undoing action, EX 1.32–1.33
      working in Edit Mode, EX 1.31–1.32
   entering information into
      entering data, B-EX 2.07–2.08
      entering dates, EX 1.21
      entering formulas, EX 1.22–1.25, B-EX 2.10
      entering text, EX 1.20–1.21
      entering titles, B-EX 2.05–2.06
      entering values, EX 1.21–1.22
      in general, EX 1.20
   footers, B-EX 2.33–2.35
   formatting
      background, EX 3.23–3.24
      hiding rows and columns, EX 3.22–3.23
      merging cells into one cell, EX 3.21–3.22
      opening Print Preview window, EX 3.32–3.33
      tabs, EX 3.24–3.25
   formulas. *See* formula(s)
   headers, B-EX 2.33–2.34
   in general, EX 1.05, EX 1.33
   inserting in workbook, EX 1.34
   layout, B-EX 2.24–2.30
   moving, EX 1.35
   navigating between, EX 1.11–1.12
   navigating in, EX 1.08–1.11
   planning, B-EX 2.04–2.05

previewing, B-EX 2.30–2.32
printing, EX 1.36, B-EX 2.34–2.35
   creating page breaks, EX 3.37–3.40
   defining page setup, EX 3.33–3.35
   headers and footers, EX 3.35–3.37, B-EX 2.33–2.34
   previewing, EX 3.32–3.33
   setting print area, EX 3.37–3.40, B-EX 2.35
renaming, EX 1.35, B-EX 2.17
spell checking, B-EX 2.24
testing, B-EX 2.23

worksheet cells
   contents. *See* cell content
   ranges. *See* cell range
   references. *See* cell reference

worksheet column(s). *See* **column**

worksheet data, formatting, in general, EX 3.02–3.05

worksheet labels, entering, B-EX 2.05–2.07
worksheet rows. *See* row
worksheet window, EX 1.07
World Wide Web (Web), WEB 1

X values, EX 4.06

YEAR function, B-EX 2.19

Zoom button, Print Preview window, B-EX 2.31

TASK REFERENCE

TASK	PAGE #	RECOMMENDED METHOD
Absolute reference, change to relative	EX 2.14	Edit the formula, deleting the $ before the column and row references; or press F4 to switch between absolute, relative, and mixed references
Action, redo	EX 1.33	Click
Action, undo	EX 1.32	Click
Actions, redo several	EX 1.33	Click the list arrow for , select the action(s) to redo
Actions, undo several	EX 1.32	Click the list arrow for , select the action(s) to undo
Auto Fill, copy formulas	EX 2.16	See Reference Window: Copying Formulas Using Auto Fill
Auto Fill, create series	EX 2.18	Select the range, drag the fill handle down, release mouse button, click , click the option button to complete series
AutoFormat, apply	EX 3.31	Select the range, click Format, click AutoFormat, select an AutoFormat design, click OK
AutoShape, add text to	EX 4.37	See Reference Window: Inserting Text into an AutoShape
AutoShape, insert, reshape, resize and rotate	EX 4.35	See Reference Window: Inserting an AutoShape
AutoSum, apply	EX 2.25	Click the cell in which you want the final value to appear, click the list arrow for , select the AutoSum function to apply
Background color, apply	EX 3.18	Select the range, click the list arrow for , select a color square in the color palette
Background pattern, apply	EX 3.18	Open the Format Cells dialog box, click the Patterns tab, click the Pattern list arrow, click a pattern in the pattern gallery, click OK
Border, create	EX 3.15	Click the list arrow for , select a border in the border gallery
Border, draw	EX 3.16	Click the list arrow for , click , draw the border using the Pencil tool
Cell, clear contents of	EX 1.27	Click Edit, click Clear; or press Delete
Cell, edit	EX 1.31	See Reference Window: Editing a Cell
Cells, delete from worksheet	EX 1.27	Select the cell or range, click Edit, click Delete, select a delete option, click OK; or select the cell or range, click-right the selection, click Delete, select a delete option, click OK
Cells, insert into worksheet	EX 1.26	See Reference Window: Inserting New Cells into a Worksheet
Cells, merge	EX 3.21	Select the adjacent cells, open the Format Cells dialog box, click the Alignment tab, select the Merge check box, click OK
Cells, merge and center	EX 3.21	Select the adjacent cells, click
Chart axis title, add or edit	EX 4.21	Select the chart, click Chart, click Chart Options, click the Titles tab, click on the Category (X) axis text box and type the text for the title, click in the Values (Y) axis text box and type the text for the title, click OK
Chart data markers, change fill color	EX 4.27	Double-click the data marker, click the Patterns tab, click Fill Effects, click the Gradient tab, select the color and related color options, click OK

TASK REFERENCE

TASK	PAGE #	RECOMMENDED METHOD
Chart text, format	EX 4.23	Select the chart label, click a button on the Formatting toolbar; or double-click the chart label, select the formatting options using the tabs in the Format Data Label dialog box
Chart text, insert new unattached	EX 4.25	See Reference Window: Inserting Unattached Text into a Chart
Chart title, add or edit	EX 4.21	Select the chart, click Chart, click Chart Options, click the Titles tab, click in the Chart title text box type the text for title, click OK
Chart Wizard, start	EX 4.04	Click
Chart, add data label	EX 4.21	Select a data marker(s) or data series, click Chart, click Chart Options, click the Data Labels tab, select the data label type, click OK
Chart, add gridline	EX 4.10	Select the chart, click Chart, click Chart Options, click the Gridlines tab, click the check box for gridline option you want to select, click OK
Chart, add, remove, revise data series	EX 4.18	*See* Reference Window: Editing a Chart's Data Source
Chart, change 3-D elevation	EX 4.34	Select a 3-D chart, click Chart, click 3-D View, enter the elevation value or click the Elevation Up or Elevation Down button, click OK
Chart, change location	EX 4.21	Select the chart, click Chart, click Location, specify the new location
Chart, change scale	EX 4.31	Double-click a value on the y-axis, enter the minimum and maximum values for the scale, click OK
Chart, change to 3-D	EX 4.32	Select the chart, click Chart, click Chart Type, select a 3-D subtype, click OK
Chart, create with Chart Wizard	EX 4.04	*See* Reference Window: Creating a Chart with the Chart Wizard
Chart, format data marker	EX 4.27	Double-click the data marker, select the formatting options using the tabs in the Format Data Series dialog box
Chart, move	EX 4.12	Select the chart, move the pointer over the chart area, drag the chart to its new location, release the mouse button
Chart, resize	EX 4.13	Select the chart, move the pointer over a selection handle, drag the handle to resize the chart, release the mouse button
Chart, select	EX 4.12	Move pointer over a blank area of the chart, and then click
Chart, update	EX 4.14	Enter new values for the chart's data source and the chart is automatically updated
Chart, use background image in	EX 4.29	Double-click the plot area, click the Patterns tab, click the Fill Effects, click the Picture tab, click Select Picture, locate and select the background image file, click Insert, click OK twice
Column, change width	EX 1.30	See Reference Window: Changing Column Width
Column, delete from worksheet	EX 1.27	Select the column, click Edit, click Delete; or select the column, click-right the selection, click Delete

TASK REFERENCE

TASK	PAGE #	RECOMMENDED METHOD
Column, hide	EX 3.22	Select the headings for the columns you want to hide, right-click the selection, click Hide
Column, insert into worksheet	EX 1.30	See Reference Window: Inserting Cells into a Worksheet
Columns, repeat in printout	EX 3.38	Open the Page Setup dialog box, click the Sheet tab, click the Column to repeat at left box, click the column that contain the information you want repeated, click OK
Column, select	EX 1.19	Click the column heading of the column you want to select. To select more than one column, hold down the Ctrl key and click each individual column heading. To select a range of columns, click the first column heading in the range, hold down the Shift key and click the last column in the range.
Column, unhide	EX 3.23	Select the column headings left and right of the hidden columns, right-click the selection, click Unhide
Date, insert current	EX 2.28	Insert the TODAY() or NOW() function
Dates, fill in with Auto Fill	EX 2.19	Select the cell containing the initial date, drag and drop the fill handle to fill in the rest of the dates. Click the Auto Fill options button and choose whether to fill in days, weekdays, months, or years.
Drawing toolbar, display	EX 4.35	Click View, point to Toolbars, click Drawing, or click
Excel, exit	EX 1.19	Click File and then click Exit.
Excel, start	EX 1.05	Click Start, point to Programs, click Microsoft Excel
Font, change color	EX 3.10	Click the list arrow for , select a color from the color palette
Font, change size	EX 3.09	Click the list arrow for 10, click a size
Font, change style	EX 3.10	Select the text, click B, click I, or click U
Font, change typeface	EX 3.09	Click the list arrow for Arial button, click a font
Format Cells dialog box, open	EX 3.07	Click Format, click Cells
Format, apply currency style, percent style, or comma style	EX 3.03	Click $, click %, or click , or or open the Format Cells dialog box, click the Number tab, select a style, specify style-related options, click OK
Format, clear	EX 3.25	Click Edit, point to Clear, click Formats
Format, copy using Format Painter	EX 3.06	Select the cell or range that contains the formatting you want to copy, click , drag the pointer over the cell or range to apply the formatting
Format, copy using fill handle	EX 3.07	Select the cell or range that contains the formatting you want to copy, drag the fill handle down, click , click the Fill Formatting Only option button
Format, decrease decimal places	EX 3.03	Click
Format, find and replace	EX 3.26	See Reference Window: Finding and Replacing a Format

TASK REFERENCE

TASK	PAGE #	RECOMMENDED METHOD
Format, increase decimal places	EX 3.05	Click [icon]
Formula, copy	EX 2.12	See Reference Window: Copying and Pasting a Cell or Range
Formula, copy with Auto Fill	EX 2.16	See Reference Window: Copying Formulas Using Auto Fill
Formula, enter using keyboard	EX 1.23	See Reference Window: Entering a Formula
Formula, enter using mouse	EX 1.23	See Reference Window: Entering a Formula
Function, insert	EX 2.06	See Reference Window: Inserting a Function
Header/footer, create	EX 3.35	Open the Page Setup dialog box, click the Header/Footer tab, click list arrow for the Header button or the Footer button, select an available header or footer, click OK
Header/footer, create custom	EX 3.36	Open Page Setup dialog box, click the Header/Footer tab, click the Custom Header or Customer Footer button, complete the header/footer related boxes, click OK
Page break, insert	EX 3.37	Click the cell below where you want the page break to appear, click Insert, click Page Break.
Page Setup dialog box open	EX 3.33	Click File, click Page Setup; or click the Setup button on the Print Preview toolbar
Page, change orientation	EX 3.35	Open the Page Setup dialog box, click the Page tab, click either the Landscape or the Portrait option button
Page, set margins	EX 3.34	Open the Page Setup dialog box, click the Margins tab, specify the width of the margins, click OK
Pie chart, create	EX 4.14	Select the row or column of data values to be charted, click [icon], select Pie in the list of chart types, select a sub-type, complete the remaining Chart Wizard dialog boxes
Pie chart, explode piece(s)	EX 4.17	See Reference Window: Creating an Exploded Pie Chart
Pie chart, rotate	EX 4.16	Double-click the pie in the pie chart, click the Options tab, enter a new value in the Angle of First Slice box, click OK
Print area, define	EX 3.37	Select the range, click File, point to Print Area, click Set Print Area
Print Preview, open	EX 3.32	Click [icon]
Range, copy	EX 1.18	Select the cell or range, hold down the Ctrl key and drag the selection to the new location, release the mouse button and Ctrl
Range, move	EX 1.18	Select the cell or range, drag the selection to the new location, release the mouse button
Range, select adjacent	EX 1.16	See Reference Window: Selecting Adjacent or Nonadjacent Ranges of Cells
Range, select non-adjacent	EX 1.16	See Reference Window: Selecting Adjacent or Nonadjacent Ranges of Cells

TASK REFERENCE

TASK	PAGE #	RECOMMENDED METHOD
Relative reference, change to absolute	EX 2.14	Type $ before the column and row references; or press F4 to insert $
Row, change height	EX 1.30	Move the pointer over the row heading border until the pointer changes to ✥, click and drag the border to increase or decrease the height of the row
Row, delete from worksheet	EX 1.27	Select the row, click Edit, click Delete; or select the row, click-right the selection, click Delete
Row, hide	EX 3.22	Select the headings for the rows you want to hide, right-click the selection, click Hide
Row, insert into worksheet	EX 1.30	See Reference Window: Inserting Cells into a Worksheet
Rows, repeat in printout	EX 3.38	Open the Page Setup dialog box, click the Sheet tab, click the Row to repeat at top box, click the row that contains the information
Row, select	EX 1.19	Click the heading of the row you want to select. To select more than one row, hold down the Ctrl key and click each individual row heading. To select a range of rows, click the first row heading in the range, hold down the Shift key and click the last row in the range
Row, unhide	EX 3.23	Select the rows headings above and below the hidden rows, right-click the selection, click Unhide
Sheet tabs, format	EX 3.25	Right-click the sheet tab, click Tab Color, select a color from the color palette
Style, apply	EX 3.29	Select the range, click Format, click Style, select a style, click OK
Style, create	EX 3.29	Select the cell that contains the formatting you want to use as the basis of the new style, click Format, click Style, type a name for the style, click Modify, specify format options using the Format Cells dialog box, click OK, click OK
Style, modify	EX 3.30	Select the range, click Format, click Style, click Modify, change style attributes, click OK
Text, align within a cell	EX 3.11	Click ☐, click ☐, click ☐, click ☐, or click ☐; or open Format Cells dialog box, click the Alignment tab, select a text alignment, click OK
Text, change indent	EX 3.11	Click ☐, or ☐
Text, enter into cell	EX 1.20	Click the cell, type text entry, press Enter
Text, wrap in cell	EX 3.13	Open the Format Cells dialog box, click the Alignment tab, select the Text wrap check box, click OK
Web page, add page title	WEB 3	Click File, click Save as Web Page, cick the Change Title button, enter the page title, click OK
Web page, publish a workbook	WEB 6	Click File, click Save as Web Page, select the Entire Workbook option button, specify a title, click Publish, click the AutoRepublish every time this workbook is saved check box (optional), click the Open published web page in the browser check box (optional), click Publish

TASK REFERENCE

TASK	PAGE #	RECOMMENDED METHOD
Web page, publish a worksheet	WEB 3	Click File, click Save as Web Page, select the Selection: Sheet option button, specify a title, click Publish, specify the items to publish, specify the Web page as interactive or non-interactive, click the AutoRepublish every time this workbook is saved check box (optional), click the Open published web page in the browser check box (optional), click Publish
Web page, publish interactive	WEB 2	Click File, click Save as Web Page, select the Add Interactivity check box, click Publish
Web page, publish non-interactive	WEB 2	Click File, click Save as Web Page, clear the Add Interactivity check box
Web page, republish automatically with updates	WEB 4	Click File, click Save as Web Page, click Publish, select the AutoRepublish every time this workbook is saved check box
Workbook, open	EX 1.12	Click 📂 ; (or click File and click Open or click the Workbook link in the Task Pane), locate the drive and folder that contains the workbook, click the filename, click Open (or double-click the workbook file name in the Task Pane)
Workbook, print	EX 1.36	Click 🖨 ; or click File, click Print, select printer and print-related options, click OK
Workbook, save for first time	EX 1.14	Click 💾 (or click File, click Save or Save As), locate the folder and drive in which to store the file, type a filename, click Save
Workbook, save in a different format	EX 1.14	See Reference Window: Saving a Workbook in a Different Format
Workbook, save to update	EX 1.14	Click 💾 ; or click File, click Save
Workbook, save with new name	EX 1.14	Click File, click Save As, locate the folder and drive in which to store the file, type a filename, click Save
Worksheet, add background image	EX 3.23	See Reference Window: Adding a Background Image to the Worksheet
Worksheet, copy	EX 1.35	See Reference Window: Moving or Copying a Worksheet
Worksheet, delete	EX 1.33	Click the sheet tab, click Edit, click Delete Sheet; or right-click the sheet tab, click Delete
Worksheet, insert	EX 1.34	Click Insert, click Worksheet; or right-click a sheet tab, click Insert, click Worksheet icon, click Insert
Worksheets, move	EX 1.35	See Reference Window: Moving or Copying a Worksheet
Worksheet, rename	EX 1.35	Double-click the sheet tab that you want to rename, type a new name, press Enter
Worksheets, move between	EX 1.11	Click the sheet tab for the worksheet you want to view; or click one of the tab scrolling buttons, click the sheet tab

Excel Level I File Finder

Location in Tutorial	Name and Location of Data Files	Student Saves File As...	Student Creates New File
Tutorial 1			
Session 1.1	Tutorial.01\Tutorial\Lawn1.xls	Lawn2.xls	
Session 1.2			
Review Assignments	Tutorial.01\Review\Income1.xls	Income2.xls	
Case Problem 1	Tutorial.01\Cases\CFlow1.xls	CFlow2.xls	
Case Problem 2	Tutorial.01\Cases\Balance1.xls	Balance2.xls	
Case Problem 3	Tutorial.01\Cases\Site1.xls	Site2.xls	
Case Problem 4			CashCounter.xls
Tutorial 2			
Session 2.1	Tutorial.02\Tutorial\Loan1.xls	Loan2.xls	
Session 2.2			
Review Assignments	Tutorial.02\Review\Mort1.xls	Mort2.xls	
Case Problem 1	Tutorial.02\Cases\School1.xls	School2.xls	
Case Problem 2	Tutorial.02\Cases\Sonic1.xls	Sonic2.xls	
Case Problem 3	Tutorial.02\Cases\Leland1.xls	Leland2.xls	
Case Problem 4			JrCol.xls
Tutorial 3			
Session 3.1	Tutorial.03\Tutorial\Sales1.xls	Sales2.xls	
Session 3.2			
Review Assignments	Tutorial.03\Review\Region1.xls	Region2.xls	
Case Problem 1	Tutorial.03\Cases\Running1.xls	Running2.xls	
Case Problem 2	Tutorial.03\Cases\WBus1.xls	WBus2.xls	
Case Problem 3	Tutorial.03\Cases\Blades1.xls	Blades2.xls	
Case Problem 4			Payroll.xls
Tutorial 4			
Session 4.1	Tutorial.04\Tutorial\Vega1.xls	Vega2.xls	
Session 4.2			
Review Assignments	Tutorial.04\Review\VegaUSA1.xls	VegaUSA2.xls	
Case Problem 1	Tutorial.04\Cases\CIC1.xls	CIC2.xls	
Case Problem 2	Tutorial.04\Cases\Powder1.xls	Powder2.xls	
Case Problem 3	Tutorial.04\Cases\Pixal1.xls	Pixal2.xls	
Case Problem 4			BCancer.xls
Web			
Session	Web\Tutorial\Mortgage1.xls Web\Tutorial\Calc1.xls	Mortgage2.xls Calc2.xls	Mortgage3.htm Mortgage3_files\filelist.xml Mortgage3_files\Mortgage2_*30888_image001*.gif Mortgage3_files\Mortgage2_*30888_image002*.gif Calc3.htm
Review Assignments	Web\Review\Fund1.xls Web\Review\FCalc1.xls	Fund2.xls FCalc2.xls	Fund3.htm Fund3_files\filelist.xml Fund3_files\Fund2_*7971_image001*.gif FCalc3.htm

Excel Bonus Tutorial

Location in Tutorial	Name and Location of Data File	Student Saves File As...	Student Creates New File
Bonus Tutorial 2			
Session 2.1			Tutorial.02\Tutorial\MSI Sales Report.xls
Session 2.2	Tutorial.02\Tutorial\MSI Sales Report.xls (*Saved from Session 2.1*)	Tutorial.02\Tutorial\MSI Sales Report.xls	
Review Assignments	Tutorial.02\Review\MSI-2.xls	Tutorial.02\Review\MSI Sales Report 2.xls	
Case Problem 1	Tutorial.02\Cases\MJ Inc.xls	Tutorial.02\Cases\MJ Income.xls	
Case Problem 2	Tutorial.02\Cases\Airline.xls	Tutorial.02\Cases\Airline Data.xls	
Case Problem 3	Tutorial.02\Cases\Fresh Air.xls	Tutorial.02\Cases\Fresh Air Sales Incentive.xls	
Case Problem 4			Tutorial.02\Cases\Portfolio.xls

Note: GIF files will have different filenames for different users.